JOURNEY THROUGH WALES

A SUMMER ROAD TRIP OF DISCOVERY AND
SMILES

MARK PROBERT

MGP PUBLISHING

Disclaimer

This book depicts events in the author's life as truthfully as recollection permits, which he readily admits, becomes increasingly vague as the years go by. It also depicts events in the life of his fellow travellers, Mrs Janice Probert, Mrs Sarah Page, Mr Dan Silvestri, and Dr Nick Lindsay, to whom no blame should be attached for anything associated with this publication. This book is not intended to be an academic text; it aims to inform and entertain. Apart from descriptions and opinions provided by the author, this book includes information derived from many sources, including Internet research. ChatGPT and Bard have been used in the production of this book, mainly for fact verification, with all the uncertainties that contains. Many more authoritative and academic sources exist; the author's comments on historic events or current affairs provide the briefest of overviews, with the intention of providing context to the events of the journey. The information represented is believed to be correct, but that is only valid if the source and its interpretation are also correct. The publisher apologises for any errors or omissions and would be grateful to be notified of any suggestions for corrections to improve the quality of future reprints or editions of this book (please send comments via www.mgprobert.com). Occasionally, dialogue consistent with the character or nature of the person speaking has been supplemented. Some names, places, and identifying details have been changed to protect the privacy of individuals… and one seal.

'Everything you have in this world is just borrowed for a short time.'

— Welsh Proverb

This one is for you Bill

CONTENTS

ILLUSTRATIONS

'We find after years of struggle that we do not
take a trip; a trip takes us.'

– John Steinbeck

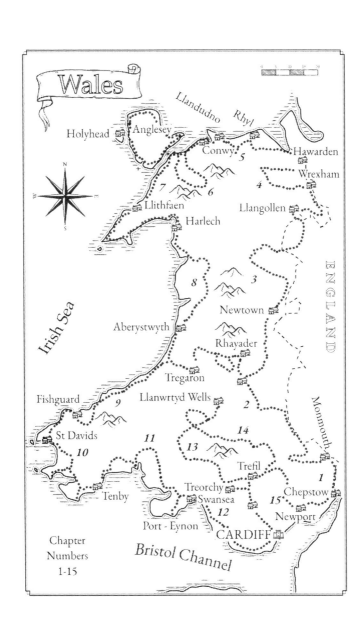

Wales

Holyhead
Anglesey
Llandudno
Rhyl
Conwy
Hawarden
Wrexham
Llithfaen
Llangollen
Harlech
Newtown
Aberystwyth
Rhayader
Tregaron
Fishguard
Llanwrtyd Wells
Monmouth
St Davids
Trefil
Tenby
Treorchy
Chepstow
Swansea
Newport
Port - Eynon
CARDIFF

Irish Sea
ENGLAND
Bristol Channel

Chapter
Numbers
1-15

PREFACE: THE IDEA

In this book, you will find a light-hearted account of a road trip taken around Wales during the summer of 2022. More accurately, it was a series of road trips which, when joined together, formed a summer-long tour of over 2000 miles. Some of the journey was made by car and some by motorcycle. If I'm being pedantic, (it has been known), some of the journey was travelled by canal boat, and 120 yards of it took place underwater in a bog.

For some of the way, I followed the route taken by the famous British travel writer HV Morton in his 1932 book, *In Search of Wales*. On his anti-clockwise car journey around Wales, the author began in Chirk, in the northeast of the country, and left shortly after passing through Monmouth, in the south. Along the way he explored various cities, towns, villages, castles, and historical sites, engaging with a broad cross-section of Welsh people. HV Morton's writing is a delightful blend of information and entertainment. His vivid descriptions and observations have a poetic charm.

Who knows where any journey will lead, or how it will end? Anything is possible. If you're on a travel adventure, that's part of the attraction. In my case, I should have known where the journey would lead because I had a map and I'd made a schedule. I even had a spreadsheet. But I knew the most interesting parts of the trip would be the ones I hadn't planned.

What follows in this book is a description of what I came across on my travels. The plan was to have an adventure. I wanted to observe a country with the eyes of an outsider, rather than taking a deep and meaningful pilgrimage 'in search of myself.' For added interest, when the opportunity arose, I could compare the Wales of 2022 with what HV Morton found and described in the book he wrote almost 90 years ago.

I hoped to discover interesting places and people, and I did. When I set out on one of my adventures, I always wonder whether crazy things will happen. They always do, as you will discover in the following pages. Over the years, the reward of experiencing those bizarre events and meeting wonderful people has fuelled the addiction that has kept me travelling. I'm not sure if I can stop.

I wanted to understand what the words 'Wales' and 'Welsh' mean today… something I regularly asked the people I met while on my journey. My trip was also a journey into the land of my fathers. Probert is a Welsh name, and my grandfather was born in the town of Pembroke Dock.

My method for planning and writing *Journey through Wales* was as follows. Being a cartographer, I naturally began with a map. I used Google Maps to plot the route that HV Morton took and the places he visited in his book. This gave me my main route, which I then modified to include other interesting things that I came across in my research.

I read several history books, including *Wales: A History* (1985) by Wynford Vaughan-Thomas, *Highlights from Welsh History* (2017) by Emrys Roberts, *The Story of Wales* (2012) by Jon Gower, and *The Celts* (1993) by Frank Delaney.

Two more books, *Wild Guide Wales* (2018) by Daniel Start and Tania Pascoe, and *Lonely Planet Wales* (2013) by Kerry Walker, Peter Dragicevich, Anna Kaminski, and Luke Waterson, provided a comprehensive guide to the classic tourist spots and some less well-known places.

I also looked at videos that described Welsh history, culture, and places of interest. Using the Internet, I looked up places of more general interest, such as the birthplaces of famous Welsh people, archaeological and historical sites, viewpoints, walks, beaches, curiosities, and night skies.

I plotted the locations I wanted to visit on my base map, along with notes for reference, and links to further information. In the end, I had a map of Wales completely covered in little blue markers. Being slightly obsessive about these things, I then colour coded the markers according to topic. UNESCO World Heritage sites were navy blue, beaches yellow etc. Some points of interest had different symbols. I say, 'in the end,' but the map kept evolving as I discovered more places to go. Despite this structured approach to route planning, impulse is often my preferred method of travel. Curiosity will often steer me around the next corner, over the ridge, or further along the road… or into trouble. People I met along the way recommended even more places to go.

The timing of my journey was based around two fixed events. I guessed the National Eisteddfod and the World Bog Snorkelling Championships would not change their dates for me, so I worked my trip around them. There was so much to see in the time I had. Visiting everywhere would have been impossible in one journey, so please be understanding if I haven't been to your favourite place.

I divided Wales into several sections, for example, The Wye Valley, The Borders, Pembrokeshire, South Wales etc., and each one of these became a separate mini-adventure or journey. I once read that it's best to travel on your own or with someone special. Using the route taken by HV Morton, changed considerably according to my planning map, I took some trips on my own, some with family members, and some with my best friend. You can meet them at the end of this book.

Because there are so many references to Welsh history in this book, and my encounters with historical events cropped up in a very random sequence during my journey, I've added a summary of Welsh history at the end of the book as a reference. It's very brief and outrageously simplified but it provides an overview that might help to keep things in context when they start to get out of hand.

As I'm writing in English, I've used the English spelling for place names. I've tried to include Welsh names in brackets when a place is first mentioned (and I apologise for any I might have missed). I'm not completely happy about this approach, but the decision is driven by a wish to be reasonably consistent. I hope to publish a Welsh language version of this book in due course. Last, being a child of the 1950s, my imperial and metric measurements are all messed up. I buy pints of beer and litres of petrol, drive for miles and measure smaller distances in metres and centimetres… or feet and inches. I suspect I'm not alone with this affliction, but I apologise in advance for the seemingly inconsistent measurement units.

Right, pre-flight checks done, let's get buckled up, and get going!

1

CHEPSTOW TO ST BRIAVELS

'Bore Da, could I have a full Welsh breakfast, please?'

I asked this, sat in a cosy little café in the heart of Chepstow, South Wales. It was an overcast Wednesday morning in May 2022, and the café had just opened its doors for another day. Only 15 minutes earlier, I'd crossed the border, stepping into the land of song and seafood-enriched early morning meals. I had chosen the words for my breakfast order carefully, a dash of the Welsh language as a nod to my new surroundings, followed by a polite request for a traditional Welsh dish.

'What's one of those?' came the quick reply from a woman midway through setting up tables. She was from Bristol.

It was my first day on a four-month long adventure, and my early morning experience was a little reminder about assumptions. Why should I expect someone in Wales to be Welsh and for a Welsh café to serve a Welsh breakfast? I'd told myself to keep an open mind, but on every journey, including life, we carry with us the additional baggage of our own assumptions, expectations, and biases. We don't even know we are carrying most of them.

The delicious eggs Benedict breakfast that followed set me up for the day and would not have been out of place in a

Master Chef final. I got to sample a Welsh breakfast later on my trip, in Swansea. It's like a full English fry-up breakfast of eggs, bacon, sausage, tomatoes, mushrooms, and beans, but the Welsh version comes with cockles and laverbread. The latter is made from seaweed and there are people who refer to it as a delicacy.

A quarter of an hour earlier, just before 8:00 am on a dull and overcast, early summer morning, I had left England behind, somewhere on the Severn Road Bridge, and begun my *Journey through Wales*. Passing over the River Wye (Afon Gwy) at about 50 miles per hour on a Royal Enfield Himalayan motorcycle, I'd arrived in a different country. I didn't feel a thing. There was no bump as I crossed the border, no customs check, not even a road sign to mark the event. That last section of the Severn Bridge in Wales looked a lot like the first part, but by then it had become the Pont Hafren.

My plan for the day was to get to Chepstow (Cas-gwent), park my motorcycle, find some breakfast, and look around the town. In the afternoon, I'd trek along the high banks of the Wye Valley (Dyffryn Gwy) up to Tintern (Tyndyrn) and then return to Chepstow by bus to retrieve my motorcycle. Depending on time, I'd then drop into some of those pretty little Wye Valley villages on my way to an overnight stop at the youth hostel (I'm a very youthful pensioner) at St Briavels, about halfway between Chepstow and Monmouth (Trefynwy). I'd planned my first day around that overnight stay – in a haunted medieval castle.

After leaving the Severn Bridge on the A466, the first clues that I was in a new country were the Red Route Clearway signs telling me 'Dim Stopio.' At the first roundabout, a large road sign greeted me to Wales and Monmouthshire (Sir Fynwy). By then, I was already feeling a tingle of familiarity. Previous generations of my family lived in the Wye Valley, and whether it's real or imagined, I always seem to experience a warm feeling of contentment when I return to one of my favourite parts of Britain. It was the obvious place for me to begin and end my Welsh adventure, and on a practical level, it was also the nearest part of Wales to my home in Dorset. If my understanding of the word is correct (always a good caveat), I might have been feeling a mild dose of what Welsh people call 'hiraeth.' The word has no direct English equivalent, but it conveys a feeling of belonging, security, and nostalgia for your home.

Five minutes after crossing the Welsh border, I was entering Chepstow and on the lookout for somewhere to stopio. Chepstow is famous for two things: having the oldest surviving stone castle in Britain, and Chepstow Races, home to the Welsh Grand National. It's a small town of just over 12,500 people on the lower reaches of the River Wye. At that point, the river is nearly at its end. It thrashes from side to side in extravagant wide loops as if struggling in its death throes before submitting to the struggle and entering the River Severn a few miles further south.

The first Welsh town on my *Journey through Wales* has had an English name from at least the beginning of the 14th century, based on the old English 'ceap stowe,' which meant 'marketplace.' The current name, Chepstow, took over from the name Striguil (or Estrighoiel) used by the Normans, based on the Welsh word, 'ystraigyl,' meaning a bend in the river. When William the Conqueror's army invaded Britain in 1066, Chepstow was soon identified as a key strategic location. The precipitous limestone cliffs that tower over the River Wye provided the excellent defensive protection that's always high on the list of priorities for any serious castle builder. Within a year, construction of the castle was underway, and it became one of the Norman's first strongholds in Wales.

The port of Chepstow lay far enough upriver to protect its people from stormy waters, but still within easy reach of the sea for anyone requiring a quick getaway. With its favourable geo-political location, it rapidly grew in importance, and by the Middle Ages it was the largest port in Wales. The castle became the southernmost of a chain of fortifications built in the hotly disputed border lands of the Welsh Marches, about which, there will be more later.

Many historians believe that British tourism began in the Wye Valley. As the first place to witness the Industrial Revolution, Britain also led the way with many social changes. With increasing wealth and free time, some lucky people could afford to travel just for fun. In the 1750s, Reverend John Egerton of Ross on Wye entertained guests with river trips and before long other people offered similar boat rides. The 'Wye Tour' became a popular route with pleasant hotels, knowledgeable guides, and stops for visitors to admire the views.

In 1782, William Gilpin published Britain's first tour guide with the catchy title, *Observations on the River Wye and Several Parts of South Wales etc., Relative Chiefly to Picturesque Beauty*. Inspired by the wonderful landscape, the tour attracted romantic travellers and artists of all types, including Turner, Coleridge, and Wordsworth. The ghostly remains of Tintern Abbey were a favourite landmark. A combination of improved roads, a cost-of-living crisis, and Napoleon's special military operations in mainland Europe made the Wye Tour a popular and much safer alternative to the Grand Tour on the continent. More than a century before a cheap week in Torremolinos became all the rage, the first package tour had been invented.

Arriving somewhere near the centre of Chepstow, I found myself in a car park bordered by the town's 13th century medieval walls. The 'Port Walls' were built to protect the landward side of the old town, which occupies a promontory that pokes out into one of those extravagant loops that the River Wye makes in its lower reaches. It was still early as I emerged onto the town's main street and there were few signs of life. I took a walk around almost deserted streets to get my bearings, while I waited for somewhere to open for breakfast. I arrived at a pleasant, tree-lined area in the centre of town. It had a friendly feel, or maybe it was a touch of that hiraeth working its magic.

A small 'A-frame' advertising sign placed on the pavement outside a café caught my eye. Complete with a mouth-watering photograph, the advert read, 'Rhubarb and Custard Slice – Custard not sold separately.' I took a few moments of philosophical contemplation as I considered the vexed history of pudding procurement that must have necessitated such a caveat.

As I pondered that mystery, for some reason, I felt myself drawn to the Ugly Mug Café. As I enjoyed my breakfast and watched the world go by, a group of six golfers on their way to a game came into the café and sat at the table next to me. There was a mixture of pre-competition nervous laughter and friendly teasing as they teed off for their fry-up breakfasts. In between mouthfuls, the boys focused on establishing a mutu-ally agreed understanding of the rules of Texas Scramble; old wounds were being opened up from previous interpretations.

A nice elderly couple came into the café. When I say elderly, I mean they were even older than me. One of the women servers greeted them with a friendly smile and asked them, 'The usual today?' The chap pulled his face mask down to his chin to reveal an unfortunate dew drop hanging from the end of his nose. I hoped it was more to do with the fresh morning air than any health-related issues. His wife removed her mask to reveal a rosy complexion; perhaps they'd walked up the hill from the river end of the town. She said little but smiled a lot. In a softly spoken voice, the husband told the waitress about the couple's latest council tax demand. The waitress listened patiently, nodding, or smiling, and sometimes both when extra reassurance seemed appropriate. To the lovely couple, her financial advice and kind supportive words were just as valuable as the pot of tea they enjoyed. Before I left the café, I asked the waitress if she thought Chepstow was a Welsh town. 'Oh yes, 100%,' she quickly replied, before going into detail to justify her scoring.

I didn't need to ask her if she was Welsh; I could hear the song in her voice.

I headed down Hocker Hill, a cobbled Roman way, towards the castle. I continued past some characterful old almshouses and alongside the Georgian frontage of Castle Terrace. Sat patiently awaiting collection outside the door of one house was something I've not seen for decades – 2 pints of milk in proper glass milk bottles. How charming! I had a brief nostalgic flashback to what seems like the less complicated and more civilised world of my childhood. Without inviting him in, I also had Ernie in my head for the next half an hour singing about the fastest milkman in the West. Perhaps I should explain – I sometimes see or hear something that triggers a tune or song from the jukebox in my head. I don't do anything to start it, it's an automatic reaction, and I often don't notice what triggered it. The tune or song then hangs around on replay for anything from 10 minutes to most of the day. I'm sure I'm not alone with this affliction, and I dare say there are support groups out there that could help (I need somebody, help, not just anybody…).

I arrived at a large car park between the castle and the museum. Before storming the fortifications, I popped into the tourist information office. Three lovely ladies were more than happy to tell me all about the town and its attractions. Before I left, I asked if they considered themselves to be Welsh. The first one declared she wasn't, she was born in England. The second said she was Welsh and Chepstow *was* a Welsh town. So far, so good. But then the third told me that in the past, the area had been neither English nor Welsh. She explained that historically (for simplicity's sake, let's say during the Middle Ages) the area was part of the Marches, which were neither English nor Welsh. Good, that's cleared that up then! We'd probably call it non-binary border fluidity these days. It's confusing, but I'll explain more in the next chapter. Before I left, I mentioned my book and asked the three women if they had any quirky things to tell me about the area. Blank expressions were shared all round. After a slight pause, one of them said 'Oh yes, there is one thing…'

What followed over the next few minutes was one of the most unusual stories that I've ever heard. It certainly qualifies as quirky. It was about a Chicago doctor named Orville Ward Owen back in the early 1900s. He was an extraordinary character, who is said to have been so obsessed with the writings of Shakespeare that he memorised the author's entire works. That formidable feat of data storage, combined with a curious analytical mind, led him to identify some unusual repetitions in the texts. He also spotted examples of what he saw as factual errors. His research led him to the many theories concerning the authorship of Shakespeare's works. Over the years, there have been many ideas put forward on this theme, some more credible than others. One of the more interesting suggestions is that the works were a collaborative effort produced by a few members of Elizabethan high society. Sir Walter Raleigh, Edmund Spenser, and Sir Francis Bacon (alleged to be the secret son of Queen Elizabeth I) have all been proposed as potential contributors. One theory suggests they embedded secret encrypted text in the works. The hidden messages related to radical political and philosophical ideas… controversial concepts at the time that couldn't be expressed openly. It sounds crazy – but wait; it gets so much better.

Dr Owen is said to have built a 'cipher wheel' made of two large cylindrical spools onto which were pasted the entire works of Shakespeare, and some other texts for good measure. Why not? He cranked the wheels, did the 'math,' and in 1893, out popped a book called *Sir Francis Bacon's Cipher Story*. This is where the craziness factor gets wound up several notches. According to the story, Dr Owen sold up all his assets in America and headed to the Wye Valley in 1909 to search for the lost works of Shakespeare – or whoever wrote and lost them. I imagine him arriving as an Indiana Jones look-alike complete with fedora, leather jacket, khaki trousers, and cracking a whip. Following instructions deciphered from his wheels, he eventually uncovered an underground vault beneath the bed of the River Wye. That alone is remarkable… such stuff as dreams are made on!

So, was it to be, or not to be? The vault was empty… a temple of gloom. It wasn't Dr Owen's finest day. But then he found more coded messages on the walls of the chamber (allegedly) and the quest continued. Some versions of this story have him finding a metal trunk on the riverbed. The disappointing upshot of all this was that the poor man eventually became financially and physically ruined by his unfruitful search. He sadly did not achieve greatness, or have greatness thrust upon him. He died, aged seventy, seen by some as a figure of ridicule, with the mystery still unresolved.

I stepped back out to the car park, glanced across to the river, and wondered what secrets might still lie below its swirling and muddy waters. The Dr Owen story was less Indiana Jones and more like a bizarre sub-plot from a Dan Brown novel. It deserves to be made into a movie. A conspiracy theory spanning centuries, mysterious codes, an illegitimate heir to the English throne, beautiful Welsh scenery, and the world's greatest ever playwright – part of me wants to believe it. I'm sure Hollywood would… Tom Hanks, where are you?

When it comes to castles, there are so many to visit. With over 600 in Wales, you need to guard against castle fatigue. After William the Conqueror invaded Britain in 1066, his army swept through an England that was largely unified under Anglo-Saxon rule. Wales was a different matter. It presented more of a challenge, with difficult terrain to overcome and a diverse collection of tribes and communities that were well used to regular fighting. The Normans knew they were up against a formidable foe, so when they built the castle at Chepstow a year after the invasion, they made it fit for purpose. Firstly, they constructed it from stone rather than from wood. Secondly, they positioned it to allow access inland into Wales and the West of England, but also to provide its defenders with a quick getaway if required – an easy escape to the sea and the safety of England or Normandy.

Chepstow Castle

As I was buying my admission ticket for the castle, a fearsome cry rang out from inside the grounds. Glancing inside, across finely manicured green lawns, I saw two medieval warriors running towards the castle walls. They were waving long swords and trying not to trip over their shields. Nothing to see there then.

A party of thirty school children sat on the grass and watched as two grownups, experts in Tudor history, described life in the mid-16th century. The mixed class of twelve-year-olds were commendably well behaved. I walked nearer and sat down on a bench to get a free history lecture. The class became quite animated when one of the experts picked out one of the kids and a young male teacher to provide a demonstration. They were then both dressed up in chain mail and helmets. The young lad was given an impressive sword, and they armed the poor teacher with a much less impressive pike. The rest of the class thought this was hilarious, and the banter was soon flying. A serious-looking member of staff swiftly admonished one lad, who shouted out, 'Come on, Adam, this might be your only chance to kill a teacher.'

I'm always on the lookout for a longest, oldest, biggest, etc, so you can imagine my delight when I discovered that Chepstow Castle has the oldest castle doors in Europe, dating back to around 1190. Anyone visiting should note that the doors currently hanging in the gatehouse are replicas. The originals are inside the castle for safekeeping. By using advanced shipbuilding techniques and iron plating, the doors were revolutionary in their day.

The castle presents its historical growth in a nicely arranged chronological order. You move through time as you walk from one addition to the next. Over the years, they just added to the existing parts using new technologies and building methodologies, rather than knocking the old bits down to start again.

After a tour of the castle, from which there are stunning views of the river, I headed for a quick look round the museum, just over the road. Ahead of me, also approaching the front door, was a man dressed immaculately in a black velvet jacket and breeches, a white tunic shirt, and black stockings. His shiny black shoes had what looked like extravagant pearl buckles – and he carried a sword. He was incredibly smart, but I couldn't let it go… I had to politely ask who he was. I felt slightly embarrassed (no change there) when he explained he was a County High Sheriff on an official visit. He seemed keen to emphasise the fact that he was visiting Chepstow with the permission of the High Sheriff of Gwent… not that I'd have been bothered if he was just dropping in for a casual cup of tea and a chat. He could have bought custard separately, as far as I was concerned, but I assume his exaggerated deference to the local sheriff was in acknowledgement of some long-standing historical protocol.

The woman at the reception desk of the museum was exceptionally helpful, patiently answering all my daft questions. When I asked her about the port's tradition of salmon fishing, she pointed me towards one of the old fishing boats, preserved in a building at the back of the museum. Apparently, you can still see salmon in the river nowadays. They seem to be the favourite meal of the seals that swim up as far as the old town bridge. I was told they were now breeding, and pups had recently been seen near the Severn Bridge. I also found out that peregrines were nesting in the cliffs near the castle.

I was keen to get started on my walk along the Wye Valley Path, but before I set off, I headed down Bridge Street to look at the river, the old harbour, and the old bridge. With my legs astride the national border in the centre of Chepstow Bridge (I'm easily amused), I was standing on the largest surviving cast iron bridge from the early 1800s. Built in 1816, the structure was once the third largest cast iron road bridge in the world. I watched as the river flowed strongly past below my feet. Only two places in the world (both in Canada) have greater astronomical tides than Chepstow and the tide rise is the fastest on Earth – it can rise 13 metres in 4 hours! I like to combine a stat attack or record breaker with my visits.

I got my boots on and made my way to the riverside start of the Wye Valley Walk. It heads north for 136 miles from Chepstow, following the river to its source in Mid Wales, on the slopes of Plynlimon (Pumlumon). My starting point seemed to be a spaghetti junction of long-distance walking trails. I was also standing on the Offa's Dyke footpath. It headed south a short distance to the River Severn, but the bulk of the 177 miles route went north to the North Wales coastal town of Prestatyn. The path follows the embankment that Offa, King of Mercia, ordered to be constructed to protect his lands from rival kingdoms in what is now Wales. The same riverside spot was also near to one end of the Wales Coastal Path, which you can follow around the entire coastline of Wales. Despite such a bewildering choice of trails, I decided to content myself with a 7-mile taster stroll, hugging the west (Welsh) side of the river as far as Tintern Abbey (Abaty Tyndyrn). From there, I'd get the bus back to Chepstow.

I followed well signposted paths and climbed the riverside route out of Chepstow towards the racecourse. Looking back at the town, in which I'd just spent a very satisfying morning, I noticed what a mixed architectural bag it is. It's not the prettiest place, but to paraphrase Nessa from *Gavin and Stacey*, 'When all's said and done… it's tidy.'

Following the trail out of town, I passed an infant's school. The children were out playing under the watchful eye of their teacher. I mustered up my very cheeriest 'Good morning,' as I passed. The teacher looked back, smiled, and gave me an equally cheery, 'Bore da.' At first, I wasn't sure if she was putting me in my place, but her smile looked genuine and her tone friendly. I was probably over-thinking it; I should just learn and use some more Welsh.

I was walking through the Wye Valley Area of Outstanding Natural Beauty (AONB). The trail was easy to follow, dry, and although there were a few steep parts, it was mostly level. The river flowed past far below on my right, at the bottom of towering cliffs. I strolled through an early summer carpet of wildflowers including bluebells, primroses, honeysuckle, buttercups, and wood anemones. The mixed forest included some oak, ash, birch, and larch, but it is the vivid green leaves of the beech trees that spring to mind when I think back to that walk. Shards of bright sunlight pierced the forest cover to provide a shower of early summer energy for my forest bathing.

Shortly after leaving Chepstow, you come across the ruined shell of the neoclassical Piercefield House. The once splendid late 18th century Georgian country house has seen better days and is now fenced off to save the inquisitive from their own curiosity. I can relate to that. Looking back over the years, I have quite a history when it comes to prohibited places… but I won't go there.

Heading back through the woods, I rejoined the Wye Valley Walk. Shortly after I'd found my way back to the path in the woods, I noticed a strange cupola-like construction in a brick wall, a few metres to my left. I went to investigate. It was something water related – possibly an overflow valve, but Victorian plumbing infrastructure isn't really my thing. Behind the brick wall was quite a large but sadly discarded ornamental pond and gardens, which must have once been part of the Piercefield Estate. Next to an area of garden flowers, including a charming patch of red tulips, a previous explorer had laid a few shards of discarded bone china on the ground. It prompted my imagination to conjure up a garden party scene from the days when Piercefield House must have been the go-to local meeting place for high-class Victorian society types. I envisaged a few thin-waisted ladies dressed in their best refinery, all flowing cotton dresses with high necklines and puffed sleeves. Perching on the edge of their seats to accommodate their extravagant bustles, they would have been admiring the water lilies on a simply splendid afternoon, each of them sipping their tea, with their little fingers extended as they chatted politely about the eligible bachelors on the Wye Tour.

I munched my way through half a dozen leaves of wild garlic as I walked – more to boost my badass outdoor woodsman image than for any calorific benefit, which I imagine would have been close to zero. I ticked off the landmarks along the way. Lover's Leap was soon followed by Giant's Cave, but the high point of the walk, and also the highest point, came just over halfway. The Eagle's Nest is a must-visit. It has to be in my top twenty views in Britain (and I've seen a lot in six decades). It's that good! In the distance, looking eastwards, you can see the River Severn, the town of Chepstow, the two Severn Bridges, and in the far distance, the Cotswolds. It's possible to see seven counties on a clear day. A huge loop in the River Wye, over 200 metres below, curls its way almost full circle, with the high limestone cliffs of Wintour's Leap in the middle distance. The poet, Coleridge, who knew a romantic scene when he saw one, described the view as 'The whole world imaged in its vast circumference.' If you're travelling on the A466 along the Wye Valley, there is a relatively short and easy walk to the viewpoint from the Upper Wyndcliff car park between Tintern and St Arvans.

My walk was all downhill from the Eagle's Nest, as far as Tintern. I had expected some high-level views of the abbey, but they never really happened because of the lie of the land and the amount of woodland. On the last stretch down to the village, you walk past a couple of 18th century limekilns. They used charcoal from coppiced woodlands and local stone to produce lime for use as a building material and for agricultural purposes.

And so, I eventually arrived in Tintern, a place that always feels magical to me, as if its historic events, perhaps in some other dimension, are still crackling away in the atmosphere. The holy hands of the Cistercian order laid the foundations of Tintern Abbey in 1131. The original structure, hewn from wood, was eventually superseded by one of stone, a monument to British Gothic architecture. But in the decade following 1536, during the dissolution of the monasteries, Henry VIII's henchmen – led by the destructive wrecking ball that was Thomas Cromwell, wrought havoc and destroyed much of the abbey. Monasteries across Britain crumbled at a rate of fifty per month, their architectural beauty lost forever. The stately remnants of Tintern Abbey serve as a sombre reminder of the Tudor power grab and the seismic shifts in the authority of the Church and the monarchy. The ruins are truly a breathtaking spectacle. Despite its destruction, the roofless shell of the abbey endures, its walls now echoing the cries of crows and jackdaws rather than the serene and lofty chants of Cistercian monks.

To see the rural calm of Tintern today, there's hardly a hint of its industrial past. It's hard to believe now, but in the 16th, 17th, and 18th centuries, the two old lime kilns I'd seen earlier were once part of a semi-industrial landscape. Numerous forges and furnaces dotted the valley. A plaque on a wall by the abbey reads, 'Near this place in the year 1568 brass was first made by alloying copper with zinc.' It seems Tintern played its part when the Industrial Revolution took off, and it was the first place to make wire on an industrial scale, including the first transatlantic cable. With those industries now long gone, it's the leisure industry again that has become important to the area – a reminder of the days of the Wye Tour.

I checked the times for the bus back to Chepstow. Perfect. A forty-five-minute wait gave me just enough time to grab something to eat and drink. Sat outside the Anchor Inn, in the shadow of the abbey, I was still buzzing from the walk as I wrote up a few notes. I was so pleased that I'd made myself walk a section of the valley for a change, instead of dashing through it by vehicle, like I usually do. It was good to slow down and enjoy the wonderful views and woodlands. I thought about Wordsworth's poem, 'Tintern Abbey,' in which he considers the timelessness of nature and the relentless cycle of the seasons. He compares it with the finite nature of our brief human existence. I grabbed my bus pass and headed for the bus-stop, suddenly aware of my time running out.

I was the only passenger aboard the bus as it headed south to Chepstow. My twenty-minute ride, by then in bright sunshine, took me back to almost exactly where I'd begun my walk 3 hours earlier.

There were one or two villages I wanted to explore before I made my way to St Briavels (sounds like St Brevvels) to stay overnight. A chance to look into my family history was the excuse to visit the quiet little village of Penallt, about 9 miles north of Chepstow on the Welsh side of the Wye Valley. Although its name derives from the Welsh for 'Top of the wooded hill,' the area is now predominantly agricultural –

and *very* quiet. The village is scattered over several square miles and Penallt Old Church, which I was heading to see, lies a mile or so from the main village centre. Halfway up a steep hill, under an old chestnut tree, I came across the base of an ancient stone cross. A notice on it told me it was a resting place – where pallbearers rested their coffin and sang a psalm as they struggled up the hill towards Penallt Old Church. I carried on and just when I thought I must have missed it, there it was. In an achingly beautiful setting, the tiny 12th century church looked perfect. Its size and proportions were faultless, and I could see the sloping graveyard had recently been a sea of daffodil blooms. The view down to the river, which meanders serenely and silently 200 metres below, is spectacular. Inside the church, I found several family history leads, including a family crest on a stained-glass window. At the opposite end of the village, as I headed back towards the river, I passed a grand-looking building called The Argoed. Parts of it go back to the 16th century when it was built by the Probert family. They say Bernard Shaw was a regular visitor and wrote some of his plays there. In the 1980s, The Argoed was owned by Robert Plant of Led Zeppelin. I wound on down the road. And it made me wonder. Stairway to Heaven would be on continuous loop in my head for at least an hour before fading away quietly and then bursting back onto the scene in Chapter Eight.

I rode my motorcycle south to Whitebrook, and as I crossed the River Wye at Bigswear Bridge, I entered Gloucestershire. From there, it was only 3 miles to the village of St Briavels. Don't laugh, but for the first night of my *Journey through Wales*, I'd be sleeping in England, although around these parts the village was probably in Wales at some point in its history. I took that liberty for the chance of an overnight stay in a moated 12th century Norman castle… and those opportunities don't come round often.

The small village of St Briavels sits on a ridge, 200 metres above the River Wye. The old motte (the small hill in the grounds of the castle) is nowadays just a tiny stump but in Norman times it would have been high enough to provide a view right down to the river. During the early 13th century, King John used to stopover at St Briavels on his hunting trips in the Forest of Dean. It was also used as an administrative and judicial centre for the area. After King John's death, King Edward I, not the most popular figure in Welsh history, re-purposed the castle into a factory to make iron bolts for cross-bows. He used the armaments for his crusades and for invading Wales in 1277. Determined to establish English supremacy over Wales, Edward I built a string of castles and introduced the English legal and administrative framework. I'll come back to that later. Over the years, St Briavels Castle changed roles several more times. It was a debtor's prison for a while, then a private residence, and now it belongs to the Youth Hostel Association (YHA). As well as providing overnight accommodation for ageing youths like me, it helps to teach real youngsters about life in Norman times. School groups tour the castle and learn history in a fun way through activities such as bread making and archery. Oh, and the castle is famous for something else… it has been described as the most haunted castle in England.

As I checked in, I asked about the castle's history and its reputation for ghosts. It seems there have been reports of ghosts in just about every room, so no one should feel left out. My room for the night was called King John's room. The friendly hostel warden, Linda, reassured me that the monarch of Magna Carta fame probably never actually slept in the room – he would have just eaten there, because it used to be part of the old banqueting hall. I think that was meant to reassure me. Linda was charming and could not have been more helpful. She kindly agreed to give me a brief tour of the castle later.

After dinner, Linda and I set off with Nigel and Gay, two more youths of retirement age, who were brave enough to stay the night. We started our tour in what is now known as the banquet hall. In times gone by, it was a courtroom. Notches carved into the stone sides of the fireplace mark the occasions when prisoners were sentenced to death. It was possible to make out seventeen such judgements – mostly for what today would be petty offences. The gibbet (a wooden structure that was used to hang people) erected outside the castle walls and conveniently opposite the church, served as a grim reminder to the local populace of the consequences of misdeeds.

Many visitors to the youth hostel have reported disturbing crying sounds coming from the old courtroom. During reno-vations, the mummified body of a baby was uncovered. One theory suggests that hundreds of years ago they sometimes placed dead babies in chimneys because a pure spirit was thought to fend off evil ones. Despite being given a proper burial, the poor restless soul continues to cry at night – allegedly. Linda told us about one overnight guest in the youth hostel, who apparently didn't know this story, but who commented on the morning after her stay: 'Thank goodness that baby eventually stopped crying last night!' There were no children staying overnight.

From the banquet hall, we made our way to the former chapel, now serving as a guest lounge, where one might relax with a brew or a soft drink. Tempting though it was, I behaved myself and refrained from asking if they served spir-its. We proceeded to the guardroom and the prison, with Linda regaling us with an intriguing blend of hair-raising ghost stories and historical factoids. The atmosphere was tense and captivating, the details almost overwhelming. Now transformed into comfortable lodgings for guests, the prison was the most eerie room of all – as if the anguish of genera-tions past had seeped into the very walls, the despair of its former inhabitants still palpable in the air. The medieval graf-fiti carved into the stones told a tale of both hope and despair. A windmill and a sailing vessel, drawn with child-like simplicity, rekindled memories of a brighter world beyond, but a quote dated 1667, etched into the window frame read, 'My days are weary, my time has come…' It was another poignant reminder of the transience of all things.

Given its legacy as a former bastion of punishment and suffering, it was no shock that the prison – more than any other part of the castle – was said to be rife with tales of supernatural occurrences. This is the most haunted room in the most haunted of castles. They say a lady in grey occupies the room… when she's not wandering the corridors. These stories had us all transfixed, hanging on Linda's every word with nervous anticipation. As she began another spooky anecdote, the enormous door to the prison slowly creaked open. We all looked round towards it and the room fell silent. I tensed myself, eyes fixed on the door as I prepared to have the life frightened out of me. Considerably less scary than the Grey Lady, it was the hostel's housekeeping supervisor, who was looking for our tour guide to ask about arrangements for breakfast.

Our tour ended down in the old kitchen. By now, we just accepted that each room came with its own set of ghostly spirits. Apparently, the one in the kitchen is called Tom, and he's friendly. He clatters about a bit and often leaves remnants of ceiling mortar on the floor overnight, although I'm inclined to think that's possibly just wear and tear. Linda showed us the old turnspit. It's a ring doughnut shaped cage that sits on the wall, just above head height, about a metre in diameter and the width of a small dog. At the time of King John, they used child labour to turn a spit over the fire to ensure the joint of meat cooked evenly. Health and Safety Officers of the time decided that these ten-hour shifts were no way to treat kids, so someone came up with the new must-have kitchen accessory of the day – a turnspit. They hoisted a special breed of dog into the metal cylinder to power the wheel. The dog would walk like a gerbil on a treadmill for hours on end (this was before the invention of slow cookers or animal welfare charities), while a chain linked to the spit slowly turned the meat for the evening meal. We were told that the dogs got to know when their ten-hour shift was up and would bark to let the chef know when the next dog was required. What an amazing tour and what an amazing tour guide!

After the castle tour, I retreated to the old chapel, where I had a very enjoyable hour chatting with fellow guests Nigel and Gay. They were from Cardiff (Caerdydd), so I was able to do some research for my book by asking them about their home city and their country. It was Nigel who explained the word 'hiraeth' to me.

You might be wondering where my travelling companion HV Morton has got to. Although he seems to have visited Chepstow and the Wye Valley according to the map in his book, he writes nothing about them. In fact, he describes very little about the last section of his tour, from Cardiff to the English border near Gloucester. He also missed out most of the east side of Wales, along the English border. We'll have to wait until Chirk, in Chapter 3 to meet up with him, but don't worry, he has plenty to say after that.

At the end of a day full of contrasting experiences I wandered off to bed. It had been a relaxing day in the Wye Valley – but I was wondering how disturbed my night was going to be.

2

ST BRIAVELS TO RHAYADER

I awoke on day two of my *Journey through Wales*, fortified by a night in a castle. Spirits were high, although I'd seen nothing ghostly during my overnight stay. The lost souls of St Briavels must have had a night off. The only sounds I'd heard were echoes of an ancient building and its ancient central heating pipes.

Breakfast in a youth hostel is something I always look forward to. A cooked breakfast is a rare treat. The Kitchen Manager at St Briavels hostel was a lovely lady, who told me all about her passion for nature and the environment. She'd embarked on an Open University course to learn more and was brimming with enthusiasm. She told me all about it as she rustled up my full English breakfast. Also enjoying the delights of a proper fry-up that morning were four motorcyclists for whom the castle was a pit stop on their tour of the Wye Valley's green lanes and byways. Their mud splattered motorbikes were resting in the courtyard outside, leaning against each other wearily, as if they'd had a hard time the day before. The bikers were middle-aged 'lads' from the Midlands, who were enjoying a laugh with each other as they also leaned against each other wearily, comparing pains, aches, and minor injuries from the previous days' off-road riding. As they hobbled to and from the breakfast buffet table, I asked one if he'd slept OK. 'No ghostly disturbances?' I asked. Raising his voice so everyone could hear, and glancing round to make sure his mates were all listening, he said, 'Well actually I *did* hear something.' With a slow and deliberate delivery, milking the moment, he said he thought he'd seen the ghost of Gloria Gaynor. With well-practised comic timing, he paused briefly before adding, 'First I was afraid, I was petrified…' As a mixture of forced laughter and groans died away, another of the boys piped up. He claimed to have seen the Grey Lady. Apparently, she'd try to persuade him the castle had a ghost in every room. He said, 'She didn't fool me though, I could see right through her.' More groans. Not to be outdone, a third member of the gang told everyone he was thinking of sending a postcard to tell his wife all about the castle, before delivering his punchline: 'I'm thinking of using a ghost writer.' Even more groans erupted as new depths of schoolboy humour were plumbed. The fourth member of the group was above all that. He sat unmoved with a slight grimace on his face as he suffered his mates' attempts at comedy. Working his way methodically through his muesli, he rolled his eyes with every punchline.

I wasn't expecting to be so richly entertained over break-fast and it put me in a good mood for the start of my second day – back into Wales again. The plan for the second day of my journey was to complete my visit to the Wye Valley and then continue on my anticlockwise route around the perimeter of Wales by skirting along part of the eastern border with England. First, though, I wanted to visit the Devil's Pulpit, a prominent outcrop on the high limestone cliffs of the Wye, quite close to the youth hostel. The pulpit is on the English side, overlooking Tintern Abbey on the Welsh side. A lazy 4-mile ride down the B4228 from St Briavels towards Chepstow brought me to the car park of the Tidenham Chase Nature Reserve. From there, a footpath heads off west, through the mixed woodlands of the reserve and then open farmland. To visit the viewpoint it's only about a mile each way and you even have the bonus of passing an Ordnance Survey (OS) Triangulation Point (199 metres) on your way. The walk there and back to the riverbank was easy-going and well worth the effort. Just before you reach the viewpoint, you come across the massive earth bank of Offa's Dyke, which at that point isn't the national border – that's further on and more than 200 metres below you, in the middle of the river.

From the flat table-top of the Devil's Pulpit, polished by many devils' feet over the years, there's a fabulous view down to Tintern Abbey, which lies upriver on the opposite bank. A noticeboard near the landmark tells visitors how, according to legend, the Devil used to preach from his 'pulpit' to seduce the monks from the monastery far below to join him. One ponders on the origins of these fables. Did they stem from a particularly boozy evening of monkish revelry on the mead? Or could it be that the abbey's human resources division put the story out there, seeking to foster a sense of foreboding in the monks, thus deterring them from succumbing to enticements beyond the confines of their devotion?

I carried on to Monmouth, a busy Welsh market town with a population of just under 11,000. It lies on the confluence of the River Wye and River Monnow (Afon Mynwy), about 2 miles inside the border with England. The town centre is steeped in history and has over 400 listed buildings. Reassuringly, it is thought to be the birthplace of Geoffrey of Monmouth, somewhere around 1095. That's mainly because he himself said he was born there, and frankly, with a name like that, you'd be disappointed if he'd been born anywhere else. Geoffrey is a bit of a mysterious character, but his books on the history of Britain provide some of our earliest sources. They combine the works of monks like Bede and Gildas, with output from Roman historians, poems from Welsh bards, and oral stories that have been passed down through generations.

Geoffrey is remembered for his romantic tales of the mystical King Arthur and his wizard sidekick, Merlin, prophet, sorcerer, and mystic messenger. Geoffrey wasn't averse to bigging up the Welsh, and through Merlin, he provided prophesies for the future. For many years, books like his Middle Ages blockbuster *Historia Regum Britanniae* (a historical chronicle of the kings of the Britons covering 2000 years) were treated as undisputed fact, but many historians now believe Geoffrey's vivid imagination may have played a large part in stitching the various sources together into a unified narrative. One part of his life that seems undisputed is his consecration as Bishop of St Asaph in North Wales in 1152. The city and cathedral of St Asaph were on my agenda for later in my journey.

Monmouth is home to Britain's only fortified bridge, the medieval Monnow Bridge and Gate. The red sandstone bridge, known locally as Pont Trefynwy, was built in 1272 to replace the former Norman timber bridge. Originally intended to defend the town, it has also been used as a toll bridge and a jail. It's an impressive sight. Although Monmouth only gets a brief mention, it was on this bridge that HV Morton concluded his book, *In Search of Wales*. I could imagine him stood on the Monnow Bridge, misty eyed as he stared into the waters of the river rushing beneath him. He was saying goodbye to a country and people who had clearly touched his heart during his long journey. Mine was only just beginning.

Henry V, also known as Henry of Monmouth, was born at Monmouth Castle in 1387. As Prince of Wales, he spent 8 years leading English armies against the rebel leader/freedom fighter, Owain Glyndŵr. More about him later. When Henry V became king in 1413, aged twenty-six, he was the first to use English as his first language. Since the Norman invasion, French had been the spoken language of the royals. He seems to have spent most of his 9 years as king scrapping with the French, and he is best remembered for defeating the French army at Agincourt, on 25th October 1415, with his band of brothers. Henry's army was massively outnumbered, but a decisive factor in his favour was the skill and accuracy of his archers, of which up to 500 were Welsh, many recruited from Monmouthshire. Most outlived that day and came safely home to be remembered.

When I was planning my *Journey through Wales*, I divided the trip into bite-size chunks. The overall pattern of the route was a meandering anticlockwise circuit of the country, similar to the route taken by HV Morton back in the 1930s. I also factored in several diversions from that main itinerary, to visit other places that looked interesting. On only my second day, I was taking the first of those detours, and it led me into the heart of Wales.

Leaving Monmouth, my route for the day took me first to Abergavenny (Y Fenni), and then up through the Black Mountains to Hay-on-Wye (Y Gelli Gandryll). Continuing northwest, my route was via Builth Wells (Llanfair-ym-Muallt) to Rhayader (Rhaeadr Gwy), where a two-night stopover would allow me time to visit the Elan Valley (Dyffryn Elan) and surrounding area in the heart of the Cambrian Mountains (Mynyddoedd Cambria).

Ignoring the A40 superhighway to Abergavenny, I took the more peaceful B4233 that runs almost parallel to the trunk road, from east to west, but a few miles further north. I felt so lucky that it was another beautiful morning, not realising then how 'glorious day' would become the default weather description for most of my trip. Nature was deploying its most vibrant colour palette. Fields of pasture had that bright and fresh, early summer look, and the hedges were showing off their best new green coat. Brightly coloured wildflowers sprinkled in a milky sea of white cow parsley decorated the roadside verges.

Sorry to spoil the moment, but... do you ever think about those colours? They're not there, are they? They're in our heads. Our brains create colours based on the light reflected from objects we see. Colour doesn't exist without us making it, just like the sound of a falling tree doesn't exist when no one is there to hear it. Other animals and insects see other worlds based on their perception of different wavelengths of light and sound. A dog's world is shades of blue, yellow, and grey, but a bat can see the ultraviolet light we can't see. Every day is a disco for them. What a strange world we live in if it all depends on our fallible senses. Our subjective experiences create our own personal worlds, and maybe mine differs from yours. I pondered these philosophical concepts for a few miles as I headed along the valley of the River Monnow out of Monmouth. The jukebox selector in my head then burst onto the scene, without my conscious input, by cueing up and playing Bohemian Rhapsody. Maybe my thoughts had prompted the opening lyrics and triggered the song, or maybe it was the subconscious thought of where I was heading.

I passed through the tiny village of Rockfield and branched left. Heading down the lane, through fertile agricul-tural country, I very nearly passed by a farm on my left. That's what most people do – go past it. There's nothing much to suggest that the farm is any different from hundreds of others scattered across the Welsh countryside… and that's how the owners of Rockfield Farm like it.

Except this is a place where rock music history has been made. A sign on the entrance from the main road makes it clear that visitors to the farm are by appointment only. The sign only became necessary in 2020, following a BBC docu-mentary called, *The Studio on the Farm*. That stirred up inter-est, and the notice is there to protect the privacy of bands and artists who stay on the farm to record music. Its guests are there to create, and they deserve to do so undisturbed. It's one of the main reasons they go there. I was lucky – having written in advance to explain my *Journey through Wales*, I'd been invited to pop in for a chat. I met up with Lisa Ward, the office manager and daughter of Kingsley Ward, one of the two brothers who established the studios in the 1960s.

Back in the day, Charles and Kingsley Ward dreamt of rock stardom and the bright lights of London's swinging music scene, but that was a long way from home for a couple of farmer's lads from South Wales. To save the expense and the trouble of travelling back and forth, the brothers had the bright idea of setting up their own recording studios on their farm near Monmouth. Their big break came when fellow Welsh singer, Dave Edmunds, recorded the song, 'I Hear You Knocking,' at Rockfield Farm. It shot to number one in the UK and eventually sold over three million copies. Although the brothers' performing careers didn't quite take off as they'd hoped, their studios certainly did. Suddenly, everyone wanted to record at Rockfield. Some of the most famous musicians in the world heard about the farm and wanted to stay there – it became the cool thing to do, and the farmhouse developed into the world's first residential recording studio.

As Lisa patiently described the farm's history, she dropped into the conversation how, back in 1975, Freddie Mercury finished composing Bohemian Rhapsody in the former tack room where she and I were sitting having our chat. The rest of the band joined Freddie, and Queen recorded one of the most iconic rock tracks of all time, as well as the album, *A Night at the Opera*. (By then, they'd already recorded the album, *Sheer Heart Attack*). The list of artists who have created rock music on the farm over four decades reads like a *Who's Who* of rock greats. It includes Oasis, Hawkwind, Robert Plant, Simple Minds, Manic Street Preachers, The Waterboys, and Coldplay. David Bowie used to hang out there and have a beer or two with his mate Iggy Pop – that's how it was. Hearing that Ozzy Osbourne's group, Black Sabbath, recorded the first demos for Paranoid at Rockfield in 1968 was special for me because it was the first cassette tape I bought. They say the Prince of Darkness christened the farm 'The birthplace of heavy metal.'

Coldplay created the album *Parachutes* in Rockfield studios in March 2000. During a recording session, they stepped outside the studio into the quadrangle for a breather. It was a clear night, and a billion stars filled the dark skies above them. As they looked up, producer Ken Nelson broke the silence, saying, 'Look up there, lads... look at the stars!' They had a first line. Chris Martin went back inside and started strumming a few chords. Sat behind the mixing desk, he looked around and saw a copy of the *Yellow Pages* phone directory. The colour gave him an idea for a song title. The chorus came to him a few minutes later. Yellow is Coldplay's most successful song, selling over 2.4 million copies in the UK and over five million copies in the United States... all inspired by a starry night at the Rockfield Studios.

Without knowing it, as she trotted out the list of bands and albums, Lisa seemed to work her way through many of the tracks on my all-time play list. As if my jaw hadn't already dropped far enough, it reached the floor when I found out that Craig and Charlie Reid (The Proclaimers) were in the next building knocking out a new album.

I wondered about the store of priceless anecdotes Lisa must have, with all those amazing bands over so many years. Yes, apparently there were more than a few eyebrow raisers, but one reason for the success of the farm is the privacy it allows its guests – those stories will never be told. I asked Lisa what it was like growing up as a little girl with world famous bands and larger-than-life music celebrities sharing her home. For her, that life of extraordinary characters and music was her normal. She explained how the business had changed over the years. Of course, digital technology had changed things, but many qualities that make the farm unique are still relevant. It's still one of the few studios where bands can get away from everything, feel at home, and immerse themselves in the creative process, a few days or weeks at a time, with nothing else to worry about. As Lisa put it, 'We know we've done our job right when we see the lead singer in their slippers.' I got the impression that Lisa was very content down on the farm. She commented: 'I have the beautiful countryside, and my lovely dog… and the big world comes to me.'

As I clunked the Himalayan into first gear and pulled away from the car park, a young chap walked across the driveway in front of me, towards the studios. It looked like he was carrying two plates of food. The lad might have already walked 500 miles, maybe 500 more, but now he was about to be the one to deliver a couple of pizzas to Craig and Charlie's door.

By the time I'd reached the main road at the end of the farm drive, my subconscious jukebox had already got me quietly singing, 'When you go… will you send me…'. I was still buzzing, thinking about what I'd just seen and heard. I guess everyone thinks *their* music, the music of their teens and twenties, was the best ever, but in my case, I'm sure it was. That's what made Rockfield Farm special to me.

I was soon in the market town of Abergavenny, one of several places that considers itself the Gateway to Wales. That label tells you why the town developed in the first place – because of its strategic location at the entrance to central Wales. Invading Romans built the fort of Gobannium on the mouth of the River Gavenny (Afon Gafenni) to subdue the local Silures tribe who had the temerity to occupy the area before the new invaders arrived. The location also led the Normans to build a castle there when they too muscled in, and the town became the focus of a string of turf wars in the medieval period.

At least today the fuel is Welsh. As I topped up the motor-cycle's tank in Abergavenny, I saw a sign telling me, 'Texaco quality fuel, made in Wales,' which I guess is from the refinery at Milford Haven (Aberdaugleddau). From Abergavenny, I took a brief diversion up to Crickhowell (Crug

Hywel) before doubling back to take the high road to Hay-on-Wye. My fourteen-mile detour to the elegant Georgian town of Crickhowell was to visit the birthplace of a fellow surveyor. There aren't many famous surveyors, but the name of this one is known all over the world. In 1790, a boy called George Everest was born in the Manor of Gwernvale, on the northern outskirts of Crickhowell. When he grew up, he became a surveyor in the British Army, and by 1830 he'd risen to the position of Surveyor General of India. The geographic scope of his work and challenging conditions made his detailed and accurate mapping of the subcontinent an epic undertaking, and they named the highest mountain in the world (which, ironically, he never saw) after him. On his retirement and return to Britain, Queen Victoria gave him a knighthood.

I found his birthplace, the Manor of Gwernvale (now The Manor Hotel), at the end of a long sweeping drive just off the main A40 road north of Crickhowell. The bright white building stands proudly, chest puffed out with a hint of regency superiority, on a man-made terrace high on the northern side of the Usk Valley (Cwm Wysg). I ascended the winding drive and, after establishing base-camp in the car park, I pushed on by foot, without oxygen, to look around Sir George's former home. Inside the hotel's foyer, there are several photos and mementos celebrating its famous former occupant. The view from the hotel was phenomenal. The Usk Valley swept left and right in hues of green under a clear blue sky. Sitting contentedly in the left middle foreground was the picturesque town of Crickhowell. Beyond, forming a spectacular backdrop, was the high mountainous ridge that stretches between Mynydd Llangatwg and Mynydd Llangynidr.

I trundled back down to the main road. A short distance from the end of the hotel's driveway, immediately next to the A40, a handful of metre-high ancient stones rose apologetically at random angles through the long grasses of the roadside verge. They are the restored remains of the Gwernvale chambered tomb, a Neolithic long barrow (a long barrow is a type of prehistoric tomb, typically made of earth and stones, long and narrow in shape. They were built by Neolithic people, who lived in Britain and Ireland from about 4500 to 2000 years ago). If the verge hasn't been cut for a while, it's very easy to miss them. Described as a monument of national importance, it was once a 45-metre long, stone-built cairn that contained four stone-built chambers. Archaeological excavations undertaken in the 1970s, prior to road improvements, suggest the cairn was part of a small settlement, one of many in the area. It's a sad sight today, however! Successive road builders have trampled the place, including the Romans, who literally drove many coaches and horses through the graveyard. Looking at the handful of metre-high stones today, one can only feel sorry for the 4000-year-old occupants who have their rest disturbed day and night by vehicles rumbling up and down the A40.

It had been a worthwhile diversion, but I needed to get back to my main route, so I headed back to Abergavenny and hung a left onto the A465 towards Hereford. After 5 miles, I arrived at the village of Llanvihangel Crucorney. Surrounded by attractive mixed farmland, the village lies at the southern end of the beautiful Vale of Ewyas (Cwm Ewyas). The valley sweeps northwards into the eastern edge of the Black Mountains and is an area popular with climbers and walkers. The Offa's Dyke Path, and the border with England, run along the ridge on the northeastern side of the valley.

Llanvihangel Crucorney was built on a mound of soil and rock that was pushed down the Vale of Ewyas at the front of a glacier at the end of the Ice Age. The small village contains many listed historic buildings, but the one I was heading for was The Skirrid Mountain Inn. As a public meeting place and inn, it has existed for over 900 years, and it is claimed to be the oldest pub in Wales. That sort of claim will always grab my attention. A few legends must have appeared in nearly 1000 years – I was eager to find out.

As I parked my motorcycle in the pub's cobbled courtyard, I felt pleased I'd bought a stylish Welsh dragon sticker for the windscreen. That courtyard was the very spot where (they say) Owain Glyndŵr rallied his men to rise against Henry IV. I popped inside for a swift drink, as I imagined the legendary Welsh leader would have done around 600 years ago, although that's where the similarities between our day's activities probably ended. A day rallying Welsh folk against oppressive English rule would be slightly out of my comfort zone, although I'd give it a go. I'm not sure how the 15th century Prince of Wales would have fared riding a 400cc motorcycle for 100 miles around South Wales... although the logistical advantage could have been a game changer for his recruitment drive.

Walking into The Skirrid Mountain Inn, I immediately felt a change of atmosphere. Wood panelling, low ceilings, and sagging oak beams confirmed I was entering somewhere with a bit of history. But it was more than that. Information boards on the walls helped me to discover some of the inn's colourful background, and the friendly woman behind the bar helped to fill in a few gaps. Some of that history is quite dark. During the early 17th century, they used the upstairs part of the inn as a courtroom, and 180 men were hanged there, mainly for stealing sheep. A rope and noose still hang down the centre of the inn's stairwell as a chilling reminder.

HV Morton was undoubtedly one of the most popular travel writers of the 20th century. I am a huge fan of his writing but Michael Bartholomew's 2004 biography of the writer, called *In Search of HV Morton*, shows him to be a complex and controversial figure. The book describes a dark side to the man, in which he is seen to be a white supremacist, extremely right-wing, and a bit of a snob. His beliefs were influenced by the political and social climate of his time, of course, when racism, sexism, and other forms of discrimination were commonplace. I wonder how he would have felt about the sheep stealers of Monmouthshire.

The amount of death and misery suffered in The Skirrid

Mountain Inn inevitably leads to tales of ghosts and restless souls, and the place has a fine collection. The infamous Judge Jeffries (the hanging judge) is said to be a regular return visitor, along with a former hangman, a priest, a barmaid, and countless victims of hanging. With reports of beer glasses being thrown across the room, disembodied footsteps, and mysterious whispering, it didn't surprise me to learn that the inn has been the subject of several paranormal investigations.

But my mood had dipped. Although there was a pleasant atmosphere in the pub, with plenty of customers enjoying their food and drink, the stories of hardship and death had left me feeling flat. They were a sombre reminder of the austere and violent times centuries ago. I didn't want to hang around. While the tales of prisoners and hangings might seem intriguing through the eyes of history, those times would have been severe and cruel for most of the population. I returned to the courtyard to issue a blood-curdling cry in the style of Owain Glyndŵr and continue northwards to my next stop.

I headed up a small lane (a 'narrow yellow' on an OS Landranger map) into the steep-sided Vale of Ewyas, heading for Llanthony Priory (Priordy Llanddewi Nant Hodni), about 5 miles up the valley. After visiting the remains, my plan was to continue to the end of the valley and head over the Gospel Pass before descending to Hay-on-Wye. Gospel Pass is the highest road in Wales, which is why I was there; I'd seen it described in glowing terms in motorcycling magazines. I was also travelling along Sustrans route 42. Sustrans is a charity that manages a network of long-distance cycle paths. I fully expected to see plenty of bikes of one sort or another in the valley. In the event, I saw few of either.

The Welsh name Llanddewi Nant Hodni translates to 'a community associated with St David (Sant Dewi) next to the river called Hodni.' Over time, the Welsh name became shortened and corrupted to Llanthonddye or Lanthoni.

The reference to St David is important to the story of the

priory. St David was the most important of several Welsh saints of the 6th century who sought remote places in which they could worship in peace. He lived in spiritual seclusion in Llanthony for a while in a cell (from the Latin word *cella* meaning small room, and related to the Latin *celare*, meaning to hide or conceal). It is likely there were also several devoted followers in other cells surrounding a church within a llan (an enclosed religious community).

Fast forward a few centuries and we find William de Lacy out hunting in the valley. The knight is said to have come across the ruined chapel of St David during a storm, and taken shelter there. The experience completely transformed his life. He gave up his military career, devoted himself to religion, and became a hermit in Llanthony. His solitude didn't last long because within a few years, Ernisius, chaplain to Queen Matilda (daughter of King Henry I of England), joined him. Together, they established a religious place that was consecrated in 1108 and dedicated to St John the Baptist. In 1118, their fledgling project expanded when a group of around forty canons (priests living in a community, dedicated to poverty, chastity, and obedience) arrived from England. They adopted the Augustinian Order of the Catholic Church. Being canons, not monks, they played a role in the surrounding area by taking services and preaching in local churches. Eventually, the community became known as Llanthony Priory. Venturing out into the local area was challenging because of the tensions that existed between the Welsh and the English. In 1135 the local 'barbarous people' destroyed the original priory, forcing the canons to retreat to Gloucester and Hereford.

Some consider the spectacular Gothic – Norman style priory that was built in its place in 1217 to be one of medieval Wales' greatest buildings. Although it existed for over 300 years, the priory was just another on the long list of beautiful buildings trashed by Henry VIII's cultural and religious vandals in 1538. On the positive side, a relatively substantial amount of the priory has survived – enough to provide visitors with a good impression of its former grandeur. I was surprised, and at first disappointed, to see there was a hotel within the confines of the priory. This isn't as alarming as it sounds. The Grade I listed building is quite discreet and as strange as it may seem, I don't think it detracts significantly from the overall atmosphere. Once I'd looked around the remains of the priory, I hurdled the stone wall on its northern side (alright, I gingerly clambered over it) and walked a short distance up the valley side towards Hatterrall Hill. I forced myself to stop, look, and listen to appreciate the beauty of the scene below – the remains of the priory sitting peacefully in the tranquil wooded valley. Although my travel journeys veer towards the whistle-stop end of the speed scale, I have learned to stop occasionally to take time to think about where I am, and to soak up the atmosphere. Llanthony is one of those special places where you must do that.

It was the small Church of St David's – a relic of the 12th century – which impressed me most and left a profound impact on me. More so than the remnants of the priory. The simple stone church building was built on the site of the saint's original cell, and it has been an important place of pilgrimage for hundreds of years. As I pushed open the heavy wooden door, I was enveloped by the stillness of the small but hauntingly atmospheric space. I was alone, and for a fleeting moment, the relentless buzz of my thoughts – my worries about health, family, finances, and the fragile state of Southampton FC's league position – were silenced. I was consumed by a feeling of tranquillity. Was it a mystical location that connected me to the past – a spiritual portal to a different time? Or was it simply the serene presence of the ancient building and its surroundings? The rational part of me inclined towards the latter, but the innate human desire for significance urged me to believe the former. Regardless, I emerged from the church with a renewed sense of calm, and a glimpse into why the place had been such an important destination for pilgrims for all those years.

It was time to take the high road, and this one really was. I was about to ride over the highest paved road in Wales (550 metres above sea level). Within 5 miles of leaving the priory, the valley splits at Capel-y-ffin, and the road begins its climb up the hillside to the Gospel Pass. I say road, but by now the single track with passing places was becoming just that – a track. I think I had the perfect transport for the job: a motorcycle that wasn't averse to some off-road riding. The surface metalling was badly broken in some places, and in others, it was just gravel. In some stretches, the road was so narrow it was impossible for a car and a motorcycle to pass. Maybe that was why I had seen so little traffic.

The origin of the name, Gospel Pass, is unclear. One theory suggests that St Paul entered Wales over the pass when he brought the gospel to Wales. Another explanation is that the name comes from English crusaders passing through on fundraising missions before sailing off to pick fights with people in the Middle East.

The road keeps climbing and as it does so, the views get better and better – and they are stunning. Fortunately, the roadside hedges thin out and then disappear as you climb higher, so there are plenty of places to pull over and take in the view. When you reach the summit of the pass, it's worth stopping to admire the panorama. It stretches towards the Cambrian Mountains in the north, with the peak of Twmpa to the left, and Hay Bluff to the right. It's breathtaking.

Builth Wells in wonderful afternoon sunshine was a completely different prospect to the same place I'd seen 3 years earlier, through a curtain of watery stair rods. This time, I took a few moments to ride up the main street, and it presented itself as a very pleasant place. The market town expanded in the 19th century as a spa resort, assisted by the development of new road and rail networks. In recent years, it has become famous as the permanent home of the annual

Royal Welsh Show – a four-day event with livestock and equine competitions, forestry and horticultural activities, crafts, and countryside sports. Unfortunately, the show wasn't on during my visit, but I did see the 18th century masonry bridge, with its six wide arches over the River Wye – a handsome sight, especially in the sunshine. I remembered that last time I was in town, I stopped in the pouring rain to admire the dramatic mural of the last days of Llywelyn ap Gruffydd, the last native-born Prince of Wales. This time, it felt more significant because I know a little more about Welsh history now and, therefore, the significance of Llywelyn. So much so that this time I rode 3 miles out of town on the A483 to visit his memorial in the village of Cilmery (Cilmeri).

Llywelyn ap Gruffydd was the Prince of Gwynedd, the northern lands that were the centre of Welsh power in the 13th century. An ongoing fight to drive out the English invaders dominated his life, and he probably came closer than anyone to achieving full independence for his country. Although he came close, and he was the only Welsh ruler to be officially recognised by the English as Prince of Wales, some historians believe that he did not truly unite Wales. Within a year of his death, his beloved Wales was under English rule.

The memorial to Llywelyn ap Gruffydd, the last Prince of Wales, was erected in 1956. It marks the place where he is believed to have been slain by English soldiers in 1282. There are many theories about his death, including the possibility that it was the result of a trap set by Roger Mortimer, a close ally of King Edward I. Another theory is that he was slain by soldiers who did not even know who he was. A large block of granite from Llywelyn's home county of Caernarfonshire stands tall on a low mound in Cilmery. The small, fenced grass area surrounding the memorial has a sombre and dignified atmosphere. When I visited, a Welsh flag, a few small wooden crosses, a shield, a candle, and a handful of flower bouquets had been respectfully placed at the base of the monument. This is clearly someone who still holds very strong significance for many Welsh people.

This might be a good moment to mention the Welsh Marches. The national border we see today wasn't established until 1536. The word 'March' is derived from the old English word for boundary, which was 'mearc.' William the Conqueror set up the Welsh Marches in the period after the Norman invasion in 1066. In effect, William and his immediate successors set up a military buffer zone between England and the people of Wales. Over 150 of the king's family, best mates, and loyal supporters were given what amounted to mini kingdoms to rule, however they saw fit. The Norman-Angevin lords (the Angevins were the first three Plantagenet kings of England: Henry II, Richard the Lionheart, and John) could create their own laws, build castles, plunder the native lands, and do pretty much whatever they liked – independent from the English Crown. The benefit for the English king was that the border area, wherever that was, was no longer a headache, and military resources could be deployed elsewhere, like on the pesky Scots.

The road from Builth Wells to Rhayader took me through typically 'lumpy bumpy' Welsh countryside. I began using this technical topographic description while exploring the Welsh/Shropshire border country around Oswestry a few years ago. My wife and I enjoyed 4 years living there before moving to Dorset in 2021. The Borders landscape around Oswestry is very similar to the Rhayader area – agricultural and undulating, with lots of sheep and lumpy bumpy bits. The hills are self-contained, steeper sided, and there are more of them, when compared, for example, with the rolling chalk downland of Dorset or Hampshire. As a cyclist, I notice these things.

I was travelling along the green and fertile valley of the River Wye, working my way north towards its source. As I approached Rhayader, I noticed the landscape changing once again. It became more rugged, with more forest and mixed woodland. Looking at the map afterwards, I could see why. I was bumping up against the eastern edge of the Cambrian Mountains. The similarity with the Oswestry area then made sense – both are transition areas, where the landscape changes between lowland and upland areas, dictated by the geology.

I almost stopped in my tracks when I saw a red kite soaring over the road. It was a rare and magnificent sight, with its reddish-brown plumage, broad wingspan with sergeant's stripes on each wing, and its distinctive long, forked tail. It seemed to have spotted some roadkill and was hovering remarkably low and in good view – probably just waiting for me to get out of the way. I felt lucky to spot it. That was, until I saw another one shortly after, and then another one… and then another. They were coming thick and fast and, as if to re-enforce the point, a flight of three flew past me in close formation. When I looked at the map later, I discovered the spot where I'd seen the first kite was a few hundred yards from the Gigrin Farm red kite feeding station. I'd probably passed right under the main flight path that up to 600 regulars feeders use for their take-away collections. By the end of 3 days in Rhayader, I realised how common the birds are in the area. Anyone wanting to see a red kite should head to Rhayader – you can't go wrong (cue brain jukebox… Let's Go Fly a Kite…).

Rhayader is a small market town within the historic county of Radnorshire. It's the first town the River Wye comes across after it sets off from its mountain source, about 25 miles further north. I motored through the town to its northern fringe and pulled over to the side of the road. I needed to retrieve the scrap of paper I had somewhere in my back pocket, on which I'd written the instructions for finding my accommodation for the next few nights. A woman and chap emerged from a drive and looked at me as if expecting a question. I told them I was just looking for my place to stay… it was owned by a woman called Caroline. 'Oh, that's me,' she said. 'You've arrived!'

It had been a long day's ride, but after a shower and change, I was keen to explore the town, and it was only a five-minute walk from my accommodation to the centre. It's difficult to describe Rhayader. I wasn't sure if I liked it to begin with, but as I saw more, I warmed to it. I saw more similarities with Oswestry – Rhayader is also a small market town that serves a wide rural community. With the steady decline in agricultural incomes over the years, its most prosperous days are probably behind it, but the town is finding a new identity and a new economic model to sustain itself in the future. Rhayader now markets itself as the outdoors capital of Wales. With plenty of hospitality and easy access to the surrounding mountains and lakes, this is a reasonable claim, although I'm sure it has some strong competitors for the title.

Rhayader is quite attractive, but not quite pretty. The town seems to punch above its weight, however, with a range of facilities you might expect from a much larger town. It has a leisure centre, museum, public parks, river, castle (remains of), post office, market, library, and even police and fire stations. For those normally confused by town layouts, Rhayader keeps things reassuringly simple. Bordered on the west and south, by the River Wye, the town huddles around a central crossroads that has a 19th century clock tower. The four roads that radiate from the centre aren't quite aligned Milton Keynes grid style, but they have an uncomplicated layout, with the names North, South, East, and West streets.

I didn't hear any Welsh being spoken on my perambulation of the town, but there was clearly a strong Welsh identity, with lots of flags and Welsh signs in evidence. In the window of one house was a plate commemorating the life and achievements of Owain Glyndŵr. On the gates of another house were two magnificent red Welsh dragons. Someone a few doors up had gone one better. Three characters from history were depicted on the 5-metre-wide metal double gates of the drive. Two women (or as it turns out, men dressed as women) were wielding pitch forks, while another person was swinging an axe while mounted on a rearing horse. Above them were the words, *AND THEY BLESSED REBECCA.* I'm not shouting – that's how the words appear on the wrought-iron gates. A neighbour told me it was the site of the town's old northern toll house.

Toll House in Rhayader

Students of *The Bible* and / or Welsh history may recognise this as a reference to Genesis, Chapter 24, Verse 60 – the blessing of Rebecca. There are varying interpretations of the original text, but many of them refer to Rebecca, wife of Isaac, being told, 'May you become the mother of thousands of ten thousands; And may your descendants possess the gates of those who hate them.' The crucial bit here is the reference to gates – and this is where we need a very brief summary of Welsh rural society during Victorian times.

Life for the farming people of south and Mid Wales in the mid-19th century was incredibly hard. They might say it still is, but even if that's true, it's still nothing like it was in those days. For most, it was barely subsistence farming. For those rearing livestock, market prices gradually decreased, and those growing cereals suffered from a succession of poor harvests. Landlords charged high rates, and the Church kept increasing tithe payments. The final straw came with the charges demanded by the private operators who ran the turnpike trusts on the new roads, making it costly for farmers to carry produce to market using a horse or horse and cart. Although these problems existed over wide areas of Wales, Rhayader became famous because it had so many toll gates – six surrounded the town – making it difficult to avoid them.

Tensions eventually resulted in violence and the toll gates were the obvious target. It's not clear how it started, but tenant farmers and workers came up with the idea of using Rebecca and her daughters (from the Bible quote) as a disguise. They dressed up in women's clothing and attacked the Rhayader toll gates in September 1843. Within months, many people had stopped paying tolls. With the attacks continuing for another year, a detachment of soldiers and London police were drafted in to restore order. The Rebecca riots ended when the authorities promised to enquire into the grievances, and eventually the turnpike trusts were abolished.

My tour of the town took me down South Street, where just beyond the Bethel Baptist Church, in the golden evening light, I found the small but perfectly formed South Street Toll house. A blue plaque on the wall dates the building to 1799 and includes an image depicting the riots. Surrounding a scene of tooled up violent looking women in full riot gear are the words: 'South Gate – Rhayader's only toll gate to survive intact after the Rebecca riots, 1843.' That evening, I looked up the relevant passage in *The Bible*. I think, on reflection, the rioters might have been selective with their interpretation of the text, probably for logistical reasons – the next verse says that Rebecca and her servants were mounted on camels.

Rhayader isn't large, and it didn't take me long to walk around most of it. Walking back to my lodgings via the town's pleasant riverside walk, I stumbled upon the site of the old Rhayader Castle. Castles always seem to be placed in the perfect location and this was no exception. The fenced-off area, where the castle once stood, occupied a prominent crag overlooking the River Wye, giving it a sound defensive position and a good view of any potential attackers. The castle was built in 1177 by Lord Rhys, Prince of Deheubarth, but after a period of typically fluid owner-ship, Llywelyn ap Iorwerth finally destroyed it in 1231. We will never know, but if the original design had specified stone instead of wood for its construction, there may have been more than just a grass playing field to see now. I rummaged briefly and fruitlessly, looking for some defen-sive ditches which, according to the information board, still survive. I gave up the search because I was disturbing the concentration of Arthur, a Hungarian Vizsla puppy. He was still on page one of his initial training, which covered the very important commands, 'sit' and 'stay.' After a perfectly executed sit and stay, Arthur spotted me. To the disappoint-ment of his owner and family, their puppy promptly bound over to say hello, all legs and waggly tail. Despite his over enthusiasm for social connection, he was still a very good boy.

The next day, my plan was to head out to the Elan Valley (Cwm Elan), to meet Jenny Hall and Paul Sambrook, two professional archaeologists, who had kindly agreed to tell me about the region and their work.

After breakfast on my first whole day in Rhayader, I headed west out of town for my meeting with Jenny and Paul. We had arranged to meet at the Pont ar Elan bridge, about 5 miles out of Rhayader. As I headed out, the landscape soon changed once again. After just a couple of miles, I was riding into whale-backed hills that reminded me of the smooth and rounded tops of the Scottish Southern Uplands. The road narrowed and the landscape grew more desolate as I rode along the old Rhayader to Aberystwyth toll road.

Looking at a map of Wales, the Cambrian Mountains are the wide expanse of uplands that run almost north-south like a spine down the centre of the country, in the gap between Snowdonia and the Brecon Beacons (the Brecon Beacons National Park has been rebranded Bannau Brycheiniog National Park). The geographer in me could easily quibble with that description, but it provides a simple way of visualising the area in the big picture of Welsh geography. 'Cambrian Mountains' has been used as a generic name for all areas of upland Wales for many years, but nowadays the name is used for a specific area of Mid Wales uplands (over 300 metres high), referred to in Welsh as Elenydd. The sparsely populated area has been described as the 'Green Desert of Wales,' and 'Wales' last true wilderness.' Although parts appear like a wilderness, it is also an incredibly rich habitat for wildlife.

This vast natural landscape is also one that man has influenced. These days, forestry and tourism exist alongside the farming that has taken place for centuries. And then there are the reservoirs, to which I will return later. People I spoke to in Rhayader told me that the equilibrium of the area is currently under threat from two recent developments. Firstly, financially vulnerable farmland is being bought up to create large-scale coniferous forests to produce timber and to offset carbon emissions. Secondly, the energy crisis is fuelling demand for more upland areas to be used for wind farms. If the Cambrian Mountains are going to remain Wales' last true wilderness, they need to be protected from too much change. A charity called the Cambrian Mountains Society is campaigning to promote and preserve the area. They advocate that the area should be an AONB.

I rode out to the Pont ar Elan bridge on what was until then the hottest day of the year. It was 27 degrees but felt hotter. The bridge lies in that famous location, 'in the middle of nowhere.' A small single-track road to the left of the Rhayader to Aberystwyth road zigzags 50 metres down the hillside. It then crosses the River Elan at the Pont ar Elan, and then wearily snakes its way up over the hills towards the dams of the Elan Valley. A small car park, big enough to accommodate about a dozen cars, lies next to the bridge and the waters of the River Elan. The river is relatively small as it flows past the car park, ranging between about 4 to 8 metres wide in the 100 metres either side of the bridge. In the places where the river widens out, it looks to have almost stopped flowing, but in some of the narrow and steep sections, it froths wildly as it forces its way through narrow and elaborate rock formations. The peaty brown water is beginning a long journey to the people of Birmingham, almost 70 miles away, via the Elan reservoirs.

I arrived for my rendezvous about an hour early. Under the mad-dogs' heat of the midday sun, a dozen millennial fun seekers of various shapes, sizes, and states of disrepair poured out of four vans of a similar description. Giggling and over-excited, they ran around the car park and riverbank out of control for several minutes, taking countless selfies. It was all good-natured stuff, and they seemed a pleasant bunch. They eventually remembered why they were there and started changing into their wet suits. The guy who appeared to be the leader took them over to the river and one by one they all immersed themselves in a relatively slow flowing section. More selfies. They then got out and walked upstream about 50 metres. One by one, with lots of whoops and screams, they started jumping off a high part of the riverbank into the river, about 4 metres below. The distance didn't look too scary, but the uncertainty over what lay beneath the surface of the peaty coloured river was presumably what gave them their adrenalin rush. Guided by the leader, who carefully pointed out the safe landing zone, they all survived the drop and then stayed in the water (more excited giggling, more selfies), before drifting their way downstream towards the car park and the bridge. This took them through a rocky rapids section, which looked great fun, and I was quite envious of them in the water, while I sweltered a few yards away in the car park.

Jenny and Paul turned up on time and we sat around a picnic table for the next hour and a half, discussing the history and prehistory of the area. Their work has involved verifying hundreds of existing archaeological and historical records of the Elan Valley, and adding new information as they find it. Paul took me on a rapid journey through the timeline of the surrounding uplands. We were sitting in the perfect place for the lesson: in the middle of magnificent rolling hills that stretched as far as the eye could see. For most of the time, we were on our own, in the silence of the land-scape, and it wasn't hard to visualise the past worlds that Paul and Jenny recreated.

In the surrounding hills, there are countless ancient sites, burial mounds, summit cairns, and standing stones. Most of these were cleverly concealed from view. Moving swiftly through the Iron Age and Roman periods, Paul explained that farming had always taken place, but evidence of its scale and extent was scarce. The Romans had mined in Cwmystwyth, yet little evidence of that remained either. However, Jenny and Paul had made another exciting find, a potential Roman Marching Camp. As Paul reached the post-Roman period, his enthusiasm heightened. He leaned forward and spoke a little faster, showing a genuine passion and deep knowledge of the medieval period. Following the Norman conquest, the region we sat in – the Elan Valley and mid-Cambrian Mountains – fell under the authority of Strata Florida (Ystrad Fflur) Abbey, located just beyond the hills to the west of our location, near Pontrhydfendigaid, in Ceredigion. It was a time when religion held great importance. The Church and State were inter-twined, with bishops and influential monastic leaders involved in governing the country. Consequently, the Church and monastic system gained immense power. The monks of abbeys like Strata Florida developed a symbiotic relationship with the aristocracy. In a sort of medieval life assurance policy, the monks' prayers secured the nobility's fortune in life and guaranteed them a place in heaven after death. In return, the wealthy bestowed vast land areas upon the monks. It seemed like a good deal, just in case.

The Catholic Cistercian monks, who occupied at least sixteen abbeys in Wales, especially prospered under this arrangement. In the eastern Cambrian Mountains near Strata Florida, they established a vast farming support network that generated considerable income from wool. The use of unpaid lay brothers, who received spiritual support from the abbey, minimised expenses. As the wool trade thrived, the monks also enjoyed the advantage of tax exemption on exports. This convenient arrangement, facilitated by the Pope, ensured British rulers received favourable treatment from God, while the monks were excused from wool taxes.

In medieval Welsh law, farming was divided between the lowland Hendrefi settlements and the high moorland Hafodydd huts. Jenny and Paul discovered these timber-framed houses up in the hills, along with small stone structures believed to be medieval cold storage boxes for preserving milk and cheese. The remains of the prototype fridges act as indicators of nearby medieval house sites.

The dissolution of the monasteries in the 16th century brought significant societal changes. Land previously owned by abbeys was distributed among Henry VIII's mates, resulting in a manorial society with large country estates. Farmers began producing more than just essentials, taking surplus cattle to markets along drove roads. The seasonal Hafod and Hendre system transitioned to a new year-round Lluest system, leading to permanent settlements on the mountains occupied by shepherding families.

Jenny and Paul had also discovered long linear mounds, remnants of late medieval rabbit farming. Paul pointed up to the hills and showed me the outline of some man-made burrows, which were quite clear, once pointed out. Another intriguing find in the Esgair Rhiwlan area is hundreds of what were previously thought to be Bronze Age cairns. They turned out to be artillery shell holes from a pre-World War I firing range. When they found evidence of a gun battery site over another nearby hill, the pieces began to fit together. According to stories told by nearby residents, the army conducted artillery experiments in the area before World War I. There was a summer camp held regularly in the area and the Royal Artillery came to the Elan Valley area for training exercises. Jenny and Paul came across a photo that showed rows of tents in the valley, and even a tethered balloon, positioned between the battery and the target area, used for range finding. Good luck with that job!

By the time we had said our farewells, the wild swimmers had also departed, slightly less wild than when they'd arrived. They'd dried themselves off on the riverbank, enjoyed a picnic, and gone on their way – leaving the car park as silent as it was before they'd arrived. I grabbed my swimming trunks and a towel from one of the pannier bags and headed upstream along the riverbank. At a spot near to where the millennials had done their dangerous diving, the rocks on the riverbank formed a small vertical wall. It screened that bit of riverbank from the car park, which was empty anyway, so I quickly got changed. I went for the less adventurous, tippy-toe water entry method rather than the double somersault and pike from 4 metres. It seemed a bit of a cop out, but I suspected there could be huge benefits from having a complete set of bones for the rest of my journey.

The water was gorgeous. It was unexpectedly warm and refreshing. The river was quite shallow where I'd entered, but it soon deepened. As I drifted downstream, the river squeezed through a fairly narrow section of rocks not much wider than my body width. I bobbed along like a cork as the flow suddenly increased and shot me through the gap. The river then opened out into my own wild swimming pool, about 20 metres long and 5 metres wide. It was glorious and relaxing, with just enough flow to drift along downstream, but not enough to be a problem swimming in the opposite direction. I lay on my back as still as I could, listening to the sounds of the river – and nothing else.

After 20 minutes, I got out to get changed. I stood still on the riverbank to listen again and take in the moment – absolute silence… apart from the contented chuckle of the river and the high-level song of a skylark. It felt like I was the only person on the planet – there was nothing and no one for miles around. That's quite a thought. Even after cooling off in the river, it was still a scorching day. I looked at my big heavy motorcycling jeans, complete with Kevlar lining and knee and hip protectors. They were going to be hot, but I had no option if I wanted to stay safe. Besides, the road-using public and nervous pedestrians of mid-Wales would not thank me for continuing my journey in my underpants alone. I imagined that the Rhayader chapter of Hells Angels would run me out of town for less. I enjoyed another minute or so before getting togged up again, making the most of being the only person for miles around in those hills.

'I hope I'm not interrupting your peace and quiet,' boomed a deep Welsh voice from the river, as a chap bobbed around in *my* private pool. It sounded like Sir Tom Jones making his way upriver. And why not? …It's not unusual.

'Oh, no, no problem,' I lied. 'I was just getting out, anyway.' This second person on the planet turned out to be Chris from Llandovery. He'd arrived at the car park a few minutes earlier on his Ducati 800 Scrambler motorcycle. Not that I'd heard anything. It must have been while I was being shot through the noisy part of the rapids. I think he must have seen me swimming when he arrived and thought he'd try it as well. Chris was a Welshman (sounds like a famous rhyme) and he knew all the classic Welsh motorcycle routes. Instead of giving me a rendition of Delilah, I got this Born To Be Wild swimmer's top ten bike rides round Wales. A route across the Cambrian Mountains had appeared in a recent copy of one of the motorcycle magazines – now everyone was trying it out!

I got packed up and made my way from the car park and back up the zigzags to the main Rhayader to Aberystwyth road. It seemed to get even hotter. I rode northwest towards Devil's Bridge (Pontarfynach), riding out of Powys and into Ceredigion. The landscape became quite open and wild and when the narrow road topped out at the highest point, it reminded me of Hardknott Pass in the Lake District. Before long, I came to the long strung-out village of Cwmystwyth. I'd marked this village out before I left because OS had identified it as the centre of Wales. I love a geographical extreme, highest point, most remote spot, etc., so it was good to tick this one off. To be pedantic, the actual centre point is on a hillside above the upper reaches of the Afon Ystwyth in Cwmystwyth – but my geo-nerdiness has some bounds and it was too hot to hike, so the road through the village would have to do.

What I hadn't expected, however, was the village's historic mining background. Having ridden through miles of unspoiled hills and moorland, it felt incongruous to suddenly be surrounded by the centuries-old ghosts of an industrial past. For a few hundred yards, the road takes you through the centre of an old mine. To one side are the old spoil heaps and on the other side are the remains of the old mine office, the mine entrance, smithy, and old miners' barracks. The Afon Ystwyth cuts its valley through rich mineral-bearing rock formations. Four thousand years ago, enterprising Bronze Age miners were cutting horizontally into the valley side to extract copper. The Romans also mined there, and later the site was used by the Cistercian monks from Strata Florida Abbey. Over the centuries, silver, lead, and zinc were mined at Cwmystwyth, rising to a peak in the 19th century, when the mines were amongst the most important producers of lead and zinc in Wales. From the 1870s onwards, cheaper imports made the mines uneconomic, and they gradually fell into disuse.

The mines at Cwmystwyth were another piece in the natural resources jigsaw, along with copper, coal, slate, and iron, that made Wales enormously significant in the Industrial Revolution. I stopped to walk around the old mine buildings, thinking of them in their dirty, smelly, and poisonous heyday, when the average miner's life expectancy was just thirty-two. Today, the mine's legacy is harmful metals that seep into the River Ystwyth and subsequently into Cardigan Bay. The significant advances of the Industrial Revolution are rightly celebrated, but the high price, in terms of human suffering and environmental damage, is rarely discussed. Broken shards of rock scattered over the dusty surface everywhere I looked were shimmering in the baking sun as I pulled away and headed for Devil's Bridge, which lay a few miles further north and only 12 miles from the coast at Aberystwyth.

I was soon putting the motorcycle on its stand in the free car park at the village of Devil's Bridge or Pontarfynach, which translates to 'bridge over the Mynach' (Welsh for monk). Artists and poets such as Turner and Wordsworth have visited the village over the years. The chief attraction is the spectacular and unusual sight of three bridges stacked on top of each other, spanning the steep gorge of the River Mynach (Afon Mynach). There are woodland walks through parts of the gorge, allowing visitors to view the 100-metre-high waterfalls. The monks of Strata Florida probably constructed the first bridge in the 12th century on the route between their abbey just outside Pontrhydfendigaid and the church at Ysbyty Cynfyn, a few miles from the bridge. I suspect that the famous legend about the first bridge has evolved to boost visitor numbers. It involves the Devil trying to trick an elderly woman so he could gain the soul of the first living thing to cross the bridge. The canny old lady was wise to the scam and played her own trick on the Devil. He didn't gain a human soul, but it didn't end well for the old woman's dog! The second bridge, a stone construction, was built in 1753, and the top bridge was put in place in 1901. I took my time to walk to the bottom of the gorge and look up at the three bridges. A double scoop vanilla and chocolate ice cream later, I was on my way again, heading for the abbey at Strata Florida.

It's a lovely twisty ride through beautiful undulating scenery as you head down the B4343 from Devil's Bridge to the village of Pontrhydfendigaid and the road to Strata Florida. On the way, you pass through villages with names that would be incredible scores in Scrabble if the rules allowed place names and there were enough tiles in the box. Ysbyty Ystwyth, for example, could earn you up to 158 points (triple word and all seven tiles used), but it would require a change of rules, two and a half boxes worth of the letter Y, and a very understanding playing partner.

I stopped at an interpretation board in the small village of Ffair Rhos, which was little more than a scattering of buildings around a crossroads. The name goes back to medieval times, when the village was the site of annual wool fairs held by the monks of Strata Florida. When the abbey was abandoned, the annual gatherings continued as cattle and horse fairs, and the village became a crossroads of drovers' routes, used to take livestock east to England. In the 19th century, Ffair Rhos became a mining village housing families that worked the Esgair- Mwyn lead mine, just under a mile to the northwest. Looking at the map today, you can see a scattering of old mines, pits, quarries, and disused mine shafts.

In the notes I took when I stopped at the side of the road, I described the village of Pontrhydfendigaid as having a quirky humpbacked bridge, lots of old miners' cottages painted in a variety of colours, and a *very* red pub. From the village, I turned onto the appropriately named Abbey Road, a name that suggested something long and winding. In fact, it was less than a mile before I arrived at the ruins of Strata Florida. It's a strange name, conjuring up images of an exotic cocktail or maybe a stripy ice lolly, but the name derives from the Latinisation of its Welsh name Ystrad Fflur; or 'Valley of Flowers' in English, which is a much nicer image. The abbey was founded in 1164 and is deeply significant in Welsh history. The abbey church was the largest in Wales at the time of its construction. Generations of Welsh princes are said to be buried there. What's left of the abbey is tucked away safely in the folds of the Cambrian Mountains.

After parking the motorcycle, I tucked in behind a group of visitors, who were following a guide. I thought it would be a good way of finding out more until I realised the guide's loud and detailed description of the site was being given in Welsh. The abbey was built in the Cistercian style, which is characterised by simple lines and the use of local materials. Sadly, there is little of that to see now, except an impressive arch and the lower sections of several walls and buildings. Interpretation boards explain the layout of the abbey, its history, and the life of the monks. One of them explains the designs on the elaborately decorated floor tiles you can see in the remains of some of the buildings. Strata Florida may not be on the same level as the grandeur of Tintern Abbey or Llanthony Priory, but that's not the abbey's fault. The blame for its destruction is down to Henry VIII, although it should be noted that Henry IV also used the abbey as a military base during his battle against Owain Glyndŵr; he had already stripped the site of much of its wealth a century before the dissolution of the monasteries in 1536.

The cultural and religious significance of Strata Florida Abbey reached new heights in the Middle Ages. Through the acquisition of vast swathes of farmland and the exploitation of the mineral wealth of nearby mountains, the monks of the abbey amassed great wealth and transformed it into a beacon of culture and learning. They preserved the history of Wales, compiling a library of national records, ancient Welsh customs, myths and traditions, as well as the works of bards and genealogies of prominent Welsh families. The abbey also played a pivotal role in politics, hosting a council of Welsh princes, led by Llywelyn ap Iorwerth, also known as Llywelyn the Great. Despite its prestige, the abbey faced relentless persecution from the English for its steadfast support of the Welsh princes.

Earlier this year, I was lucky enough to find a signed copy of a book called *Up the Claerwen,* written by Sid Wright in 1948. The book describes five routes for crossing the Cambrian Mountains from Rhayader or Builth Wells to Aberystwyth. Sid Wright's account of the abbey's demise is a powerful reminder of the loss of Welsh independence and culture during the 16th century. The abbey was a symbol of Welsh identity and pride, and its destruction was a blow to the Welsh people. He writes:

> But with the dying freedom of Wales perished also the glory of Strata Florida; the pen of her monks refused to chronicle the successes and triumphs of the conqueror; her altars were no longer frequented by the descendants of those who had raised them; the rude magnificence of an almost barbaric regal line was no longer displayed at solemn seasons in her holy fane; she had enough to do to save a remnant of her vast possessions out of the 'lion's mouth,' until, year after year, broad manors and extensive tracts of country were forcibly wrenched out of her grasp, her influence drooped as her lands and wealth dwindled away (Wright, 1948, p66).

Strata Florida Abbey is a significant part of the rich history and culture of Wales, and Wright's words remind us how important it is to ensure that such rich heritage is not forgotten.

Some surviving records and relics from the abbey can now be found in the National Library of Wales, in Aberystwyth, which I had on my schedule for later in my *Journey through Wales*. The relics include the Nanteos Cup, a simple wooden chalice rumoured to be the Holy Grail. Just stop for a second and let that sink in... the Holy Grail!

It was mid-afternoon by the time I'd found my way back to the Elan Valley, but the beauty of travelling in summer is the long hours of daylight, so I still had plenty of time for a relaxed 60-mile cruise around the reservoirs. I'm sure Chris from Llandovery would back me up when I say that riding around the winding roads of the Elan Valley on a motorcycle on such a day is a real treat. You keep coming across amazing dams and reservoirs… it's like a Welsh Lake District.

The Corporation of Birmingham built the six Elan Valley Reservoirs in the late 19th century, transforming the landscape of Mid Wales. The first to be built was the Caban Coch dam, which was constructed between 1892 and 1904, and the last one, also the largest, is the Claerwen Reservoir, constructed between 1949 and 1952. Claerwen Reservoir is about 3.7 square miles in size. In the late 19th century, as industry and cities spread across the midlands of England, the need for clean water became dire. The poor living conditions and water-borne diseases in Birmingham led Joseph Chamberlain, mayor of the city, to act. In a bold move, he orchestrated the acquisition of several water companies and brought in the consultant, Robert Rawlinson, to find a solution. The Elan and Claerwen rivers of Mid Wales had the catchment area, high rainfall, and elevation to make them the top choice for providing clean water. It was a controversial choice; 300 people had to move because of the construction of the reservoirs. Despite their contentious history, the Elan Valley Reservoirs have created a breathtakingly beautiful landscape. These reservoirs in the Cambrian Mountains offer a serene and picturesque experience, even when the water levels are low. The reservoirs are a statement of our ability to transform the environment (in this case someone else's), but also a symbol of nature's resilience in adapting to those changes.

It was one of those afternoons when you just cruise along, taking in the sights and sounds of the world around you. I spent a few hours exploring the Elan Valley Reservoirs, taking notes, snapping photos, and enjoying the peace of the place. As I left the reservoirs behind me, it was Roger Waters that the jukebox in my head cued up for an unexpected but very welcome performance of 'Pigs'… maybe triggered by a subconscious connection with water. As I cruised slowly back for another night in Rhayader, my mind reviewed the amazing variety of things I'd experienced that day, from archaeology to wild swimming, copper mines to the Holy Grail, and not forgetting the 19th century water infrastructure. The random variety of things along the way was mind-boggling, and the next day would probably be the same – although it was also going to include some cultural input in the form of a William Shakespeare play. Its bonkers, but as the little voice in my head reminded me – it's *As You Like It.*

After covering some serious mileage over the previous days, my second full day in Rhayader was more sedate. I popped into the tearooms by the crossroads in the town centre for a relaxed breakfast. It gave me some quiet time to catch up with my notes and look forward to that appointment with Bill Shakespeare in the afternoon. For almost an hour in the café, I had a front-row seat watching streams of criss-crossing traffic: people on their way to work, visiting, or off to do the shopping. For most of that time, red kites soared in the airspace above the clock tower, like stacked planes awaiting landing permission.

After the waitress had disappeared with my breakfast order, I heard a sudden stream of melodic conversation coming out of the kitchen. Yes! At last, I'd found someone speaking Welsh. When she reappeared, I told her it had taken me the best part of 2 days staying in and around the town to hear a Welsh person speaking in their native tongue. She smiled and said she was from Liverpool. Her mum, out in the kitchen, was from Turkey, so they conversed in Turkish, with the odd word of Welsh and English thrown in. What I'd heard was her telling her mum that they needed to bake some more rock cakes.

The second waitress *was* a Rhayader girl. She told me how things in the town had changed over the years. Recently, locals had been selling up, encouraged by soaring house prices, with so many retired 'outsiders' moving in. The balance of the population was changing – as it is everywhere. She told me the café's customers were mainly a combination of elderly locals and tourists, especially walkers, cyclists, and motorcyclists.

A couple of American tourists came in and sat at the table next to me. After they'd finished a heated debate over whether or not their eggs could be correctly described as over-easy, the conversation turned to the latest wave of COVID to hit California. Apparently, the Yellowstone National Park could be closed for years. The rest of their conversation seemed to involve bunches of this and bunches of that, stuff that was sick, and a few things that were awesome. A group of three elderly ladies came in for their cappuccinos and relived the highlight of their weekend – a day trip to the bright lights of Cardiff.

I downed the last of my tea and headed for a couple of hours' research in Rhayader's excellent library. The friendly librarian showed me the section dealing with Wales and local history. One book that caught my eye was called, *In Search of Birds in Mid Wales*. It took me back to my teenage years, although my search wasn't so geographically restricted. I wondered how many people had opened that book up expecting to find something more racy than Cambrian ornithology. There was a steady stream of users who clearly appreciated the many facilities and friendly service available

– note to Powys Council, please keep this hugely valuable community resource open!

I wrote up some notes and lost myself in books about the local area for a while, before I set off for my afternoon at the theatre. Stepping out of the pages and back into reality, I took the A470, on another glorious sunny afternoon, to a turning about 4 miles south of Rhayader. Signs directed me down a small track to a car park in a field. This was clearly no ordinary theatre I was heading for. The Willow Globe, or Y Glôb Byw, as it's known locally, is an open-air theatre made entirely of living willow. Planted in 2006 by local volunteers headed up by a small charity, Shakespeare Link, it is a scaled down willow version of the Globe theatre in London.

I bought a ticket and a beer from a helpful volunteer called Louise, in a barn that doubled up as the box office and bar. In the hubbub of people coming and going around the box office and heading for the theatre, Louise pointed out some members of the theatre company and told me a bit about its background. Since planting the theatre they've run Shakespeare-related productions, festivals, and workshops on the site every year, with the season beginning on 23rd April, the date traditionally celebrated as Shakespeare's birthday, and running through to mid-September. The timing of my visit to Rhayader was just fortunate: it coincided with the Willow Globe Theatre Company's production of *As You Like It*. Louise had tickets to sell, so I left her to it, but before I made my way to the theatre, she added 'Oh, don't forget to pick up a cushion before you find a seat, and there's plenty of mosquito repellent in the basket by the entrance. Help yourself.' Good advice, and not the sort you'd get at many West End theatres.

I followed a steady stream of people wandering towards the theatre, which at first sight looked like a sizeable green thicket or small copse in a field. I'd guess the circle of branches, open to the sky, must be about 15 metres in diameter, stretching up about 4 metres at its highest. Sure enough, at the theatre entrance, there was a basket of assorted sprays and roll-on insect repellents. It was on a wooden bench, next to a pile of cushions and a notice warning theatre-goers to be aware of rabbit holes. Once inside, I took my place on a fairly rustic wooden bench in the second row. The seats in front seemed to be within touching distance of the stage, which looked like an area of decking about the size of a garden patio. I could tell it was the stage because written on the front were the words, 'All the world's a stage.'

It was a bizarre and magical experience even before the play started. The bushy willow branches woven together to create the theatre walls give the building a sense of organic movement, as if it's a living, breathing entity – and it is. Opposite me, on the far side, a small band was warming up, partially hidden by branches and leaves. There was a very mixed audience. Some people were dressed for a night at Covent Garden, some looked like they'd just finished milking down on the farm – and then there was me in my motorcycle over-trousers and jacket. Louise took a seat on the next bench, ready to provide prompts if needed. The play got underway, and it was a mesmerising experience – I loved it. The smell of fresh willow and the sound of birds singing in the background added to the special atmosphere of the place. During the quiet moments, you could hear the high-pitched mewing of a red kite circling high above the stage, or the rhythmic baa-ing of sheep in the next field giving their opinion on the performance so far. Willow warblers hopped from branch to branch as if gate-crashing the performance to see what all the fuss was about. The play itself was absolutely delightful – I didn't know the story before I went, but it was easy to follow, and hugely enjoyable. The cast were just amazing and hats off too for the acting, the singing, the humour, the costumes, the music, the cushions, and everything to do with the production: it was an absolute delight. And I didn't even need the insect repellent.

There was a chance for another drink after the show and I

loved how the cast mingled with the audience to share a chat, a joke, a glass of wine, or a cup of coffee. I headed back to Rhayader still buzzing from the show, and wondering what the next day was going to bring that could possibly match the last couple of days in Mid Wales.

3

RHAYADER TO TREVOR

Continuing north from Rhayader, my route roughly tracked the boundary between the Welsh hills to the west and the English lowlands to the east. Before we get any further, let's talk about that border. Chepstow, at the southern end of the River Wye, and Flint (Fflint), on the Dee estuary (Aber Dyfrdwy), are the approximate ends of the land border between Wales and England. The distance between them is just over 112 miles, according to the UK Racing Pigeon online distance checker. This very helpful point-to-point distance measuring website resists the temptation to use 'as the pigeon flies' miles as its units of measurement, opting for the more traditional crow-based version. Pigeons that opt to walk the land border, however, if they had a fear of flying, for example, will find they have to travel 160 miles; over 40% further than the direct line distance. The significant discrepancy between the two distances is because of the border's unpredictable undulations, akin to the agitated tail of a Welsh dragon, which contorts and twists in a serpentine manner. As it bumps past Gloucestershire, Herefordshire, Shropshire, and Cheshire, the boundary twists one way, and then seemingly on a whim, it doubles back again the other way. In places, the convulsions make sense because the border follows the course of a river, as it does on parts of the River Wye or River Severn. In other places, the randomness seems to defy logic.

I shimmied along the border with England as I rode northward, doing the hokey cokey, one leg in, one leg out, hopping in and out of each country without even realising it. Road signs would suddenly appear, welcoming me to Wales, and I'd think, 'Wait, when did I leave?' It's a real head-scratcher. We all know how Wales lies to the west of England but between Bishops Castle (Shropshire, England) and Montgomery (Powys, Wales), you can go east into Wales and west into England. In Llanymynech, the border runs down the middle of the street, dividing the main road in two. At the local golf course, you can drive in Wales and putt in England. But that's the nature of the crazy border, it's like a rollercoaster, twisting, and turning, taking you for a wild ride – bordering on the outrageous.

After bidding farewell to Rhayader, I took a little detour down to Llandrindod Wells. I picked up the A483, which took me north to Newtown (Y Drenewydd) and then onto Welshpool (Y Trallwng). Just to get our bearings, the A483 is one of those top-to-bottom roads that run the length of Wales, like a spinal cord. It starts in Chester and ends in Swansea (Abertawe), 153 miles later. There's also the A470, which runs from Llandudno to Cardiff, 186 miles in total… if you can have two spinal cords. The two roads cross at Builth Wells. Anyway, I carried on northwards, taking another diversion into the Cambrian Mountains, before finding my way back to the A483 near my old hometown of Oswestry.

Riding a motorcycle north from Llandrindod Wells to Welshpool, if the weather is fine, is pure joy. The views are spectacular, and the road is a never-ending ribbon of gentle curves, winding this way and that. There are spectacular views out to the west as you approach Newtown from the south on those lovely, twisty roads. I'd been to Newtown many times, passing up and down the A483, but more precisely I'd passed around the town. Since 2019, the latest bypass completely avoids the town altogether, so this time I was going to head for the centre and have a good look around. But first I was going just a few miles further north to the visit the remains of Dolforwyn Castle, near the village of Abermule.

Back in the 13th century, this was the wild frontier. To the south and east were the Welsh Marches and England. To the north and west were the native Welsh lands under the control of Llywelyn ap Gruffydd. In 1267, King Henry III signed the Treaty of Montgomery, which confirmed Llywelyn ap Gruffydd as the Prince of Wales. Wales was officially an independent country, united under Llywelyn's leadership – almost. Llywelyn had fought hard to bring most of Wales under his rule, defending his country, and taking the fight to the English, just like his father and grandfather had done before him. He built Dolforwyn Castle, the last great Welsh castle, between 1273 and 1277, on a high ridge (231 metres) that provided commanding views down the Severn Valley. It was the administrative HQ for the lands he controlled to the north and west, and it would act as a lookout on the edge of his territory. The town that grew around the castle, provided work and protection for the people living there. Unfortunately, that protection was short-lived. When Edward I became king in 1272, it was bad news for Wales – and anyone else who wasn't English.

Edward I might be known as the Hammer of the Scots, but he was equally ruthless with his treatment of the Welsh. On hearing about Llywelyn ap Gruffydd's Dolforwyn Castle project, he ordered work to stop immediately. Llywelyn replied that he didn't need planning permission to build on his own land, which didn't go down well with the new king. Edward I gave permission for Roger Mortimer, a local Marcher Lord, to sort things out. Dolforwyn Castle was eventually over-run in 1277 and as a reward, the castle and all the seized lands were granted to Mortimer. The king commissioned him to build a new market town in the nearby Manor of Cedewain, to act as the new English administrative centre in the strategically important region of Mid Wales. And so, they built Newtown.

We'll come across Edward I later on the *Journey through Wales*. He's hard to avoid in Wales, but in brief, between 1277 and 1283, he invaded the country with three major campaigns, using resources on a scale that overwhelmed the Welsh opposition. King Edward I built his famous 'ring of iron' castles to maintain control over the native population and he created 'planted towns' (new administrative centres, populated mainly by English incomers), such as Caernarfon, Conwy, and Harlech.

Less than a mile west of the little village of Abermule, there's a parking area at the side of a small lane. I left the bike there and took a leisurely fifteen-minute stroll up the winding path that leads up a hillside to the ruins of Dolforwyn Castle. Spotting a possible tasty take-away, two buzzards soared and circled above me as I plodded up the last steep section of the path. The cool breeze blowing through the trees was a welcome relief from the heat of the climb, and soon I found myself standing alone in the ruins of Dolforwyn Castle. The birds left, disappointed. The remains of the ancient walls were only a metre or so high in most places, but the plan outline of the castle and its internal walls were clear to see. There was no one else in sight or earshot. I walked around, read the interpretive panels, took notes and photos, and then rested a while, taking in the magnificent views out to the east, and down the Severn Valley. I tried to imagine what it would have been like to be holed up in the castle, surrounded by hundreds of hostile forces, and running short of food and water. It reminded me I was short of food and water, so I headed back to the bike and continued down the road to Newtown.

Newtown sits about 7 miles from the border with England and is the largest town in Powys and Mid Wales. The local joke is that Newtown has been a new town since 1279 although, confusingly, it was also awarded New Town status in 1967 as part of a regional development plan.

I'd visited the town briefly a few years earlier during a motorcycle ride from Land's End to John o'Groats (described in the book *Another Journey through Britain*). The town enjoyed its boom times in the 18th and 19th centuries, growing wealthy on the town's textile and flannel industries. The steam driven Cambrian Mill became the largest woollen mill in Wales, and for a while, Newtown was known as 'the Leeds of Wales.' I'll leave you to decide if that's a good thing.

On this trip, I'd come to see something else, a link to a remarkable past that's not widely known about. I parked in the town's main street, at one end of Long Bridge, (which I'm glad to report was a long bridge), which spans the River Severn. I found myself opposite the old Flannel Exchange, once the grandest building in town. Flannel, in this case, is the soft woven cloth produced from wool, not the slang word for flattery and nonsense, nor the small squares of double-napped cotton you use to wash your face and more difficult-to-reach parts of the body. Two hundred years ago, Newtown was the largest flannel production centre in Wales, possibly Britain, and the Flannel Exchange was the marketplace where it was traded. The size and architectural style of the building echo those glory days, except that now, it's a cinema and the 'Steam Mill' – two floors of pumping bass, pulsing lights, and guest DJs. The name is a nod to the heady days of the Cambrian Mill. I imagine, to this day, there's still a fair amount of flannel talk on a Saturday night.

I walked up the town's wide main street, satisfyingly named Broad Street, looking for something to eat. They still hold an open-air market there every Tuesday, a practice that goes back to the town's original charter in 1279. I found myself drawn into the porch of one of those attractive looking 17th-century black and white, timber-framed buildings. It turned out to be a Wetherspoons pub called the Black Boy. Inside, the bar walls were decorated with photos, prints, and painting, showing the history of the town – plenty of images of sheep, the markets, wool mills, marching bands, and of course, John Roberts, the Romani Gypsy harpist who was once the country's leading performer on the Welsh triple harp. Eating in the pub gave me an opportunity to talk to the people working there. I couldn't help but wonder about the pub's name. Wasn't it a bit inappropriate these days? The bartender informed me that the name had been around for ages, and it actually referred to a chimney sweep – in this case the junior version. The pub owners had even held a public vote on the name a few years ago and the majority had voted to keep the traditional name. I wandered aimlessly up Broad Street to nose around further before continuing my journey, and I'm glad I did. It was as though fate had told me to stay a while longer. I came across the Robert Owen Museum and spent a very enjoyable half an hour learning more about someone who I knew little about.

Robert Owen is the town's most famous son and a true visionary. Born in 1771, he grew up in a community that valued social justice and mutual support. He found great success in the textile industry but despite his wealth, Owen was horrified by the inhumane conditions faced by factory workers, including young children. He decided to do something about it. He moved to Scotland and transformed the New Lanark Mills in Scotland into a model factory and community. Under his leadership, the mills became a shining example of fair working practices and education for all. Owen is credited with opening Britain's first infants' school at the mills in 1816 – that is 21 years before the first kindergarten in Germany, and 44 years before anything similar was established in the US. His legacy lives on to this day – the New Lanark Mills are now a UNESCO World Heritage Site.

But Owen wasn't the only notable figure to come out of Newtown. The friendly woman behind the reception desk in the Robert Owen Museum told me about other famous residents like Laura Ashley OBE, David Davis, and Pryce Pryce-

Jones. In fact, she proudly pointed out that the town had even named four new roundabouts on the bypass after those notable figures. It was Pryce-Jones, who I wanted to find out about. Few people will have heard of him, but back in the mid-19th century, he created the business model for buying goods by mail order. That industry is now a global one worth about £75bn – imagine what Pryce-Jones, the Jeff Bezos of his day, could have done if he'd had access to the Internet!

Pryce-Jones left school aged twelve and worked in a drapery shop. When he took over the business 10 years later, it grew rapidly through a combination of good service, high quality, and innovative ideas. Many of his customers lived in the scattered towns and villages surrounding Newtown, so instead of waiting for them to come to him, he contacted them. He sent patterns, leaflets, and brochures out to his customers, showing his range of products made from local Welsh flannel. His customers would then send in their orders, and he sent the goods back. At first, he used the post office and sometimes the stagecoach to distribute his goods. Later, he was also able to use the railway. He had started the mail order industry.

The awards Pryce-Jones won at the National Eisteddfod of Wales added to his reputation and by the 1870s, his A-list customers included Florence Nightingale, Queen Victoria (who knighted him in 1887) and most of the crowned heads of Europe. As custom grew, he had to move to bigger premises and in 1879, he built the Royal Welsh Warehouse, opposite the Newtown train station. Britain's expanding rail network helped Pryce-Jones to increase his sales and marketing reach, and by 1880 he had over 100,000 customers, some as far away as the US and Australia. He built another factory in 1895 and six years later, he needed to add a post office to cope with demand.

The birth of mail order home shopping in Newtown is a remarkable story, and not one you might associate with a little market town in Mid Wales. The Royal Welsh Warehouse and the factory buildings are still there, and that's where I was heading next. They're easy to find – just locate the station and you're there. The two red-brick and stone buildings, four and five-stories high respectively are still impressive sights. On the front of the main building are the royal crest and two stone plaques embossed with 'Paris 1878' and 'Vienna 1883' to mark the company's attendance at two prestigious international expositions. I was reminded of the enormous Amazon distribution warehouse I'd passed on my way up to Wales, next to the M5 at Severn Beach, Bristol. It's the modern-day equivalent of the Royal Welsh Warehouse. Nowadays, the two original mail order buildings in Newtown have been split into a variety of businesses. There's a gym, a business start-up centre, a ten-pin bowling alley, a carpet shop, and a breakout room – whatever that is. I wandered into each of the two buildings and looked around as much as I could. Some of the surviving details showed the luxurious standard to which the buildings had been constructed, with elegant parquet flooring on the stairwell landings and lovely honey-brown tiling on the walls. I took a few notes, a few photos, and decided to break out – it was time to head up the A483 again towards Welshpool and on to Lake Vyrnwy (Llŷn Efyrnwy).

The weather continued to be kind as I tracked westwards into the northern end of the Cambrian Mountains and the Berwyns – a little known yet spectacular mountain range. I rode under almost cloudless skies through more 'lumpy bumpy' border farmland, like the area south of Rhayader. I was heading towards a small hamlet called Pennant Melangell, but first, I wanted to revisit Lake Vyrnwy on the way. When my wife Jan and I lived in Oswestry not so long ago, the lake and the village of Llanwddyn were a short drive or ride out and we often popped over for a walk, a visit to the RSPB bird hide, a coffee in the café – or even all three if we were feeling particularly reckless.

Like the Elan Valley Reservoirs further south, Lake

Vyrnwy is a Victorian creation. It was built in the 1880s to provide fresh water to Liverpool, 66 miles away as the pipe-line flows. The lake and dam, in their beautiful mountain setting, were a magnificent sight when I arrived. I always feel calm and relaxed there, but then I've only ever seen it on warm, peaceful days. With its shimmering blue waters almost completely surrounded by tall pine trees that come down to the water's edge, the lake has quite a Nordic vibe. It's also an engineering masterpiece. The 44-metre-high dam was the first large stone-built dam in Britain and was the first to carry water over its crest instead of down channels at the side. The surface area of the lake is 1.8 square miles, or the equivalent of about 600 rugby pitches, which is an important comparison for some people, especially if they're Welsh. Lake Vyrnwy is a designated nature reserve and around ninety species of bird have been recorded as breeding there.

The Lake Vyrnwy reservoir was surrounded by contro-versy when it was built, like its Elan Valley counterparts, and many others in Wales. Construction involved flooding the original village of Llanwddyn, whose residents had no say in the matter. Despite the uproar created, the decision makers in Westminster repeated the trick again in the 1960s when they permitted the creation of the Tryweryn reservoir near Bala. Liverpudlians must have got even thirstier, so the decision was made to dam the River Tryweryn and flood the village of Capel Celyn. Like Llanwddyn before, the residents, other members of the public, and Welsh MPs had little say in the matter. But Capel Celyn was different. It was the 1960s and 1970s, a time when Welsh people felt their language and traditional culture was under threat. There was indignation over the Tryweryn reservoir scheme throughout Wales and perhaps people weren't so deferential to authority as they had been in Victorian times. Tryweryn symbolised a way of life and a language being overwhelmed and drowned out by the English. The words, 'Cofiwch Dryweryn' (Remember Tryw-eryn) were painted on the wall of a derelict cottage by the side of the main road between Aberystwyth and Llanrhystud, and the words became a rallying cry for Welsh patriots. The name, Tryweryn, has become iconic in Welsh culture and politics, and lives on through art, poetry, and music.

Leaving Lake Vyrnwy, I skirted the southern edge of the Berwyn mountains, riding some spectacular B roads through dense coniferous forest for most of the way to Pennant Melangell. At the small village of Llangynog, I turned onto a narrow lane that weaved alongside the upper reaches of the Afon Tanat in a landscape that was scoured out during the last Ice Age. Snowdonia National Park was less than 2 miles away. The tiny country lane was lined with thick green hazel hedges, and almost at the end, at the head of the pretty Cwm Pennant, I found St Melangell's Church, which houses the restored shrine of Saint Melangell. It's reputed to be the earliest surviving Romanesque shrine in Northern Europe (Romanesque architecture was a style that lasted from around AD 1000 until the Gothic-style in about AD 1150). I was keen to visit Pennant Melangell because I'd seen it described as one of the holiest places in Britain.

Pennant Melangell Church lies in a quiet and green part of the narrow valley floor. The Afon Tanat meanders slowly past, its gentle babbling providing arriving pilgrims with a soothing melodic background of watery liturgical chanting. The valley towers up steeply on three sides to around 550 metres, wrapping itself around Pennant Melangell as if to protect it and confirm it as a place of sanctuary. Apart from the church, there's just a handful of other properties, including the St Melangell Centre. To call it a hamlet is a bit of an exaggeration. This is a church without a local congregation – a Pilgrim's church.

Surrounding the simple Norman, 12th century church is a circular churchyard, and just inside the boundary wall is a ring of ancient yew trees, suggesting the site goes back to the Bronze Age. Next to the churchyard, a car park occupies the old common land that was used for centuries as a meeting place. It still is…. already in the car park when I arrived were at least a dozen other dusty looking motorcycles. Their riders stood around drinking coffee and sharing banter and experiences. It turned out that they came from near my home in Dorset and they were on a two-day off-road and green lane experience holiday. It was great to meet and chat with them, but I was also happy when they rode off, restoring the peace and silence that seems more appropriate for Pennant Melangell.

Saint Melangell (or Monacella) lived in the 7th century and is the patron saint of hares. Her story, in various versions, is found in medieval writings. She was the daughter of an Irish king who wanted to marry her off to one of the noblemen in his court. She was having none of it, so she did what anyone would do – she fled to remote Wales, to live like a hermit in the Tanat Valley. It is said that she didn't see the face of a man for 15 years. Like many of these stories, it involves a prince. This one, Brochwel Ysgithrog, Prince of Powys, is described as either dashing or dastardly (I suppose he could have been both) depending on your source. One day, in the year 604, Prince Brochwel was out hunting in the valley near to where Melangell was quietly in worship. His hounds chased a brown hare into a thicket, where Melangell was praying. The hare found sanctuary under Melangell's cloak, and when they saw her, the hounds ran away, howling. Impressed by her compassion, courage, and sanctity, Prince Brochwel generously gave her the valley to live in as a place of sanctuary. Melangell founded a small religious community there and became its abbess (a woman in charge of a convent). Following her death, her memory continued to be honoured and Pennant Melangell became a place of pilgrimage. A shrine was erected to her in the 12th century but was dismantled during the Protestant Reformation. Her bones were hidden from those doing the reforming, but they were eventually returned to the rebuilt shrine in the 20th century.

I took my time to look around the church and the shrine. I

felt a special atmosphere, a feeling of serenity, peace, and safety. It was the same calmness that I felt at Llanthony Priory and it's difficult to put it into words. Was it really there, or did I want it to be there? It was clearly a spiritually charged place in a beautiful setting that had witnessed the emotional outpourings of thousands of pilgrims over centuries. Scores of messages left at the base of St Melangell's shrine, many with pictures of hares, were evidence that this is still considered a very holy place, and still a place of sanctuary for pilgrims from all over the globe. Whatever was going on, I felt uplifted, and I was glad I'd put Pennant Melangell on my list of places to visit.

My next stop, Pistyll Rhaeadr (in English, spring of the waterfall), was a couple of valleys away to the northwest. It was about 4 miles as the crow flies, but three times that distance as the crow rides a motorcycle. It's another place I'd visited regularly when we lived in Oswestry and I couldn't pass the opportunity to take another look at the highest waterfall in Wales, and Britain's tallest single-drop waterfall. At 73 metres, the drop is greater than that of Niagara Falls, but nothing like as wide. From the village of Llanrhaeadr-ym-Mochnant, I turned onto the reassuringly named Waterfall Street. It's then a 4 mile ride up the valley of the Afon Rhaeadr, which pokes a wedge into the steep sides of the Berwyns. It's a very narrow roller coaster of a lane. At busy times, with up to 2,000 visitors per day, it can become grid locked; you're forever coming across vehicles coming the other way and having to back up to find a passing place. I was glad to be on my motorcycle this time – and especially on such a perfect day.

Pistyll Rhaeadr is referred to in the 'Seven Wonders of Wales' poem, which according to most sources, was written by an anonymous poet, who was possibly English. The rhyme lists notable Welsh landmarks, and my plan was to tick them all off over the following few days to see just how wondrous they were.

Pistyll Rhaeadr and Wrexham steeple,
Snowdon's mountain without its people,
Overton yew trees, St Winefride's wells,
Llangollen bridge and Gresford bells

When I'd ridden almost as far as possible, I parked on the verge next to the river. It was just before the car park at the end of the road, which by early afternoon was almost full. From where I parked, it took less than 5 minutes to walk to the base of the falls. If you have the time, there are lovely paths that wind their way through the woods to the top of the falls, with stunning views back down the Tanat Valley (Dyffryn Tanat). Standing at its base, Pistyll Rhaeadr is an awesome sight. The River Disgynfa cascades off the Berwyns in three stages, to a plunge pool at the base of the falls. Thick green curtains of trees, grasses, and mosses have been pulled back on either side of the falls to let it cascade through and down in a scene that looks like something from the Amazon jungle. The Afon Rhaeadr emerges from the plunge pool at the bottom of the falls and heads down the valley to contribute to the waters of the River Severn, via the Afon Tanat and River Vyrnwy. It was the briefest of visits and I felt I was working my way through the scenic sights tick-list again as I walked back to the bike to head 3 miles down the road to Llanrhaeadr, and then on to Sycharth, before my overnight stop in the village of Trevor (Trefor).

I think most people who live in the border area around Llanrhaeadr-ym-Mochnant just call it 'Llanrhaeadr.' Jan and I certainly did when we lived about 11 miles away, near Oswestry. I stopped off at the village church there because it's another location that holds a significant place in Welsh history, confirmed by the sign that greets you as you enter the village. It reads, 'Welcome to Llanrhaeadr-ym-Mochnant church, birthplace of the Welsh Bible.'

William Morgan was the vicar of the parish (and rector of Pennant Melangell) when he created a Welsh language version of *The Bible* in 1588. Its influence on Welsh literature, culture, and education cannot be overestimated. It was no straightforward task, however, because until then, there was no standardised version of Welsh. The revised version of his work, published in 1620, remained in use in Wales for over 200 years and has been credited with saving the Welsh language. It was the main tool used in the circulating schools of the 18th century (described later in Chapter Six) and enabled almost 70% of the population of Wales to receive schooling. I walked around inside the church, read the interpretation panels, and saw a hand printed copy of the 16th century Bible as translated by William Morgan (on loan from the University Library of Wales, Aberystwyth).

By the time I reached Sycharth, about 6 miles further east, I was feeling punch drunk from the barrage of big-hitting historical sites I'd visited over the last few days. Sycharth is right up there among the big ones, though, because it was the 13th century home of Owen Glyndŵr, a towering figure in Welsh history, whose legacy still resonates today.

A majestic oak tree at Sycharth Castle

Sycharth Castle lies nestled in the picturesque Welsh

borderlands just a stone's throw from the border itself. It's another one of those places that somehow exudes an aura of historical significance. The remnants of an ancient motte and bailey are a short walk across a field from the small car park. Though the castle walls have long since crumbled, I found them easy to visualise as I sat on the circular mound that remains. The ditch surrounding the inner mound is watched over by a pair of majestic oak trees, standing sentinel like guardians of the past. An artist's illustration of the castle on an interpretation board shows a walled courtyard surrounding the castle on top of the inner mound, with a bridge over a water-filled ditch leading to a larger fenced compound.

Just how grand the castle was is difficult to say, but that wasn't the point. Sycharth Castle was a symbol of Welsh independence and a centre of culture and politics during Owain Glyndŵr's time. Here, he held court, received ambassadors, and made speeches to his followers. Today, the site of Sycharth Castle may be just a hilly mound, but its significance to the Welsh people endures. It stands as a symbol of Welsh heritage and culture, and a reminder of the country's ongoing fight for independence. As I departed, I was glad to have *felt*, as well as seen, such an important icon of Welsh history.

From Sycharth Castle, it was only a 7-mile ride to Oswestry, my home for nearly 4 years until 2021, so the area felt very familiar. I popped into England briefly, but then after a quick dart up the A5, I was in Chirk, back in Wales. Now, at last, I was travelling in the footsteps of the writer HV Morton. He begins his book *In Search of Wales* in Shropshire, easing his way into Wales via Ludlow and Shrewsbury. He thought Shrewsbury was glorious and romantic (HV Morton, 1932), but he starts his quest for Wales in earnest when he arrives at the Welsh border town of Chirk. To get to Chirk, HV Morton followed Thomas Telford's historic stagecoach route that runs from Shrewsbury to Holyhead, a route taken nowadays by the A5 trunk road. Thomas Telford built solid roads using substantial foundations, like the Romans had done before him. They were expensive but built to last. Another design feature of Telford's Shrewsbury to Holyhead road was its maximum gradient of 1 in 20. This was for the welfare of coach horses, but I think I speak on behalf of generations of cyclists in thanking him for that gentle incline through the mountains of North Wales. From Chirk, my route took me a final 5 miles to the large village of Trevor in the Vale of Llangollen. The name is an anglicised version of the Welsh name Trefor, meaning large village.

I arrived at the canal marina in Trevor by early afternoon in time to meet my wife, Jan, who'd driven up from Dorset. We loaded our luggage and ourselves onto a 55-foot narrow boat that was going to be our home for the next four nights. We were going to explore the next part of my route, and a small corner of Wales, by water. The hire boats are custom made for holidays and very comfortable – a 6-foot-wide waterborne home from home, including kitchen, bathroom, sleeping quarters, and lounge. The marina is located right next to one of the canal junctions. If you go straight ahead as you exit the marina, you're almost immediately going over the famous Pontcysyllte (sounds like pont-ku-suhlt-uh) Aqueduct and into England. Turning sharp right takes you to Llangollen, about 12 miles away as the narrow boat chugs. And that's where we were heading, to get to the town that evening so we could have a whole day there exploring the day after. We were keen to get going before the canal got too busy. The canal has become one of the most popular cruising grounds in the country and the stretch between Trevor and Llangollen is particularly narrow, even for a narrow boat. There are parts where it's impossible to pass a boat coming the other way.

The afternoon was pleasantly warm as we cast off and turned a sharp 90 degrees right in the canal basin towards

Llangollen. It's quite a tricky three-point manoeuvre in a 55-foot boat, especially as it's needed within the first few minutes that you're in charge, so I was glad to get round without incident. Watching people negotiate the turn as they come in and out of the marina is quite a spectator sport. It can be quite entertaining as you sit outside the nearby Telford Inn on a pleasant afternoon or evening. I'm surprised the onlookers don't have Strictly Come Boating paddle boards to score people's attempts as boats are eased or scrunched around the tight corner of the canal.

We were soon on our own – just us, the boat, the canal, and nature all around. As we glided along slowly, serenaded by the quiet rhythmic thud-thud-thud of the diesel engine, the water of the canal was like a mirror, reflecting the lush green trees that lined our route, and the landscape beyond. Our journey passed through gently rolling fields, which gradually became steeper on either side of the wide valley floor, as we progressed westward. Small groups of cows and sheep with mature lambs filled many of those fields. Some lambs didn't realise they were mature and still insisted on the occasional playful spring in the air. Although the fields came right down to the side of the canal from time to time, the banks were more often lined with hedges. Large hawthorn trees arched over the water in places. The blossom was at its peak and from time to time the light breeze, which was blowing at 90 degrees to the canal, would blow an extra little puff and send a shower of white confetti over us.

The good thing about travelling by canal boat is you can't go anywhere fast. Your boat doesn't know the meaning of words like 'rush' or 'hurry,' and you soon find yourself slowing down, synchronised with your lethargic progression through the water. Although the distance from Trevor to Llangollen is only 12 miles, it took us over 3 hours to get there. As we chugged along, we were travelling back in time, using a means of transport that was in its heyday in the late 18th century. The Llangollen Canal was built at a time of canal mania, to connect the River Dee in the north with the Ellesmere Canal in the south, allowing for the transport of goods such as coal, limestone, and agricultural products. The construction of the canal was a major engineering feat, as the design required it to be built with no locks (which was good for us) through difficult terrain. In 2009, the canal was recognised as a World Heritage site by UNESCO because of its exceptional cultural and natural significance.

The canal was teeming with wildlife, from playful swans and ducks to the occasional heron standing statuesquely at the water's edge. Sheep and cows grazed in the lush green fields either side. In places, groups of cows came down to the water's edge to take a cool drink. As we neared Llangollen, the landscape changed. The towering limestone cliffs of the Eglwyseg Rocks loomed in the distance, and looking back to the east, we could see the impressive Pontcysyllte Aqueduct stretching across the River Dee. After we'd moored up in the marina on the outskirts of the town, we congratulated ourselves on our marvellous feat of navigation and seamanship over a brew of coffee. I leafed through HV Morton's book *In Search of Wales* to see what he had to say about the town, and immediately felt intimidated by his brilliant turn of phrase.

4

TREVOR TO HAWARDEN

Llangollen marina turned out to be a great choice for our overnight stop; not too far to walk into town and quite handy to walk to the Horseshoe Falls (Rhaeadr y Bedol) in the opposite direction. Our plan for the day was to follow HV Morton's footsteps to visit those waterfalls, then go to Valle Crucis Abbey (Abaty Glyn y Groes), and finally Castell Dinas Brân. We started our 8 mile walk by following the canal towpath through the outskirts of Llangollen on the Dee Valley Way. It took us past the Royal International Pavilion, which hosts the Llangollen International Musical Eisteddfod each year, and into the open countryside. Our first stop was the Horseshoe Falls, the weir built by Thomas Telford to control water flow from the River Dee into the canal system and provide water for local industries. It's only a half-hour walk to get to the falls from the marina and as you get closer, the canal narrows, the muddy waters become clearer, and the flow speeds up. We spotted small fish swimming among the reeds in the shallow waters. Every now and then, they'd gamble on a feast, vaulting from the water in a hopeful, acrobatic lunge at unsuspecting flies.

Before we knew it, we were there, at the falls. The weir sweeps in a gentle arc across the River Dee like a half-metre high dam. Above the weir, the river looks inky black and as smooth as glass, hardly seeming to move. Then it reaches the weir, drops over the edge, suddenly in a hurry, and spills into the next section of the river, foaming, and slightly angry. The weir definitely adds a touch of man-made beauty to the natural scenery. There's a flat field to one side, and the gently sloping meadow that tumbles down to the riverbank on the other side looks as though it was tailor-made for summer picnics.

We retraced our steps back along the canal path for a short distance, then cut up to the left, up the Eglwyseg River Valley to find Valle Crucis Abbey. The buildings are now ruined, but when the abbey was founded in the 13th century by Cistercian monks, it was one of the largest and most prosperous monasteries in Wales. The footpath took us through lush fields, full of bleating sheep. The gentle lullaby of the sheep has reverberated across the valley for centuries, since the days when the hoody-wearing brethren of Valle Crucis Abbey first ushered in the era of fleece-based commerce in this region of Wales. We arrived at the abbey by going down a steep set of steps next to the river and crossing a small bridge. It wasn't possible to look around the site because it was closed for the day, but we could see plenty of the ruins from the perimeter fence. The friendly guy cleaning the visitor centre was kind enough to give us some leaflets from which we were able to discover that this historic gem of Welsh architecture boasts the only surviving monastic fishpond in Wales! The monks were forbidden from eating meat, so their food intake consisted mainly of fish along with fresh vegetables and herbs. Their pescatarian diet would have been a much healthier one than most of us have today.

HV Morton considered the short walk from Llangollen to Valle Crucis Abbey to be one of the most beautiful in Britain. It is certainly very pleasant, especially the parts alongside the canal. His description of the abbey ruins is typically vivid and descriptive, but while he saw the evening sun gently illuminating the abbey and its surroundings in hues of gold (Morton, 1932), we found the place closed off, and positioned between a caravan site and a group of camping pods.

We walked back along the same path and took a detour to climb up to Castell Dinas Brân, known for years to my wife's family (and I suspect many others) as Crow Castle. The views were amazing even from only halfway to the top, and as we climbed, we were serenaded by the occasional crow, and by some noisy sheep, excited by a farmer on a quad bike, far below us, going from field to field with the sheep's breakfast. We met a woman with her dog, Merlin. She was originally from Oldham but came to Llangollen as a teenager on her motorbike, met a local lad, and never left. There were lots of incomers in Llangollen, she told us, and buying property was nearly impossible because of the inflated prices and demand from out of the area. It's a story you hear in many places around Wales.

It's a long haul to Castell Dinas Brân, but well worth the effort because when you reach the top, the ruins are dramatic and awe-inspiring. As defensive positions for castles go, it is as good as it gets. The view from the top, at 321 metres high, is stunning. To the north are the impressive limestone crags of Creigiau-Eglwyseg, laid down in the warm waters of the Devonian period, 340 million years ago. Jan and I discussed how it is almost impossible to imagine that timescale, as we climbed to the summit in approximately the same length of time. It's not a long walk, but it is very steep. To the east, the view was equally impressive down the Vale of Llangollen to the Pontcysyllte Aqueduct. It stirred memories of my GCE physical geography – the wide glaciated valley, now occupied by the river, used for the communication routes – two main roads, the canal, and to the west, the railway. The castle lies on top of an ancient Iron Age fort and is thought to have been built in the 1260s by Gruffydd ap Madog, a powerful lord. I hope he included food and water in his design considerations because it would have been one hell of a trek down to Llangollen and back to top up supplies. Like most Welsh castles, it was the subject of semi-permanent turf wars for centuries, trapped in a cycle of destruction and reconstruction by warring tribes and nationalities. In 1402, Owain Glyndŵr was inevitably one of those involved. Jan and I had a modest swig of water to celebrate our successful ascent before making our way back to the town. As we descended from Crow Castle, a black crow flew in front of us – right on cue – as if aware of a contractual obligation to appear. It let out a loud 'caw' that echoed around us, leaving us with a memorable sight and sound.

Jan and I headed back to Llangollen and treated ourselves to a classic Welsh gastro experience at the Wharf Tea Room. We sat outside and stuffed ourselves with Welsh rarebit, Welsh cream teas, and Bara Brith (Welsh fruit cake). Not quite the healthy diet enjoyed by the monks from Crucis Valle Abbey. We watched a big strong horse called Sonic pulling a canal boat full of happy looking people upstream towards the Royal International Pavilion. Handicapped by our over-indulgence, we somehow still managed the short walk to the far side of the town to see Plas Newydd, somewhere else visited by HV Morton. On the way, we crossed the town's 14th century bridge, ticking off another of the Seven Wonders of Wales. It's a lovely view, particularly looking west from the bridge, as the waters rush beneath you. Charming, black and white half-timbered buildings hug the sides of the river, steam engines toot-toot in the station on the north bank, and the steep-sided green rolling hills provide a picturesque backdrop. The town is famous for its white-water canoeing or kayaking competitions, but when we were there, the river was low and cluttered with tree trunks, branches, and debris. I had to disappoint Jan by telling her my demonstration of shooting the rapids would have to wait for another day.

The town was busy with tourists but then I've never been to Llangollen when it's not been busy with tourists. It was a 15-minute walk up to Plas Newydd… which was closed. I should have done more research on my visit timings. The building appeared in the 15th century, but over time, the original humble cottage was transformed into a Gothic black and white architectural masterpiece, adorned with elaborate stained glass and intricately carved oak. Apart from the stunning architecture, the house is famous for two things – its gardens, and the 'Ladies of Llangollen.' Not able to go inside, Jan, and I could at least enjoy those beautiful gardens and the views.

The Ladies of Llangollen were two women named Sarah Ponsonby and Eleanor Butler, who lived together in the late 18th century, attracting the attention of visitors, and becoming something of a social phenomenon in their time. HV Morton was clearly taken with their story and devotes over four pages of his book to the ladies. Back in the late 18th century, the ladies' eccentric lifestyle and ambiguous relationship represented a challenge to the strict norms of society. In today's more liberal times, they wouldn't cause such a stir. Their eccentric lifestyle might have been more easily embraced and even celebrated; they'd probably make regular appearances on television game shows, have a regular video blog, and their own series on Netflix.

By the time we were back at our boat, we'd done quite a bit of walking for oldies, so we decided to rest and have a lazy afternoon. Jan had a sleep. I wrote up my notes… and then had a sleep. You don't get this level of nuanced real-life detail in every travel book.

The next morning, Jan and I slipped the ropes from our mooring at 8:00 am and chugged our way back to Trevor at a leisurely pace in glorious sunshine, retracing our previous day's journey. The warm breeze occasionally bathed us in sweet fragrances from the meadows either side of the canal. From time to time, wafts of vanilla and almond scents drifted across from dense patches of hawthorn blossom. Other aromas that assaulted our nostrils from time to time weren't so sweet smelling, but the poor cows couldn't help that.

By late morning we were back at Trevor, where a disappointingly small crowd of spectators were on hand to see my perfectly executed ninety-degree right turn onto the Pontcysyllte Aqueduct. I had the tiller in one hand and my camera in the other, ready to capture all those perfect scores on the Strictly Come Boating paddle boards.

Pontcysyllte Aqueduct stretching across the River Dee

The iconic Pontcysyllte Aqueduct is a landmark of British engineering. As the UK's longest and highest aqueduct, it towers over the Dee Valley at a height of 38 metres and 307 metres long. This remarkable feat of architecture and engineering was constructed between 1795 and 1805 by the legendary Thomas Telford, one of the key figures of the Industrial Revolution, and the guy hogging the civil engineering headlines on my *Journey through Wales* over the last couple of days. A boat ride over the Pontcysyllte Aqueduct is a 'must do' once-in-a-lifetime experience for many canal enthusiasts. Designated as a Grade I listed building and part of the UNESCO World Heritage Site, the aqueduct is a breath-taking sight. The scariest part of going across by boat is the moment you realise you're in a very long cast-iron trough, not much wider than your boat – and the sides of the trough appear to be less than an inch thick! To your left is a walkway, but on your right, beyond the boat, is about a foot of water, then an inch of cast iron – and then thin air! Try as you might to prevent it, it's impossible to stop the boat clanging loudly into the side of the trough every now and again. It felt like one more hard nudge on the side of the thin iron trough would send us and several million litres of canal water tumbling into the valley below. I kept telling myself that thousands of boats have crossed the aqueduct before, so why would it collapse now? Perhaps for reassurance, I tugged on my lifejacket halfway across, making sure it was secure. That made Jan laugh. 'It's not *drowning* you want to be worried about pet,' she said. 'If you fall off the boat now, you'll need a bloomin' parachute!'

It's an old cliché, but when you're gliding serenely across an aqueduct, it really is like floating along a river in the air. For a few moments, the feeling is so special that you forget all the statistics and just enjoy the experience. And just as that begins to sink in, you're on the other side and having to steer past the queue of boats coming the opposite way. For the next mile or so we passed clusters of moored boats on long-term residents' berths. They were probably just as annoyed at all the tourist traffic as I was with all the chicanes they had set up, which made life interesting when boats came in the oppo-site direction. Approaching Chirk, the canal was almost completely covered for several hundred metres by a tall arch of trees. The sun was blocked out in places, but in others it found its way through in golden shafts that illuminated the lower branches and leaves. The whole effect was stunning. Nature was proving that its green colour palette can provide an almost infinite variety of hues and shades. I thought I spotted an overtly olive, proud peacock, and tranquil dawn –

but then I realised my brain had retrieved the Dulux colour chart I was using when decorating the kitchen before I left home.

Jan and I proceeded through this dappled, verdant tunnel in a forest bathing trance. Having to negotiate two long tunnels brought us swiftly back to reality. The Whitehouse and Chirk tunnels were both constructed in 1801. The latter, at 421 metres, is the longest on the Llangollen Canal and, remarkably, the first in Britain to boast towpaths. Prior to that, boats were 'legged' through tunnels – with the crew lying on the roof of the boat and walking along the ceiling brickwork of the tunnel to push their vessel forwards.

Although the Llangollen Canal was owned by an English company, 90% of the canal was in Wales and passing the border into England made me think about what the canal had done for Wales. Well, quite a bit. It was a transport lifeline from rural Wales to the rest of Britain and led to significant economic growth when it was built. Nowadays, as Jan and I were discovering, it's a fantastic asset for the Welsh tourist industry, something that its original builders could never have dreamed of.

The short stretch of canal we were enjoying, from Trevor to Chirk, packs quite a punch, boasting a UNESCO World Heritage aqueduct, two tunnels, a lift bridge, and an extra aqueduct for good measure – all without any locks to deal with. We pulled into the Poachers pub, midway between Chirk and St Martins, for a three-hour lazy break. Sat in the shade outside, we watched other peoples' canal boats glide past in the sun. We continued our journey for another hour before stopping for the night, miles from civilisation, with quiet fields either side of the canal. You can moor almost anywhere, within reason, if there's a suitable gap on the canal bank, and as we stopped one more time, Jan and I felt we were slowing down to the canal pace of life. As the engine died (blissful silence), a herd of Guernsey cows ambled over to inspect us for a couple of minutes before ambling away again. Presumably, we'd passed the 'suitable neighbours' test. Jan and I chatted over coffee on the boat, watching the slow-moving waters in the fading light, as a pair of Canada geese and their goslings settled down for the night on the bank opposite us.

The following day, we retraced our route back to Trevor, where we moored in the marina overnight ready to hand the boat back in the morning. We'd done this routine before and didn't want the last-minute panic of bringing the boat back in the morning. We had a lovely meal in The Telford Inn over-looking the marina while watching, with barely disguised smugness, a succession of boating disasters unfolding on the ninety-degree bend on the now familiar canal junction in front of us.

Very early the next morning, we were woken by the loud metallic crashing sound of another canal boat mooring beside us. Thanks guys; we needed an alarm call! We had our last breakfast aboard and decanted our belongings back into our car. We settled up our bill while the traffic in the marina reached its rush-hour peak. Everyone was bringing their boats back at the same time to hand them over. There was much clanging of boat on boat, and boat on stone dockside, and a lot of highly stressed exchanges of views. Fortunately, the narrow boats are tough old things.

The water-borne part of my *Journey through Wales* was over. Leaving the marina, Jan, and I drove west, just over 7 miles along the A5 to Glyndyfrdwy Castle, also known as Owain Glyndŵr's Mount. It's just before you get to the village of Carrog. Nowadays, all that remains is a grassy mound, roughly 7 metres tall, and 15 metres in diameter – very similar to the one at Sycharth. It lies where the flat valley floor of the River Dee is about half a mile wide, snuggled into a gap between the river and the busy A5 road. The Llangollen

Railway line also passes within a few feet of the ancient site. Tightly framed by that relatively modern transport infrastructure, it takes a leap of imagination to picture it as the spot where Owain Glyndŵr's supporters proclaimed him Prince of Wales on 16th September 1400. In the notes I wrote at the time, the academic historian in me described it as being like a giant sandcastle – a green speckled one, part covered with sheep droppings. Looking at the photos I took, it looks more like a giant green pincushion with pine trees sticking out at all angles... but this image is probably distracting from its historical significance. Although the mound is similar in appearance to the one at Sycharth, the sites had different purposes. This one is strategically positioned, high on a river cliff with far-reaching views along the river valley. It feels like it has a military purpose. Sycharth seems more like a family home, which it was, tucked away in the landscape for privacy. From the side of the A5, it was just a short walk across a field of inquisitive sheep, and a hop over a stile, to get to the mound. I stood on top, looking down the valley (a fantastic view), and tried to imagine that scene in 1400, when around 300 of Owain Glyndŵr's followers gathered to hear his rousing speech and call to arms. At least he didn't have to struggle to be heard over the traffic from the A5.

Our next stop was going to be 'something completely different.' We were heading for the Yew trees of Overton, or to give the village its full name, Overton-on-Dee (Owrtyn). The trees were next up on the list of the Seven Wonders of Wales after I'd seen Pistyll Rhaeadr and the Llangollen Bridge. That would just leave Wrexham steeple, Snowdon's mountain without its people, St Winefride's wells, and Gresford bells.

The village of Overton-on-Dee is about 7 miles south of Wrexham, and as the name suggests, it's beside the River Dee. It lies surrounded by picturesque countryside, forests, and farmland. The churchyard of St Mary the Virgin contains the ancient, gnarled trunks of twenty-one yew trees... the ones featured in the rhyme. We soon found the place and looked round the churchyard. Some of the trees are estimated to be over 2000 years old. I ran a hand over the dark, mottled brown of the bark, almost black in some places. As I did so, the jukebox in my head kicked in with a line from the old Casablanca favourite 'Yew must remember this…' I'm sorry, that's awful, but it's just what happens.

They are impressive without doubt but for us, the jury was still out on whether they deserved their place in a Welsh wonders top seven list, and we set off for Wrexham to see how its steeple would measure up.

Before I continue with the account of our trip, our visit to Wrexham prompts me to briefly acknowledge a couple of key moments from the history of Welsh football. The Racecourse Stadium, Wrexham, is the oldest continuously used international football stadium in the world. It was there that Wales played their first international home match in 1877, although it didn't really end well for them: they lost 2-0 to Scotland. Wales won their first game against England in February 1881.

But back to the road trip – we were in Wrexham to check out that steeple on the parish Church of St Giles. It wasn't difficult to find because the church dominates the centre of the town. It was built in 1492 and the famous 41-metre-high steeple was completed in 1506. The medieval church was pleasant enough and had some impressive arched windows and stained glass. I only had one issue with it – that famous steeple is a tower. I imagine this was because the writer of the seven wonders poem needed a tall church architectural feature to rhyme with 'people.' After we'd spent some time looking around the church, Jan and I moved on to the village of Gresford, just a few miles further north.

We arrived just before midday and parked outside the village's All Saints' Church. The light red sandstone building mainly dates from late 15th century, and like many others, its churchyard is also home to a collection of ancient yew trees.

But it was the bells we'd come to hear. We only had to wait a few minutes, and they began to chime. They were OK, but to me they sounded much like any other church bells, not that I claim to be an expert in the field. Jan thought we should give them the benefit of the doubt and wait to hear them again. I think it was just her way of getting me to buy her a slap-up lunch from the bistro du fritto over the road. While we waited for our order, which I described to Jan as *Poisson Pané et Frites Gourmet* fried one way, the owner of the chippy advised us to come back on a Tuesday evening for bell ringing practice. Tourists come from far and wide just to hear the bells, apparently. I mentioned the 'seven wonders' poem and asked if that's what drew people – or was it perhaps the bells' purity of tone? He told me another reason, one that I'd not come across until then. The Gresford disaster of 1934 was considered to be one of the most devastating coal mining accidents in British history. An underground explosion caused the deaths of 266 miners and the bells of St Giles Church rang out as a symbol of mourning. The bells are still a poignant reminder of the disaster and it's perhaps more for that reason they are considered one of the most famous sets of church bells in Wales. I checked HV Morton's book to remind myself of the seven wonders – that just left Snowdon and St Winefride's well to tick off. After a long day, we headed to the Welsh village of Hawarden to find a library to sleep in.

Gladstone's Library is one of a kind. It is not only a residential library with twenty-six bedrooms and 150,000 books, but also the only Prime Ministerial library in Britain. The library was founded in 1894 'for the pursuit of divine learning' by William Ewart Gladstone, one of Britain's greatest political figures and a man who enjoyed being Prime Minister so much, he tried it four times. It attracts visitors from all over the world who come to read, write, and reflect. And, as a bonus, you can also eat and sleep there. In appearance, the building is like a small Oxford college, and that style continues inside. The reading rooms are spacious and well-lit.

They are a silent celebration of erudite nostalgia and a physical manifestation of Gladstone's ponderings. The spines of thousands of volumes create a colourful tapestry of literary history, and the air is heavy with the musty scent of leatherbound tomes and aged paper from a bygone era, when knowledge was an endeavour best pursued through ink and quill, or at worst the printing press, rather than with those pesky digital devices of today. The furniture speaks of long hours spent in contemplation. It feels like a sanctum, a place of refuge where the present recedes and the past reigns supreme. I took an instant liking to Gladstone's Library and after two nights, I was ready to move in. Of the many quotations that appear in the corridors of the library, the following seems appropriate to my journey:

With the traditions and history of Wales,
with the language of Wales,
with the religion of Wales,
with the feelings of Wales,
I affirm that Welsh nationality is as great as English nationality.

Paraphrased from Gladstone, W.E. 'MR. Gladstone at Swansea' [Press Clipping]. London: 1887

Fifteen miles from Hawarden lies Ruthin (pronounced Rithin), where HV Morton was particularly impressed with the prominent town square (Morton, 1932). The town square has survived centuries of war and destruction and can still be seen, surrounded by winding streets and half-timbered buildings. One of those buildings, a former courthouse, is the oldest timber-framed town house in Wales, built in 1435. Jan and I found our way to Ruthin Castle, a 13th-century fortress with a rich history as a castle, but now a hotel. The castle, surrounded by beautiful gardens, is rumoured to be haunted by several ghosts, including the Grey Lady (another one). There are two conflicting accounts to explain her identity. One claims she was Joan, the Lady of Wales, and wife of Llywelyn ap Gruffydd, the last Prince of Wales. According to that legend, she was imprisoned at Ruthin Castle after Llywelyn's death in battle and died of a broken heart. The other version portrays her as a woman who murdered her romantic rival with an axe and was subsequently executed. Whoever she was, her remains are believed to be buried within the castle walls. During our visit, Jan and I took a leisurely walk through the hotel's beautiful Italian gardens, managing to avoid any ghostly encounters, before moving on to Flint.

As we set off again, I reminded Jan of our agenda for the rest of the day. Our route through Flint, Holywell, St Asaph and Pontnewydd was going to include another castle (obviously), 'The Lourdes of Wales,' and a cave where some of the oldest known Neanderthal remains in Britain were found. I wasn't 100% sure how to interpret Jan's brief sideways glance at me, but after over 40 years of marriage, I could tell it was something like 'Thank God I'm here for my holiday rather than having to put up with a boring Caribbean cruise like some wives have to.'

We parked next to Flint Town United's football ground when we arrived in the town (another little treat for my wife) and walked the short distance to the remains of the castle on the banks of the Dee Estuary. Flint Castle has a simple fortress design like a schoolchild would draw. There's a circular tower in each of the four corners, joined (or they would have been) by stone walls. We were less than 2 miles away from England on the opposite bank of the river. The international border was somewhere out there in the middle, amidst the shifting sands. As well as looking directly towards the Wirral, we'd come face-to-face with Edward I again. He enjoyed a relatively easy ride when he inherited the English throne in 1272, with most barons falling into line. Llywelyn ap Gruffydd, Prince of Wales, was different though and so, in the year 1277,

Edward I invaded Wales, determined to quell any dissent. Flint was selected by the English king as a crucial bridgehead. Its castle was one of many fortresses built by Edward I as part of his 'ring of iron' project – a chain of fortifications erected along the coast of Wales, designed to conquer the Welsh, and impose English rule. The castle has since featured in the works of some of Britain's most acclaimed artists. It was a key setting in Act III of Shakespeare's play, *Richard II*, and in 1838, it was captured in watercolour by JMW Turner. Jan and I clambered up to the highest point we could get to and took in the fantastic views up and down the Dee estuary and across to the Wirral. As always, those castle builders had an eye for a grand-design location, although in those days it wasn't just a matter of being easy on the eye – it was more a matter of life and death.

The ancient holy site of St Winefride's well, in Holywell, has been referred to as 'The Lourdes of Wales.' It has been a place of pilgrimage for over 1,300 years, making it one of the oldest pilgrimage destinations in Britain. There's a small chapel on the site, and a visitor centre that provides information about the history and significance of the well, but of course, it's the well that people are keen to see. The well is a natural spring that bubbles up from the Earth, and it is said to possess miraculous healing powers... and why is that? Well, St Winefride was a Welsh saint who lived in the 7th century. According to legend, she was a beautiful and virtuous woman who was sought after by many suitors. Along came Prince Caradog. There often seems to be a prince involved in these stories, and although there is no mention of whether this one was dashing or dastardly, his actions point towards the latter. Caradog attempted to force Winefride to marry him, but she refused and was immediately beheaded. Let's be honest, that was a bit extreme, but without Caradog's violent reaction, we wouldn't have the rest of the story... miraculously, her head was restored to her body, and she rose back to life. Winefride dedicated her life to God and retired to a convent, where she lived in contemplation and devotion until her death. The story is why visitors come from all over the world to partake in the well's restorative waters and to pay homage to the patron saint of the well. As if to re-enforce the claims of miracle cures, we saw twenty-five discarded crutches and walking sticks in one corner of the visitor centre.

It was less than 5 miles from Holywell to St Asaph in rural Denbighshire, on the River Elwy, about 3 miles inland from the seaside town of Rhyl. Its position is roughly 20 miles from Chester or Liverpool. HV Morton was both surprised and amused when he visited St Asaph, thinking it was more of a village than a city (Morton, 1932). You will see it described as the smallest city in Britain, but there are a few other contenders for that title, including St Davids in Pembrokeshire. The roots of the city of St Asaph can be traced back to the 6th century saint and missionary St Kentigern, also known as St Mungo, who began his evangelism near the River Clyde, on the site of modern-day Glasgow. When he was forced to leave the area, he moved to Wales, staying for a time at St Davids, and then moving north to present day Denbighshire, where he founded a cathedral at Llanelwy (church on the Elwy). Asaph ap Brochwel, a descendant of Saint Kentigern, was appointed the bishop of St Asaph in the early 7th century. The cathedral is one of the oldest and most historic buildings in Wales, and it has been a centre of religious and cultural life in the region for centuries… so that's where we were heading first. Continuing a familiar trend in the narrative – we got to the cathedral at 4:30 pm to find it closed. The programme of services showed there would be one at 6:00 pm, however, so we decided to come back then.

Instead, and changing topic completely once again, Jan and I headed for the Pontnewydd Cave (sometimes referred to as The Bontnewydd palaeolithic site), a scheduled monument just 5 miles up the River Elwy from the cathedral. After navigating some very tiny lanes to get to where we thought the cave was, we parked on the roadside verge and started to look around. We were in a tranquil rural backwater that felt a long way from anywhere. It took a while for us to find the cave in the cliffs high up the valley side, but there was no mistaking it, when we finally discovered it. A serious-looking metal door in the bricked-up entrance to the cave stopped us going any further, but there was a hole through which we could see quite a way inside – mostly at graffiti-decorated cave walls. We spent a few minutes trying to imagine the scene nearly a quarter of a million years ago, but really? It's almost beyond comprehension.

The 30-metre-deep cave, situated 55 metres above the Elwy Valley floor, was occupied by Neanderthals around 230,000 years ago. Well-preserved fossils of our early human relatives have been found in the cave, including teeth, jaws, and limb bones. The fossils are among the oldest known Neanderthal remains in Europe.

As we walked back to the car, we passed a small cottage and met a chap sweeping his drive. I asked about the cave and he told me he saw and heard visitors regularly, some serious archaeologists, some curious like us, and some just looking for somewhere for a party. The guy had moved down from Liverpool (talk about culture shock), and whether or not he was a keen historian, he certainly gave that impression. He told us that the brick wall dates from World War II, when the cave was used for storing munitions. We speculated on how the cave was formed and how the Neanderthal remains had found their way inside it. He favoured the 'glacier scouring the valley and depositing remains into the cave' theory… but then again there might have been Neanderthals living in the area… and sabre-toothed tigers. Jan and I had to get back to St Asaph, and as we drove down the tiny country lanes, we discussed how whacky our day had been, once again. Little did we think when we got out of bed that morning that we'd be discussing Neanderthal lifestyles and sabre-toothed tigers with a scouser later in the day.

It was just before 6:00 pm by the time we got back to St

Asaph, as luck would have it, but we couldn't see any signs of movement around the cathedral. I left Jan in the car while I popped over to check whether anything was happening. I did a complete lap around the outside of the building and saw no one. I stood at the edge of the churchyard, looking at the main entrance, and waited a few minutes in case someone turned up. Nothing. The bells chimed 6:00 pm. There was still not a soul to be seen – it was just me and an eerie stillness. In an instant, however, things changed. I stood transfixed and mesmerised as the most wondrous choir of angels burst into song – what in the name of creation was happening? I checked my pulse – yes, I was still among the living. The divine choir persisted; it was a thing of unearthly beauty. I scanned my surroundings for the shining tunnel and the ghostly figure that ushers the dead to their final place of rest. Was this the reaper making his 6:00 pm round up?

It was then that I realised the building I was standing right next to was the St Asaph Cathedral Song School, and looking through the window, I could see the cherubic faces of the young choristers, as they followed the notes on their sheet music. Ah, how it all made sense! I lingered for a while longer, basking in the serenity of the moment on that warm summer evening. There was no service that evening and the cathedral remained shut. I told Jan about my embarrassing twilight misunderstanding while we drove back to Hawarden for the night. And sadly, that was nearly that for our week on tour together. After a minor logistical shuffle in the morning to retrieve my motorbike from the marina at Trevor, we'd be going our separate ways again, Jan back to Dorset by car and me continuing my Journey through Wales on my Royal Enfield.

5

HAWARDEN TO CONWY

I was determined to visit the smallest ancient cathedral in Britain, so I retraced the route that Jan and I had taken the previous evening to St Asaph, and it turned out to be third time lucky. There was no service taking place when I returned, but the cathedral doors were open, and I was able to look around at last. All the usual suspects seem to have had their 15 minutes of fame at St Asaph. Founded by the Normans in the 12th century, Edward I, Owain Glyndŵr, and the Roundheads all make guest appearances in its timeline. The Reverend William Morgan, who we came across in Llan-rhaeadr, was appointed Bishop of St Asaph cathedral in 1601, and died in the city in 1604. There is a copy of the Welsh Bible he worked so hard to make possible inside the cathedral, and there's a splendid Gothic style translator's memorial in the churchyard outside. The interior of the cathedral was digni-fied and serene. I picked up a fact sheet near the entrance to help me understand what I was looking at and got chatting to a volunteer who was tidying up. He told me a bit about the history of the place, including the story of Felix Powell. Felix and his brother George attended St Asaph Cathedral back in the early 1900s. George was a chorister, and Felix became the cathedral's organist when he was only twelve. They went on to become music hall favourites, and together they wrote the World War I favourite, 'Pack Up Your Troubles in Your Old Kit Bag,' in 1915 (Felix wrote the tune, George wrote the words). Felix must have been a bit of a lad because you can still see his carved signature on one of the the the church pews. When I'd finished my tour and taken a few photos, I packed up my troubles and headed to the Translator Tearoom. I think my attention to historic detail was waning by then because looking back at my notes, I wrote, 'Tearoom... posters of William Morgan... lemon drizzle cake... one of the best.'

My journey continued north towards the coast. My plan was to turn left before I hit the sea at Rhyl (Y Rhyl), and then head for an overnight stop at Conwy via the seaside resorts of Towyn, Colwyn Bay (Bae Colwyn), and Llandudno. I was going to make a big diversion inland to Llangernyw on the way, to see the oldest living thing in Britain. This will come as a big shock to those of my friends who consider me to be the oldest living thing in Britain.

Although Rhyl is only a 10-minute ride from St Asaph, this is Wales, so there's always time to fit in another castle – and this time it was in Rhuddlan. In this corner of Wales, you won't be surprised to read it's another one built by Edward I. This one was constructed at about the same time as the one in Flint and it looks like they've come from the same blueprint – four circular towers, one in each corner. More of the Rhuddlan version has survived. Once again, the setting is exquisite – high on the banks of the River Clwyd, near to a crossing place, and with great views up and down the valley. There was one small problem with this site when it was first chosen, however; the river wasn't deep enough to get boats of sufficient size from the sea to the castle. No problem! King Edward I conscripted hundreds of locals to dig the river straighter and deeper.

The magnificent castle, built in 1277, was built to help Edward I consolidate his control over Wales. In 1284, he issued the Statute of Rhuddlan, which established a new system of government for North Wales, effectively annexing Wales to the Crown of England and creating the system of governance that would remain in place until the Laws in Wales Acts (also known as the Acts of Union) of 1535-1542. I parked my motorcycle in Castle Street (I see what they've done there) and walked across to take a brief look at the castle and its magnificent setting before moving on to Rhyl.

HV Morton liked Rhyl, although he found it rather windy (Morton, 1932). I can't say this seaside hotspot is one of my favourites, but I'm sure it has plenty of loyal fans without me. I know that because the Rhyl Sun Centre is one of the largest holiday parks in Britain. On my drive through, I saw a boating lake, plenty of amusements, and more fast-food outlets than there were grains of sand on the beach. I may have exaggerated that last bit. For decades, thousands of summer visitors have flocked annually to what they refer to as the 'sunshine coast.' There, they will have waded in warm waters before migrating back to their more regular feeding grounds in the great industrial cities of northwest England, when the weather became cooler. An eclectic architectural tapestry of seafront buildings provides an almost infinite variety of styles, and as I drove out of the town, I noticed a few survivors from the town's late 19th and early 20th century heyday. Those regal-looking Victorian guest houses have seen it all, summer season after summer season. Nowadays, they're still waiting… arms folded and feet tapping, ready for the annual convoy of charabancs to arrive from Merseyside. They stare as if hypnotised, peering out across 5 miles of the Irish Sea, to the gracefully turning blades of the North Hoyle Offshore Wind Farm. That's thirty more big fans of windy Rhyl.

I was soon riding along a stretch of coast that HV Morton considered to be purposely designed for crowds of holiday makers (Morton, 1932). I didn't stop in Towyn either, but the impression I got while riding through was that there were more static homes than normal ones. It was, in effect, a holiday-parkopolis, and although I wasn't drawn to the place, that number of static caravans shows that many people are.

A 20-mile drive inland from Towyn took me to Llangernyw. It was a lovely ride through more of the lumpy, bumpy landscape of rural Wales, with cattle and sheep dotted around steep-sided hills of rich green grass. I rode nervously past a sign saying, 'Road Closed…' and fortunately it wasn't. Further on, there was another a sign saying, 'Scenic Drive…' and fortunately it was.

Llangernyw is a quaint and picturesque village nestled in the rolling hills towards the top end of the Elwy Valley. It's a charming and unassuming place that exudes an air of peaceful serenity and timelessness. I'd file it under the 'hidden gem' or 'well-kept secret' sub-category of charming Welsh villages. There's a pretty collection of white cottages, a pub, a post office, and an antiques shop. At its heart lies St Digain's Church, its ivy-covered walls and ancient yew tree lending an aura of spiritual reverence to the village. And it was the tree that I'd come to see – the oldest ancient tree in Wales, and possibly the world according to some descriptions. At first sight, the yew tree looks as big as the church – it's enormous! It looks more than a single tree, but when you get up close, you can see how multiple trunks have grown from the base of the tree and spread outwards. If you clamber around the base, as I did, of course, it seems like you're actually inside the tree. For many years, people have seen the yew tree as a symbol of death and the journey of the soul to the afterlife. Celtic druids thought the yew was sacred and planted it close to their temples for death rituals. Their ancient pagan sites were often eventually taken over for Christian worship and churches were built in the same places. Despite being associated with death, the yew tree's longevity also makes it a symbol of eternal life. Whatever its background you can't help but admire the Llangernyw Yew, a reminder of the unrelenting resilience of the natural world within the cyclical nature of existence.

I enjoyed looking around the church and churchyard of Llangernyw; it felt very calm and restful, but I had more places to tick off my list before my day was done so I dropped the Royal Enfield off its stand and headed back to the coast. Re-joining the coastal corniche (cliff) road at Abergele, I rode through Llanddulas, Colwyn Bay (Bae Colwyn), and Rhos-on-Sea on my way to Llandudno. Rhos-on-Sea was a pleasant-looking place, which had some major sea-defence works underway when I passed through. I hadn't included the small coastal town on my itinerary for its civil engineering works, though. Continuing the spiritual theme from Llangernyw, I was there to visit the tiny St Trillo's Chapel, believed to be one of the smallest Christian chapels in Britain and one of the oldest Christian sites in Wales.

St Trillo's Chapel, the sea and the Lleyn Peninsula

The chapel is on the seaward side of the road that sweeps westwards in a gentle arc from Rhos Point towards Penrhyn Bay. A wide pedestrian promenade runs parallel to the road to its right, about 7 metres below it. The chapel is tucked into the side of the steep slope between the road and the promenade, making it almost invisible to passing traffic. I nearly missed it, but I'm glad I didn't. The simple, rectangular chapel, constructed of stone and timber, dates from the 7th century. The interior of the chapel is plain and unadorned, with a single altar and a few wooden pews. My notes from the visit read, 'Lovely peaceful chapel with seating for six – on the promenade – easy to miss.' There's not much known about the man himself, but he is considered a local patron saint and is revered by many in Wales for his piety and devotion. It's thought that he died a martyr and was buried at the church he established, which later became known as St Trillo's Chapel. When I visited, there was hardly a cloud in the sky and the sea was Mediterranean blue. There was no one around and the scene was one of pure serenity.

Llandudno is the largest and most popular holiday resort in Wales and has been for many years. HV Morton wrote relatively little about the place back in the 1930s. Less than a page. What he saw clearly impressed him though, because he compared the sweep of Llandudno Bay to that of Naples (Morton, 1932). Other creative wordsmiths have labelled the resort, 'The 'Welsh Riviera,' or 'The Cannes of the North.'

Llandudno got lucky with its magnificent setting. It lies on a peninsula that juts into the Irish Sea a mile or so from the general east-west alignment of the North Wales coastline. Two large headlands of carboniferous limestone point northwards. Sheltered between them is a saucer shaped bay containing 2 miles of sand and shingle beaches. To the west, the imposing craggy dome of The Great Orme (Y Gogarth) is by far the largest of the two headlands, rising to 247 metres and pointing towards the northwest, as if answering the question 'Which way to Anglesey (Ynys Môn)?' Snuggled below its protective headland, on its west side, lies the town's second and slightly quieter beach.

For clarification, because I found it confusing, the names

'The Great Orme' and 'Great Orme's Head' (Pen Y Gogarth) are often used interchangeably. The OS map shows that the former refers to the entire headland, while the latter refers to the northernmost tip of the headland.

In the early 19th century, Llandudno was a small village with a population of just of a few hundred. A nearby copper mine was the biggest employer, and the rest of the villagers scratched a living from agriculture and fishing. The only buildings on the seafront were a few fishermen's cottages and a couple of inns. All that changed when the Chester and Holyhead Railway opened its line to Bangor in 1848. The Mostyn family, who owned most of the land in the area, saw an opportunity to develop an unproductive area of marsh-land into a fashionable seaside resort… and Llandudno was born. A few years later, they built a new station, which made the sunny seaside town even more accessible to thousands of workers from the newly industrialised north and midlands of England. Thousands of holidaymakers from those areas and others have made Llandudno their favourite seaside resort ever since. The Queen of Welsh resorts is a lovely, old-fashioned seaside destination, and was named Britain's second favourite in a *Which?* poll in 2022. I would place Llandudno in my personal top three, along with Swanage, and Largs, although Llandudno is much larger than those two.

After finding somewhere to park the motorcycle, I took a relaxing walk along the resort's unusually wide pedestrian promenade, which runs parallel with the beach. I decided to go for the full Victorian seaside experience: a walk along the prom, an ice cream on the pier, and a tram ride to the top of The Great Orme. Starting next to the Craig-y-Don beachside paddling pool, a mile or so to the east of the town centre, I ambled westwards along the prom towards the pier. I had all the time in the world, or at least all afternoon and early evening, before I had to get to my youth hostel in Conwy. I could take my time and relax. It was another beautiful summer's day, blemished only by the very stiff breeze that scurried off the sea and rushed up the beach as if in a hurry to make landfall. It was perfect for forcing ozone into visitors' lungs, but not so good for toddlers playing ball games or frail elderly folk attempting to manoeuvre around deck chairs. Out in the Irish Sea, towards the horizon, that fresh north-easterly was doing another job… spinning the 185 turbines of the Gwynt y Môr (Welsh for sea wind) and Rhyl Flats wind farms. The summer sunlight glinted on rows of 150-metre-high windmills that looked like lines of soldiers on marching drill. The ever-changing light patterns gave the wind farm the appearance of a distant art emplacement.

The spotlessly clean promenade was bustling with happy visitors of all ages. Perhaps it was the warm weather, but even the dogs ambled along like relaxed tourists. At that stage, my visitor sample size was small, but I'd only heard northern English accents, and amongst those, plenty of scousers. Young couples larked around and flirted while simultaneously trying to look cool, taking plenty of photos of how crazy they were for their friends to like. Stressed mums and dads steered over-excited children around ice-cream stalls and other merchandise opportunities, while seagulls on routine patrol cackled to each other, passing on intel about potential pickings. Elderly couples strolled along in quiet contentment, arm in arm down the same stretch of prom they'd ambled down this time last year, the year before, and countless summers before that.

The beach road runs to the landward side of the prom, beyond rows of immaculately manicured flower beds, and beyond that is an impressive line of tall pastel-painted hotels, guest houses, and private houses. Most are grand in scale and design, dating from the second half of the 19th century, when the resort was in its first flush of youth. It's easy to imagine Victorian ladies strolling along the promenade in extravagant summer dresses, carrying parasols, walking arm in arm with gentlemen sporting thick striped blazers, straw boaters, and over-developed moustaches. The initial development of the resort was meticulously planned, and subsequent growth has been carefully controlled by the same landowner for generations. This has allowed Llandudno to keep most of its original buildings in good condition and for the town to expand in a co-ordinated way, avoiding the random tackiness of resorts less fortunate.

Llandudno ticks all the seaside holiday boxes. They still have donkey rides on the beach, and Britain's oldest Punch and Judy show has brought processed meat products and tales of Italian domestic violence to Llandudno promenade since 1864. At 700 metres long, the town's Grade II listed pier is peerless in Wales and the fifth longest in England and Wales. It's no surprise to discover it's a former pier of the year. It deserved more than a quick dash to the end and back, so I told myself to take my time and enjoy the stroll. Stalls selling a bewildering array of fast food lined the first section of the pier. Hooked above them was a line of small loudspeakers, pumping out Needles and Pins by the Searchers, and a medley of similar hits from the 1960s. Someone had correctly identified the target audience and a wave of nostalgia rippled through me. The jukebox in my head decided it was a good idea to put Sweets for my Sweet, also by the Searchers, on repeat play for a few minutes. Somehow resisting the temptation to purchase a frozen pornstar Martini and a cheeseburger, I dragged myself past the fast-food outlets and continued my slow amble away from the land.

Perhaps with their typical visitor in mind, the authorities have installed plenty of benches along the pier, and I stopped at one about halfway down for a quiet sit down. I thought I'd mingle with some visitors and find out what drew them to Llandudno… while I finished off a top-heavy softy ice cream with a chocolate flake. As luck would have it, I sat next to a local gentleman, a retired factory worker from Chirk. Gareth turned out to be a lucky find. He gave me a potted history of Llandudno and The Great Orme, and he was in no rush. I don't think I was the first visitor to benefit from his encyclopaedic knowledge of the resort, but at his pace of delivery, it concerned me that he'd started his story back in the 1850s. (I didn't have the heart to tell him I had to be in Conwy by 8:00 pm.) He told me how, back in the day, they built most of the town in the winter months, so summer visitors wouldn't be disturbed. Some builders went to America to keep working over the summer period and that's why you come across so many place names like Bala, Caernarfon, Swansea, Newport (Casnewydd) and Cardiff on the east coast of America. Gareth was a great guy, he taught me a lot, and I'm very grateful that he forced me to slow down and listen to his stories.

The view from the end of the pier was superb all around. Far out to sea, the art installation continued to flicker and glint in the afternoon sun. The gentle arc of Llandudno Bay swung round from Little Orme's Head (Creigiau Rhiwledyn) in the east, to the town end of the pier, edged by a thin line of sandy beach and the elegant line of holiday hotels and guest houses. The pier was bathed in glorious summer sunshine, but looking back behind the town, to the south, white and grey cumulonimbus clouds billowed upwards high into the sky and provided a dramatic backdrop to the line of beach-side hotels. Shafts of sunlight pierced through in places like theatre spotlights, picking out their favourite locations, as if hinting at places worthy of a visit. The mighty expanse of The Great Orme dominated the view to the north side of the pier, and the top of that headland was where I was heading next.

The word 'Orme' is believed to be derived from the Scandinavian word for worm. According to historical accounts, a Viking raiding party stumbled upon The Great Orme and mistook it for a serpent (an easy mistake to make), leading them to flee in terror. The Great Orme peninsula is almost 2 miles long and just over a mile wide, with its summit standing at a towering height of 247 metres – that's a very large lump of carboniferous limestone.

I headed through the shaded back streets of Llandudno to

find the base station of The Great Orme Tramway, the only funicular tramway in Britain that travels on public roads. I considered going up to the summit by tram and back by cable car, or vice versa. The cable car passenger ride, which stretches just over a mile, is the longest in Britain. The 5 minutes it took me to walk from the pier to the tram ticket office were long enough for me to carry out a detailed analysis of the pros and cons of each option but in the end, it was an easy decision – the guy in the ticket office told me the cable car wasn't working because of high winds. I tried not to look too outraged, but the wind didn't seem that strong to me. I bought my return ticket. I was sitting in the tram and on my way within 5 minutes.

Since it first opened in 1902, the tramway has trundled thousands of visitors to the summit, through The Great Orme Country Park and Nature Reserve. The tram has a lovely old-fashioned feel to it – you feel as though you're travelling on the original 1902 version. Its carriages are mainly made of wood, with open holes where you might expect to find glass windows. The paint looked so thick in places that you could imagine someone had trowelled on twenty layers of thick Devon cream. As we eased our way through the final built-up parts of town, the tram paused while a flock of sheep ran along the road in front of us. I started chatting to an elderly woman sat opposite me with her husband. I fully expected her to be Betty from Bootle or Sharon from Stockport, but I must have found the only other southerners on the tram: Sue and Graham from Surrey. They put me to shame by saying they were going up to the headland to bird-watch and then they'd be walking back down. Those open windows were certainly keeping us well ventilated, especially as we approached the top, when I had to grudgingly admit it was nearly blowing a gale – strange on a sunny summer's day.

It's a short walk from the terminus station across to the OS triangulation point on the summit of The Great Orme. The old surveyor in me felt compelled to inspect the condition of the combined triangulation point and GPS station, after which I felt reassured enough to take in the breathtaking views. To the southwest were the sparkling blue waters of Conwy Bay, with the town of Penmaenmawr beyond, backed by the mountains of Snowdonia. On a good day, the views stretch to Anglesey, the Isle of Man, Blackpool, the Lake District, and beyond. Looking around, it feels like someone has dumped a sizeable chunk of the Yorkshire Dales onto the North Wales coast – you're surrounded by large rolling fields of close-cropped grass, with occasional patches of yellow speckled gorse. There's a sheep farm and long stretches of grey limestone pavement… it was like looking at the moors above Malham Tarn.

The excellent visitor centre at the top provides plenty of information about the history and wildlife of the headland. A whiteboard displays the flora and fauna spotted by visitors, and on the day I visited, the list included common rockrose, field gentian, harebell, Western and European gorse, ling, chough, cormorant, fulmar, guillemot, peregrine, razor bill, and no less than twenty different species of butterfly. All that natural beauty was cleverly counterbalanced by a building called the Summit Complex. I suffer from something similar, but I've always thought it was just a bad head for heights. The café and crazy golf didn't add to the natural beauty of the headland – but let's be generous and say it caters for all tastes… and that's fair enough.

Before I was blown off the headland, I got the tram back to town. The highlight of the journey down was seeing a pod of porpoises and some seals out in Llandudno Bay. Passengers shuffled in their seats to avoid the wind that was whistling through the openings that might have been windows. Most of the carriage was kept entertained by a couple with strong Lancashire accents who speculated, all the way down, on whether the holes in the side of the tram could be called windows if they didn't have glass. It was like the guy was giving us a free 'live from The Great Orme' Peter Kay tribute show with his wife providing the perfect deadpan partner. I wish I'd recorded it in hindsight, but the bit I remember halfway through the discussion, which doesn't seem half as funny as the real thing, went like this:

Peter Kay look-alike husband: (Holding his head in his hands for comic effect) 'You can't be serious, love. You can't have a window without glass, that's just bloody ridiculous! … it's just a bloody hole!'

Mrs Deadpan wife: (Arms crossed) 'I'm telling you; you don't need glass for it to be a window.'

Peter Kay look-alike husband: (Throwing his hands up in frustration for comic effect) 'Well, what do you call that thing in the wall that lets the light in?'

Mrs Deadpan wife: (Smiling) That's still a window, love, whether it has glass, or not.

Peter Kay look-alike husband: (Scratching his head for comic effect) 'Well, I never. I always thought you needed glass to keep the bloody rain out!'

Mrs Deadpan wife: (Giggling) Not always. There are plenty of windows that don't have glass.

That no one joined in the couples' entertaining exchange of views probably means we didn't know much about windows either. I looked it up later and apparently a window can be called a window, even if it doesn't have any glass (she was right).

When we reached Victoria Station back in Llandudno, I headed back to find my motorcycle, via yet another ice cream on the promenade, and then rode all the way back up The Great Orme again to find the next on my list of 'must visit' places.

There is a danger I might overuse the expression 'hidden gem' on my *Journey through Wales*. Instead, let's call this next place I visited a hidden copper-iron sulphide mineralisation (which rolls off the tongue equally smoothly). The visitor attraction I was rapidly approaching may never have existed if it hadn't been for a discovery in 1987, which was made almost by accident. Ask most people what they know about The Great Orme, and they will probably tell you that it's somewhere in North Wales, maybe near Llandudno. A few people will know it has a cable car and a tram to take people to the visitor centre at the top. Fewer people will know that below the surface lies something described by Guinness World Records as the largest Bronze Age copper mine in the world.

To set the historical context, the Bronze Age in Britain is generally considered to have taken place between 2500 BC and 800 BC. During this time, The Great Orme copper mine was worked for eight centuries, with the period from 1600 BC to 1400 BC being referred to as its golden age. During this time, the mine dominated the supply of copper in Britain. However, issues with flooding and the availability of copper from other sources led to a significant decline in production. Large-scale mining only resumed during the Industrial Revolution, when advances in technology made it possible to empty the mine shafts of water using steam engines and pumps. This revitalisation was driven by a high demand for copper, which was used to clad the hulls of wooden ships, including those of the Royal Navy. Copper mining at The Great Orme was viable on an industrial scale for most of the 19th century until iron replaced wood as the primary material for shipbuilding. Around this time, cheaper copper sources became available from overseas, and the mine was once again plagued by flooding as it progressed below sea level. It was eventually closed in 1881 and lay in ruins for over a hundred years.

Fast forward to the late 1980s, when Llandudno was well established as a firm favourite for summer visitors. Easy access to the top of The Great Orme by cable car and a tram with no glass in its windows made it a popular day out for tourists. The old copper mine site and its waste tips had become a bit of an eye-sore, so the local council and the Welsh Development Agency decided to landscape the area and turn it into a visitor car park. Before any groundwork could be done, they needed to carry out an underground survey to establish how stable the site was. When the survey work began in 1987, the bulldozers soon exposed a 19th century mine shaft. Current mine manager, Nick Jowett, was one of the first people to rope up and go down to explore. He and the team descended through 145 metres of carboniferous limestone to sea level. The first half of the drop passed through the old Bronze Age workings and it turned out to be the doorway to a labyrinth of passageways and chambers. Thirty-three years later and the network of known tunnels has extended to over 5 miles, with more still being discovered. There is also an enormous open cast area on the surface, next to the visitor centre. Even after removing over 50,000 tons of mining waste, 95% of the site remains buried, so there's plenty more to explore and hopefully much more archaeological evidence to uncover. A company called Great Orme Mines Limited was established in 1990 and a year later, they opened the mine to the public.

The tidy car park and small collection of neat buildings that greet you as you approach The Great Orme copper mine sit next to the remains of the Bronze Age opencast site. The buildings look fairly modest, but an underground attraction isn't about the bits you can see on the surface. I had a quick chat with the staff in the building that houses the entrance to the mine, bought my ticket, and prepared to go 4,000 years back in time. Once you've got your miner's hat on and watched the introductory video, you're good to go. From there, the tour of the mine is a self-guided walk through about 200 metres of tunnels and a vast underground chamber. Over 30,000 visitors negotiate the small flights of steps in and out of the well-marked subterranean route every year. There are some sloping passageways, but the walk is fairly undemanding... although I'd recommend you leave your high heels behind. I'm certainly glad I did. Regularly spaced information boards describe how The Great Orme miners developed the mine thousands of years ago, and the information is pitched at about the right level – it's presented in a fun way with a few cartoons to appeal to the youngsters but also plenty of hard facts and scientific detail.

At about the same time as the guys down the coast at Preseli were hauling bluestones to Stonehenge, other settlers were exploring The Great Orme. They discovered surface deposits of green malachite, a mineral formed by a combination of water, carbon dioxide, and copper ore. How did they know what it was? And what to do with it? Perhaps there were Irish, Iberian, or Middle Eastern copper consultants doing the rounds along the western seaboard trading routes of Britain on the lookout for new ore deposits, and maybe they passed on their knowledge and skills in exchange for a percentage of the material found? We'll never know. The Great Orme settlers dug out a large opencast pit before it became too difficult to go any deeper. They then became miners as they followed the veins of malachite underground, opening up holes in the ground and tunnelling further into the limestone. Although they didn't know it, these guys were living in the middle of the first Industrial Revolution, when new metal materials replaced stone to produce more efficient and effective tools and weapons.

On its own, copper is relatively soft, but by mixing 90% copper with 10% tin, you get bronze – and lift off! There is little evidence of tin mining in Wales until the 12th century, so it's reasonable to assume the tin must have come by boat from Cornwall. That's over 300 miles away, so there must have been significant long-distance trading going on. At Pentrwyn, a headland near to the copper mine, excavations have uncovered the only known Bronze Age smelting site in Britain. One of my favourite parts of my visit to The Great Orme mine was the display that showed how bronze would have been produced all those years ago. Archaeometallurgists (that would be an impressive 134 points at Scrabble if you could use that many tiles and occupy one triple word square) have recreated the process, using evidence from the Pentrwyn site, to show how it was done. It still looks ridiculously complicated even with today's knowledge, tools, and materials. If they did't have those consultants, you wonder how much trial and error had to take place before they cracked it. There must have been plenty of failures along the way, but as the Bronze Age early adopters would undoubtedly have said, 'That's metallurgical evolution.'

Bronze is a harder and more practical metal than copper… and it was a game changer. The games that changed were mainly agriculture and fighting – the plough and the sword. A bronze plough was a more robust and efficient tool than handheld sticks, or brittle slabs of stone. Bronze axes were more efficient than the relatively blunt stone ones they replaced. The new tools allowed larger areas of woodland to be cleared for agricultural land. Improved tools and methods eventually led to surplus food and the accumulation of wealth, and if you have that, there's usually someone around who wants to take it off you. Tribes had to defend themselves. They developed bronze knives into longer and longer versions that gradually morphed into swords, and they used metal for more protective shields and for lethal tips for spears.

You only see a tiny fraction of the network of tunnels under The Great Orme when you visit the mine, but it's enough to get a good idea of what Bronze Age mining was like. It was tough. After the tour through the tunnels, you emerge above ground again at the oldest part of the mine – the open cast 'hole in the ground' that was first dug nearly 4,000 years ago. More information boards explain how the mine was developed over time and how the ore was extracted. Heading back to the main building, you go past the archaeology store, which, as the name suggests, is a warehouse of old things that have been found on the site. There are long racks of the hammerstones that were used for gouging out the tunnels. The mine manager, Nick Jowett, pointed me towards recent research (by R.A. Williams and C. Le Carlier de Veslud), which describes how important the mine was for over seven centuries. For 200 of those years, the mine dominated Britain's copper supply and became part of a long-distance trade network that extended to France, the Netherlands, Germany, Denmark, and Sweden. Researchers estimate that over 800 tonnes of copper were produced from The Great Orme mine – enough to produce one to two million axes – and who knows how many more they will find as they excavate the site in future decades.

It's hard to get your head around something that happened 4,000 years ago, but walking round the actual tunnels that were mined, seeing the opencast pit close up and the tools used, gives you some insight into what it must have been like. The information boards provided the context and statistics, which explained why the location is so significant. I came away having had a memorable experience and with a much better understanding of one of Britain's most important prehistoric archaeological sites.

Those who know me well know of my admiration for the YHA. As a youth of many years standing, I've enjoyed their homely hospitality for decades. The hostels are always in great locations and the staff are invariably super helpful and friendly. Take the Conwy hostel, for example: I'd checked in and been typing up my notes for an hour or two before I realised that I might miss out on an evening meal. I dashed to the restaurant to find it quite busy with a party of college kids. I asked if there was any chance of something to eat. 'Well, we're closed now,' the young volunteer helper said, 'but I'm sure the chef will find something for you. What would you like?' I had a great meal, entertained by the feeding antics and social interaction of a dozen or so teenage students (whatever), and made my way back to my room for a reasonably early night. My only problem in that hostel was having a room right next to the swing doors at the end of one of the corridors, which was also near the toilets. Every time someone went through the doors, a high-pitched squeak emerged from the door hinges, followed by a loud bang as the door shut. I didn't notice it to begin with, but a hostel full of college students generates a lot of nocturnal traffic, and a lot of squeaking and banging.

6
────────

CONWY TO LLANBERIS

The next part of my *Journey through Wales* took me further west along the north coast of Wales and into the mountains. My plan was to spend a leisurely morning looking around Conwy before making my way across to Bethesda, on the edge of the Snowdonia National Park. I was going to meet my daughter, Sarah, there, and she and I were going to spend the following week together. Sarah was going to travel with me on my adventure around Snowdonia, over to Anglesey, and then halfway down the west coast of Wales before heading back home. It's a rare treat for a dad to get so long with his busy millennial daughter and I was really looking forward to it.

I feel Conwy is one of Wales' best-kept secrets. It is just exquisite, and I wonder why so few people seem to know about it. Maybe it is well known, but it seemed quiet when I was there. HV Morton was hugely impressed by it, commenting on both its historical significance and its great beauty (Morton, 1932). It's a very pretty little coastal town, surrounded by gentle hills and rolling farmland. The impressive sight of the town's magnificent suspension bridge was what first struck me as I approached, and then the picture-book 13th century Conwy Castle, with its towering stone walls and turrets looming high above the town.

Conwy Castle was one of the 'ring of iron' fortifications built by King Edward I between 1283 and 1289, and it played a prominent role in the ongoing conflict between England and Wales over subsequent centuries. With walls over 3 metres thick, eight towers, and a curtain wall with another twenty-one towers, you would think it was impregnable, but our old friend Owain Glyndŵr briefly seized control for the Welsh in the 15th century. It was used as a military stronghold until the 19th century and is now a UNESCO World Heritage Site and popular tourist attraction. Just as I was writing up my notes from this section of the journey, I read that Conwy Castle had been named the most beautiful castle in Europe (by the travel magazine and guide, *Conde Nast Traveller*). Given that Wales has more castles per square mile than any other country in Europe, there was always a good chance it would do well, but Conwy took the very top spot – and that's a good choice.

But, amazing as castles are, there's more to Conwy than its imposing castle and fortifications; the narrow streets are a delight to wander, with their medieval buildings, shops, pubs, and hidden nooks and crannies. Oops, it sounds like I've slipped into guidebook speak. If you're feeling adventurous, there's always the option to climb the ancient 10-metre-high walls that surround the old town. The complete circuit of the medieval battlements is almost a mile long. While walking round, you can take in the stunning panoramic views looking outwards, and peer inside to look down on the old town. I *was* feeling adventurous. It took me three-quarters of an hour to walk right round, and I was surprised to find almost no one else up there. I only met two other people: a startled couple of teenage school kids. When I stumbled across them, they rapidly untangled themselves from mid-canoodle, and without any embarrassment at all, walked on. I expect they were discussing their history homework, maybe trying to experience what it was like to grapple at close quarters on the battlements. Or perhaps they were reflecting on the brilliant words used by HV Morton to describe Conwy Castle.

When the town walls led me to the river, I dropped down to the quayside to see the smallest house in Britain. The front is a dazzling post-box red, so it's hard to miss it, even though it's only 2 metres wide by 3 metres high. It's a tourist attraction now, but until May 1900, the house was occupied. It's ironic that the last person to live in the smallest house in Britain was one of the largest guys around – big Rob Jones, a local fisherman, who was 6 foot 3 inches tall.

The harbour at Conwy

With the tide out, a handful of colourful fishing boats leaned wearily against the town quay. It made an attractive sight on that sunny morning, with the castle as a backdrop and bright blue skies above. A long row of green lobster pots, a sprinkling of little orange buoys, and piles of fishing nets waiting to be repaired made for a colourful and photogenic foreground. To an accompaniment of cackling seagulls, I chatted to a couple of fishermen who were about to board their boat. Only a few boats operate from the port nowadays, they told me, and the size of their catch was nothing compared to the old days (things not being as good as the old days is a given, isn't it?) If they're lucky, they might catch some crab, lobster, mackerel, whiting, or cod, but it was usually mussels and whelks they landed. The lads told me that some of the catch goes to the local hospitality sector, but most of it gets exported to Belgium and France.

I walked across to get a close look at the Conwy Suspension Bridge, about which I'd read great things. Completed in 1826 and one of Telford's finest, it is supposed to be *the* way to approach the town. After I'd walked across it both ways, that made sense. I should have thought of that earlier. HV Morton was very taken with the bridge, writing how perfectly it blends with the castle, and it does, with the towers of the suspension bridge reflecting the design of those on the castle (Morton, 1932).

I spent what was left of the morning looking around the nooks and crannies of the charming old town, huddled securely within its historic walls. A coffee and cake later and I was on my way again, heading west, and back in the tyre tracks of HV Morton. A short distance out of Conwy, as the narrow road climbed steeply into rugged hills, I passed a sign confirming my arrival in the Snowdonia National Park. I said a quiet thank you to HV Morton for taking me on that scenic route instead of along the quicker A55 North Wales Expressway. The narrow road I was following rose ever higher into and through the atmospheric Sychnant Pass towards Penmaenmawr. According to HV Morton, this road quickly transitions from Conwy's estuarine views to somewhere resembling the Scottish highlands. (Morton, 1932). He was right. When I look back at my photos, I could easily be looking at an image of one of Scotland's west coast glens, with steep valley sides covered in gorse and ferns, and patches of bare rock and scree. The odd sheep and goat scratched around optimistically, looking for something nourishing among the few patches of short grass. Once through the pass, you're soon back to the familiar North Wales seaside landscape of long sandy beaches. One thing you cannot miss, however, is the imposing sight of the Penmaenmawr slate quarry… it's an absolute monster. It towers up on the mountainside dead ahead of you as you leave the Sychnant Pass. The slate industry in Penmaenmawr developed later than in other parts of North Wales, and although it was an important source of slate, it never achieved the same scale of production as some of the other quarries in the region. It was more about quality than quantity, however, and keen students of slate roofing will wax lyrical about the excellence and durability of the slate from Penmaenmawr Quarry. Readers familiar with the roof of the House of Parliament or perhaps The Royal Albert Hall will know that those buildings are kept dry to this day thanks to Penmaenmawr slate.

As it weaves its way sinuously towards Holyhead, the A55 hugs the small amount of level coastal land that lies between the mountains of Snowdonia and the Irish Sea. Before long, I was peeling off that main road and heading inland to the town of Bethesda. All the while I'd been navigating my course westwards over the North Wales coast, Sarah was also travelling towards Bethesda from Dorset, on her Royal Enfield Interceptor motorcycle.

Bethesda is a small town with a population of just over 4,000 people, situated in the Ogwen Valley. It's about 4 miles from the coast and surrounded by the hills and mountains of Snowdonia National Park. The town's history is all about slate quarrying, but today it's a popular destination for hikers and outdoor enthusiasts… and that's why Sarah and I were going to be based there for two nights. Our aim for our first full day in the area was to climb the peaks of Glyder Fawr and Glyder Fach – numbers four and five on the list of Welsh mountains over 1,000 metres. From experience, I knew Snowdon would be super busy with tourists in midsummer and the Glyders would be a much quieter option – but they would give us an equally fantastic day's walking in the mountains.

They have lots of chapels in Wales and it came as no surprise to discover the town of Bethesda was named after one. The main reason the town exists, however, is slate. The Penrhyn slate quarry, the largest in Britain, has kept people of Bethesda employed since the 18th century and now the main pit is about a mile long, half a mile wide, and a quarter of a mile deep. Stop and think about that for a moment; it's staggering. At the end of the nineteenth century, the Penrhyn quarry was the world's largest, employing over 3,000 people and producing over 100,000 tons of slate per year. That's about 186,000 square metres of roofing tiles, or for those whose minds work that way, and I believe there are a few, enough rock to fill approximately 26.7 Olympic-size swimming pools annually – assuming that the slate is crushed and compacted into a relatively uniform size and shape, and that it is being measured in terms of its overall volume rather than its weight or other dimensions etc. Let's leave it there. The poor conditions in which the slate miners had to work led to, 'The Great Strike of Penrhyn,' which lasted for 3 years, beginning in November 1900. This was the longest dispute in British industrial history. The other thing for which Bethesda has a claim to fame is the percentage of its people who speak Welsh. According to the 2021 census, 78% of Bethesda's population spoke Welsh, a figure higher than the average for both Gwynedd (64.4%), and Wales (17.8%) taken as a whole.

These few headline facts give you a flavour of the town and the surrounding area. It is very Welsh, has strong roots in Welsh nonconformity, and is steeped in mining history.

Chapels are a quintessential element of most Welsh villages and towns. Often, they are very simple in design, bordering on bleak, but they can also be strikingly ornate and sometimes quite over-the-top with their elaborate designs. The presence of these distinctive and iconic buildings in the rural and urban landscape says, 'You're in Wales.' A few years ago, the Royal Commission on the Ancient and Historical Monuments of Wales estimated there were almost 4,500 of them, which is an exceptionally high concentration of religious buildings for a country the size of Wales. At their peak, in the mid-19th century, nearly 80% of worshippers in Wales attended a nonconformist chapel, but nowadays many are closed and many more struggle to survive. Welsh people reading this will probably be filled with nostalgia right now, thinking about the old chapel from their childhood, but some non-Welsh readers might not know much about them. So, what are they?

First, there's that word 'nonconformist.' In this context, it means a religious group that doesn't conform to the doctrine, discipline, and practices of the established Anglican Church, i.e., the Church of England. In Wales, nonconformist churches began to emerge in the 17th century, largely because of the religious and political turmoil of the time, but the seeds that led to those breakaway groups can be traced back to Tudor times. For much of its history, Wales had been a Catholic country, but things changed under Henry VIII. In 1531, he broke away from the Catholic Church of Rome and made himself the Supreme Head of the Church of England. The surrounding story of sex, politics, and religion has fascinated us for centuries. For Welsh religion, the change was seismic and the clue to the problem is in the name 'Church of England.' Where does that leave Welsh worshippers? Things got worse a few years later. In 1536, The Act of Union firmly joined Wales to England. The law of England became the law of Wales. English was the only language permitted in the courts of Wales, and only those speaking English could hold public office. In very simplistic terms, this meant that those in charge of Welsh administration, the establishment, became English speakers, while the rest of society used the Welsh language. It was a situation that continued and became embedded over the following generations. The Welsh language was in common day-to-day use by most of the population, but formal activities, for example the law, administration, and education, had to be conducted in English. This contributed to a sense of alienation and marginalisation among many Welsh people.

Fast forward to the early 18th century. The Reverend Griffith Jones, from Carmarthenshire established his famous circulating schools. A school was set up at a temporary location, perhaps in a barn or church, where both children and grownups were taught to read and write in Welsh. They used William Morgan's translated Welsh Bible that was published in 1588. After 3 months of tuition, the circulating school would move on to a new location. The aim of the schools was primarily religious; the Reverend Griffith Jones wanted to promote literacy among the Welsh population to encourage people to read *The Bible*. However, the impact of the circulating schools on Welsh society was much broader, and by 1777, almost 6,500 such schools had been established, enrolling over 300,000 students, of which two-thirds were adults. This means that almost 70% of the population of Wales received schooling through the circulating school method, which was a significant achievement in terms of promoting literacy and education in the country.

The combined efforts of the Reverend Griffith Jones and William Morgan helped to ensure Wales had a working-class population that was literate, but also Welsh speaking. The disconnect with England, in both religious and political terms, still existed. Disillusioned with the Church of England, Wales became a nation of dissenters and into this gap stepped several charismatic preachers, people like Howell Harris, Daniel Rowland, William Williams, John Calvin, and John Wesley. Several religious movements emerged that were not part of the established church. These new religious groups included Baptists, Independents, Congregationalists, Wesleyans, Quakers, Religious Society of Friends, Independents, Calvinists, and Presbyterians. They built chapels for the Welsh people to follow these new nonconformist religion denominations. Many chapels were given exotic sounding names from locations in the books of *The Bible*. Hebron Congregational Chapel, Ebenezer Independent Chapel, and Salem Methodist Chapel are all examples of chapels named after places in the *Old Testament*.

While the official language of work and education was English, it was the chapel to which the population turned for their spiritual guidance and social cohesion. The chapels allowed Welsh people to live their lives as they wished and kept their language alive. In a broad generalisation, the Welsh-speaking working class followed nonconformist religions in chapels, and the English-speaking establishment worshipped in the Church of England. It was a polarisation that became increasingly important in society, industrial relations, and politics.

They built the Bethesda Chapel in the village of Glanogwen back in 1820, a handsome building erected to the glory of God, in a land where spiritual reverence was a source of comfort for those who lived in grinding poverty. As the years passed, the community around the chapel grew in size as the slate quarry grew in size, until eventually, they could no longer call it a village. And so, with a stroke of the pen, Glanogwen became Bethesda.

Sarah and I found ourselves in a small but cosy bunkhouse on the southern edge of the town. The Afon Ogwen flowed gently nearby, providing a melodic background sound as it danced its way towards the sea. Some of the energy from that dance is being collected to provide power to the local community. About 140 homes in the Ogwen Valley area of Bethesda have clubbed together in a collective scheme with the National Trust, which owns a hydro-electric turbine on the river. The 'Energy Local Club' began in Bethesda, back in 2016, but the technological and economic model they've developed, and the experience gained, is now being used to create similar schemes across the UK. The upshot is that members of the scheme can get their electricity for about a quarter of the cost that most users pay elsewhere. And it's not just hydro-power. The town is actively supporting the use of solar panels and wind turbines. The local secondary school has got solar panels on its roof, for example, and you'll spot wind turbines scattered across the nearby hills. It's all part of the town's forward-thinking policy of reducing its carbon footprint and doing their bit for the planet.

Our bunkhouse was owned by a lovely couple who made Sarah and me very welcome. The following day, which was Sarah's birthday, we were going to be climbing the Glyder peaks. After a second night in Bethesda, we planned to tour more of the Snowdonia area, ending up in Llanberis. We'd then look around Anglesey and have an overnight stay on the Llŷn Peninsula (Pen Llŷn), in a shepherd's hut. After that, we'd work our way down the west coast of Wales. My spreadsheet of visitor sights and appointments was primed and ready for action.

I love a day in the mountains, and I was way overdue a high-altitude fix. After breakfast, Sarah and I walked to the centre of Bethesda, stocked up with food and drink, and caught the bus up to the Mountain Centre at Idwal Cottage, about 10 miles from the town. What followed, on yet another perfect summer's day, was on reflection, probably my favourite day of the year.

The gurgling sound of the fast-flowing stream from Llŷn Idwal was our backing track as we began our walk. The first section of the walk is fairly easy-going, which is good because it got my limbs cranked up and moving before the more challenging stuff higher up. 'Let's take it easy, at first,' I said, rolling out an old family favourite that Sarah has had to put up with at the beginning of every run, cycle trip, or walk since she was a toddler.

Once on our way, we met few other people because everyone who was ahead or behind us going up the path was going at a similar pace, and at that time of day there was no one coming down the other way. We soon got to Llŷn Idwal, about 200 metres above our starting point. The shallow lake lies in a hollow that was sculpted out of the mountains by a glacier at the end of the last Ice Age. Once beyond the lake, you're into increasingly tough and steep climbing before you get to a summit plateau that stretches out at a height of around 1,000 metres between the two peaks of the Glyders. Near the top of the steepest section, before getting to the plateau, we approached a rock feature called the Devil's Kitchen. Right there, almost 1,000 metres up the mountain, we unexpectedly came across a BBC film crew – as you do. They told us they were filming for a documentary on climate change, and they were up in the clouds that day to highlight the existential threat to the tufted saxifrage (*Saxifraga caespitosa*), the rarest of several rare plant species that cling precariously to life in Cwm Idwal (the valley within which Llŷn Idwal lies). After the last Ice Age, Britain became a landscape of tundra vegetation similar to places you find nowadays in Canada, Siberia, and Norway. That environment was perfect for tufted saxifrage. Over the next few thousand years, however, the climate warmed up, other plants moved in, and soils began to develop. Dense woodland took over most of Britain and many of the old Arctic species became extinct, muscled out by faster growing, more competitive plants. The steep, north-facing slopes of Cwm Idwal are now the only place in England and Wales where tufted saxifrage is still found – but that's now under threat. We were told that a single 40-degree centigrade event like some parts of Britain had experienced that summer, and the tufted saxifrage species would be lost from Cwm Idwal.

We caught up with a delightful old gentleman who was taking a short breather, which seemed fair enough when he told us he was in his mid-eighties. I was glad of a chance to catch my breath myself. He seemed to have absolutely nailed his retirement way of life. He lived locally and he told us how he and his wife go over to Anglesey one day of the week together for a coffee somewhere, for example to Beaumaris. One other day of the week he was allowed out on his own, when he normally climbed one of the Snowdonia mountains! This was a model I noted and saved for future inspiration; in case I am lucky enough to reach that age.

The plateau on top of the Glyders range is strange. It's a long narrow horizontal street of grey broken rocks and boulders of all sizes, like a builders' yard of spare scraps left behind by some mountain building giant. The views down to the Ogwen Valley were incredible. We were looking down on slow-moving vehicles, like lines of ants, regularly spaced as they slowly crept left and right along the main road. To the north, we could see the unmistakable outline of Tryfan and to the southwest was another of the Seven Wonders of Wales – 'Snowdon's mountain without its people.' Except I knew there would be hordes of people on it, so I was glad we were on the Glyders and not over on the opposite side of the Llanberis Pass, competing for footpath space. As we skirted around the lip of The Nameless Cwm (which seems an odd name), the breeze was blowing wisps of cloud through a narrow gap, up and over the summit plateau. We passed the Castle of the Winds rock formation (always good for a dad joke) and walked on to the randomly stacked rock slabs and boulders that make up the Glyder Fach summit.

One of the dramatic features on the summit plateau is a pile of rocks called The Cantilever. Amongst a pile of huge boulders, a giant slab of rock, perhaps 10 metres long and 3 metres wide, lies horizontal, about 5 metres above the surface of the summit plateau. Two-thirds of the slab are supported by other boulders, but the rest provides a spectacular overhanging platform. Sarah and I took it in turns to clamber up and stand right on the end to be photographed in silly poses. It's what everyone up there has to do. The descent from

Glyder Fawr back to Idwal Cottage is steep and rugged, especially the first section, where it's hard to see a path amongst all the scattered boulders and scree. Picking our way down carefully, we were entertained by a search and rescue helicopter circling in the valley below us – hopefully just training.

By the time we'd got back to the main road at Idwal Cottage it was mid-afternoon, and we only had a few minutes to wait for the bus back to Bethesda. It was almost as if we'd planned it. We celebrated the day and Sarah's birthday with an Indian meal in Bethesda that evening, pleasantly exhausted but satisfied. She told me how she'd enjoyed the day, but she'd really just been expecting a long walk. She would have brought a harness, helmet, some ropes, and a few carabiners if she'd known that I was planning so much extended rock face traversing and scree skiing. I think she may have picked up a tendency for exaggeration from someone; she loved it really. The following day we were back on the bikes and off to Llanberis.

It was yet another dazzling summer's day (but you know this by now) as Sarah and I set off to ride our circuit of the Snowdonia area. How lucky were we? The route took us down to Capel Curig and then onto Betws-y-Coed before dropping down to Blaenau Ffestiniog, then north to Beddgelert before finishing our day in Llanberis. It was going to be the best part of 60 miles, and it was going to be awesome!

The A5 road out of Bethesda took us up the Ogwen Valley again, past Llŷn Ogwen. The mountains towered up either side of us and we rode alongside the Glyders that we'd climbed the day before. We were now the ants that people up on the top were looking down on. Tryfan looked amazing, and in that weather, I was wishing we had more time (as usual) to do more climbing. The A5 eventually weaved its way through the Llugwy Valley, where steep valley sides covered in coniferous trees closed in to make the valley floor very narrow. As the road twisted and turned through the dense forests and rolling hills, we swayed rhythmically from side to side. It was a good day to be on a motorcycle.

I'd stopped at Swallow Falls many times before, but it was Sarah's first time in the area, so we pulled over to take a look. They are always impressive and even though the water levels were low, the falls still looked dramatic. Dappled sunlight danced on the calm waters upstream before the river cascaded approximately 15 metres down a series of rocky ledges in a swirling, chaotic mass of foam and spray, crashing against the rocks in a deafening roar. A cool mist of spray wafted up from the watery cauldron and drifted over us, carried by the gentlest of breezes. With all that relentless power, shouldn't someone be talking to the guys from Bethesda about building a hydro-electric scheme?

As we rode down the A470 through the Crimea Pass (Bwlch y Gorddinan) towards Blaenau Ffestiniog, the landscape opened up again, revealing a desolate topography of bare and rugged mountains scarred by enormous slate quarries. We were approaching Blaenau Ffestiniog, 'The Town That Roofed the World' right at the heart of 'The Slate Mining Landscape of Northwest Wales,' another UNESCO World Heritage Site. The area is known for its rich mining history and its unique heritage railway, but we had an appointment with a slate mine. The Llechwedd Slate Quarry was one of the 'big three,' along with the Penrhyn and Dinorwig Quarries, producing high-quality slate for roofing and construction, back in the day. It would have employed over 3,000 men at the time of its peak production in the late 19th century. There are still working slate mines in Blaenau Ffestiniog today, although the industry is now a tiny fraction of what it was at its peak. The Llechwedd Slate Caverns, which were once part of the larger Llechwedd Slate Quarry, are still in operation as an underground tourist attraction, offering guided tours to view the old mine workings and learn about the history of the slate industry… and that's where we had just arrived.

Once checked in, Sarah and I were given a miner's helmet each, and with a handful of other visitors, we walked into a hole in the side of a Welsh mountain. Our guide, Liam, took us underground along dark, cramped, and damp adits (horizontal tunnels) and drifts (sloping tunnels) for an hour and a half, providing a series of mining facts and anecdotes as he pointed out the features at regular stops. Some of the stories were about the 'jackdaws'; these were young boys, typically between the ages of 8 and 12 years. They were called jackdaws because they were small and nimble, and their work involved climbing and crawling through narrow passages in the mine like small and agile birds. The lads usually worked underground as 'pickers,' separating waste rock from slate. Accidents were commonplace and many jackdaws were injured or killed, while working in the mines.

Liam clearly had a genuine interest in the history of the mines, and his deep respect for the miners was clear. At one point, we stopped to look at an enormous chamber from which slate had been excavated decades ago and he showed us a few artefacts that he and his friend had found just the previous week, when exploring an adjacent adit. There were some old cigarette packets, the remains of a woollen hat and a small tin box. Those few personal objects brought to life the reality of workers in the underground tunnels. The climax of the tour was a very moving light and sound show deep in the mine, in a huge slate chamber, partly flooded with water. As ghostly images of former miners flickered across the dark walls and shimmered on the surface of the water, we watched and listened to a tribute to the men involved. The sounds echoed around in the darkness, accompanied by the stirring harmonies of a male choir. It was 'hairs on the back of your neck' stuff. I was touched by how the tribute emphasised the lives of the people involved, rather than just providing impressive statistics about tons of slate produced and numbers of shafts dug. It was very thought-provoking, and we were a slightly subdued and thoughtful group of visitors as we made our way to the steepest train ride in Europe (with a gradient of approximately 55.6%), for the ride back to the surface.

Our final visit, before our overnight stop in Llanberis, was the charming village of Beddgelert, nestled in a picturesque valley surrounded by high mountains. It brought back happy memories of when I updated the OS Landranger map of the Snowdonia area (Sheet 115) back in the 1980s. I stayed in the village for about a month while walking the hills and bringing the map up to date. Beddgelert is a lovely place, and makes a perfect base for walking, but what Sarah and I most wanted to see, like most visitors, was 'Gelert's Grave.'

The story of Gelert is part of Welsh folklore, and it brings us back to Llywelyn ap Iorwerth again, from the 13th century. Gelert was a hound, and the faithful companion of the Welsh Prince. The legend involves the prince returning to his hunting lodge in Beddgelert after a day hunting in the mountains. Gelert had been left behind in the lodge with the prince's infant son. Llywelyn arrived home to find a scene of bloody mayhem and an upturned cot. His boy was missing and Gelert had blood around his mouth. Llywelyn may have been a bit impulsive on reflection but believing that his loyal hound had attacked and killed his son, the prince drew his sword and struck poor Gelert down. The situation, as is often the case, was more nuanced than it first appeared. The loud yelps of the dying hound awoke the prince's baby son, who until then had been covered by blood-stained sheets and blankets next to his cot. Beside the infant was the dead body of a wolf. It turned out that Gelert had been protecting the child from the wolf, which had somehow found its way into the child's room. The hound had killed the wolf to keep Llywelyn's son safe, and it was the wolf's blood that the hasty prince had seen around Gelert's chops. Blinded by his own fears, behavioural bias, and assumptions, the prince had misjudged the situation entirely, and his rash actions had cost him dearly. Full of remorse, and said to have never smiled again, Llywelyn built a final resting place for his faithful companion, and Gelert's Grave can still be seen to this day in Beddgelert. The legend is heart-breaking and poignant, but the pedant in me couldn't help but question some of the details: where was the mother, for example, and how irresponsible was Llywelyn to go off hunting while leaving his boy alone in the house with a dangerous dog? It's best not to question legends, though; their power and significance lie in their underlying message and this story has become an enduring symbol of the loyalty and devotion that is so valued in Welsh culture.

By the time we reached Llanberis, we'd almost done a complete circle around Snowdon. When HV Morton drove through Llanberis Pass on a wet spring day, he observed how forlorn it seemed (Morton, 1932). After many trips to the area, I must admit that's the default image I also have of Llanberis and the pass: a light drizzle falling from grey skies onto grey mountains and grey buildings; a drab scene seen through eyes in which all your colour receptors have been inactivated. On average, there are around 200 rainy days per year in North Wales, but those figures were hard to believe in the summer of 2022. The same climate change that's threatening the tufted saxifrage was giving us some short-term gain in the form of a long hot summer.

It had been an amazing day of mountain scenery, a sample of life underground in a slate mine, and another brush with Llywelyn ap Iorwerth. I realise my frailties at trying to be a writer, when I try to describe how it feels to be on holiday with my girl for a day's walking in the mountains and then riding in the sunshine around Snowdonia. I just don't have the words. Our accommodation for the night was another youth hostel, where once again we had a warm welcome. We'd had a great time in Snowdonia and next up, in the morning, was Anglesey.

7

LLANBERIS TO LLITHFAEN

I'm a regular visitor to Bangor. I go there every 47 years. My last visit in 1975 was with my old mate, Nick, although in those days he was my new mate. We'd met the previous year, as trainee land surveyors working for OS. In the summer of 1975, the two of us set off for a walking weekend in Snowdonia. Wandering somewhere in the mountains north of Blaenau Ffestiniog, we came across some abandoned slate mines. Being young, reckless, and irresponsible (as opposed to now, when we're old, reckless, and irresponsible), we travelled a lot further underground than we should have done, given our lack of suitable equipment – or any equipment really, apart from an old torch with dodgy batteries. The abandoned tunnels and caverns we discovered were amazing and became increasingly thrilling the further we ventured away from the safety of the surface. I'm sure we shouldn't have been there, but that made it even more exciting. Whether it was common sense (unlikely), lack of bottle (very likely), or fading batteries that made us turn around eventually, I can't recall, but at some point we realised we'd gone far enough, and it was time to find our way out. Happy days.

In that same spirit of reckless adventure, we also visited Bangor University on the same weekend. I can't remember whether we were invited to meet up with Nick's girlfriend and her pals there, or whether we just invited ourselves, but somehow, we found our way there. I can't even remember if Lesley, Nick's girlfriend from his school days at Cardiff, was even still his girlfriend at the time, but as I often can't remember what I did last week, it's a minor miracle I can recall anything about a weekend nearly half a century ago. It must have been quite special, though, to remain tucked away somewhere in my head all those years. And it was. Nick and I were treated with fantastic hospitality by Lesley, Rhiannon, Clare… and a few other lovely girls whose names escape me. We had a wicked weekend. I should clarify… that's 'wicked' in the sense of being very good fun. We visited numerous Bangor hostelries, consumed far too much booze, danced into the night, and laughed ourselves silly, as you do at that age. Nick and I crashed out in the girls' dormitory, which, sadly, sounds a lot more scandalous than it really was.

Bangor University plays a significant part in the history of Welsh further education. HV Morton writes how the people of North Wales struggled for many years to get the university built in Bangor, and about the important role it plays in the region. Nowadays, the university is a highly regarded research-intensive institution with a broad range of specialist subject areas such as psychology, ocean sciences, linguistics, and health and medical sciences… not that I gave a toss about those things 47 years ago.

When we arrived for my second visit to Bangor, Sarah and I did a couple of circuits around the city centre, looking for somewhere to park so we could visit Bangor Cathedral, (Eglwys Gadeiriol Bangor), also known as the Cathedral Church of Saint Deiniol. We turned in to the High Street, but at around 20 metres above sea level, it wasn't really that high. Perhaps they should rename it, 'Long Street' because researchers from the OS have identified it as the longest High Street in Wales (1,265 metres long). As we dismounted our bikes, we were slightly taken aback by the sight of a peacock walking down the pavement towards us, casually doing a bit of window shopping. I think we all know which fashion retailer he was looking for, but he was in the wrong street. Sarah wondered if we'd slipped into the twilight zone, but I reassured her that everything was perfectly normal. She was just on one of her dad's adventures and these things happen. It reminded me of when I came across a flock of geese walking down the middle of the A58 in Sowerby Bridge, West Yorkshire (described in *Another Journey through Britain*). When Sarah later researched online for 'peacocks of Bangor,' she discovered that the birds had probably escaped from the nearby Penrhyn Castle estate back in the 19th century. They obviously enjoy a bit of retail therapy and have now become a familiar sight in the area. We were just about to set off for the cathedral, when 'Life on Mars' boomed out from the shop doorway where we were standing, and I had to stay and listen to the end. That was going to be with me for the next two hours or so.

Bangor Cathedral is a small yet remarkable structure that was built on the site of a Welsh monastery founded by St Deiniol way back in AD 530. It's one of the oldest Christian sites in Britain. Its location and proportions kept it out of the covetous and rapacious sight of Viking raiders and helped it to survive their frequent asset liberation visits. Over time, the community grew, and the cathedral was rebuilt in the 11th century in the Norman style that was all the rage at the time. Later on, in the 19th century, the cathedral underwent major renovations, which gave it the impressive Gothic style we see today. The cathedral has been the final resting place for several kings of Gwynedd, and inside you can also pay your respects at the shrine of Saint Deiniol. The cathedral's Biblical Garden has every plant mentioned in *The Bible*, making it a lush and verdant oasis for contemplation. We met two lovely people inside who were setting up props for a children's class. They generously gave up some of their time to chat and tell us about the cathedral, of which they were clearly immensely proud. When I mentioned my book, one of them (much better educated than me, but that's a low bar) said, 'Oh you're a modern-day Giraldus Cambrensis!' I smiled and nodded, as if acknowledging a shrewd and perceptive observation. It was only later, when the manuscript for this book was almost complete, that I found out about the Giraldus he was referring to. Also known as Gerald of Wales, he travelled widely and wrote about the culture, politics, and religious practices of Wales during the 12th and 13th centuries – and one of his most famous works was called *Journey through Wales!*

Being someone who is normally guilty of planning things to death, I'm ashamed to say my pre-visit notes for Bangor were not as extensive as I would have liked. 'University town, cathedral, and pier,' is admirably succinct, but is hardly the preparation required for a fulfilling visit. Anyway, I had ticked off the university (years ago) and cathedral from that comprehensive list, so we headed for Garth Pier (Pier y Garth). Garth is a district of Bangor and the pier is sometimes referred to as Garth Pier, Bangor Pier, or Bangor Garth Pier. I'm so glad the pier found its way onto my list, and our timing was perfect. In its 125th year, the Grade II listed Bangor Garth Pier had just won the coveted 2022 'Pier of the Year' award.

Brighton, Hastings, Blackpool, Cleethorpes, Weston-Super-Mare… Rishi Sunak can you hear me... Bangor has beaten them all… your piers took a hell of a beating!

It's a great accolade for all the hard-working volunteers who help to keep such a special example of seaside Victoriana maintained and looking good. To save you looking it up, Cromer was second in 2022, followed by Colwyn Bay in third place. Bangor Garth Pier is 460 metres long, making it is the second-longest pier in Wales, and the ninth longest in the British Isles. The National Piers Society, who know a thing or two about these things, said Bangor Garth Pier 'Boasts the best panorama of views of any pier in the UK.' Well, it has a bit of a head start in that department. Jutting out into the

Menai Strait, it has the spectacular Menai Bridge to its left, Llandudno to its right, and the mountainous skyline of Snowdonia behind it. The pier is in an amazing location. Added to that, the old Victorian toll booths and a silver onion domed pavilion at the end make it the very epitome of Victorian seaside splendour. You probably know what's coming next. Sarah and I bought our tickets, bought an ice cream each, and strolled leisurely to the end of the pier and back. Grownups of all ages, shapes, and sizes, were doing the same, all politely saying hello to each other as they passed in the sunshine, while groups of excited kids ran up and down or did a bit of crabbing. Standing next to the rails of the pier and looking landward, I could make out the route Sarah and I would be taking next: about 2 miles south-westwards down the side of the narrow Menai Strait to the suspension bridge, and then another 5 miles north-eastwards on the opposite side, along the southern coastline of Anglesey to Beaumaris. It looked so beautiful on a warm summer's day and part of me wished we were going to walk the route along the Welsh Coast Path, instead of tearing round (sedately, in a safe and leisurely manner) on our motorcycles.

Making the short crossing over the sea to Anglesey from Bangor, you'll find yourself in the enviable position of having not one but two bridges to choose from. The first, Thomas Telford's Menai Suspension Bridge (Pont Menai), opened in 1826, and was the world's very first iron suspension bridge. Stretching out for 417 metres, its central span is 177 metres long and it sits 30 metres above the water to allow the tallest of ships to sail beneath it. But don't let the Menai Bridge hog all the glory. There's also the Britannia Bridge (Pont Britannia), an impressive prototype box-girder bridge, designed by William Fairbairn and Robert Stephenson, which opened to the world in 1850. Originally built to carry rail traffic, it was seriously damaged by fire in 1970 and rebuilt as a double-decked structure that now serves both rail and road traffic. Both bridges are such remarkable feats of engineering that

Sarah and I were compelled to add a totally unnecessary loop to our journey, so we could cross both of them. More accurately, I was compelled to add a totally unnecessary loop to our journey so we could cross both of them, and Sarah followed me, slightly confused about what her daft dad was up to. The Menai Suspension Bridge is particularly awesome. It's the huge iron chains and over-sized links that catch your eye as you cross over it, and when you see it from a distance (there's a great viewpoint on the Anglesey side, between the two bridges), you see what a truly elegant design it has. Thomas Telford himself crossed his bridge on horseback leading a procession to celebrate the opening in 1826. Numerous A-list celebrities of the time graced the event with their presence, among them the Duke of Wellington, who famously praised the bridge as 'a triumph of art and science.' The Menai Suspension Bridge is just that and still has the wow factor all these years after its opening. I might have to revisit that Seven Wonders of Wales poem and see if I can slip the bridge in somewhere. It's surely got to be up there. I'll think about that again at the end of my journey.

There's always something special about being on an island and I think Anglesey has a special vibe all of its own. That point was being emphasised as we rode up its coastline towards Beaumaris and looked back to the mainland. We had entered an island microclimate in which we had clear blue skies overhead, while over on the mainland, in stark contrast, there were grey clouds building over the mountains.

What *was* happening with the weather in the summer of 2022? I'd always thought that two consecutive days in Wales without rain were unusual and three would be very rare. Four dry days is a statistical anomaly, five would get the Met Office statisticians scurrying for their record books, and six would be a climate event. The summer of 2022 will be remembered as a record-breaking dry and sunny 4 months, and if there was rain falling somewhere on Wales, for most of that time, it wasn't on me.

Anglesey is the largest island in Wales, with an area of approximately 276 square miles. It is predominately rural with the only towns of any size being Holyhead, Llangefni, Menai Bridge, and Amlwch. The important ferry port of Holyhead is the largest town, with a population of just over 12,000.

In Roman times, Anglesey was known as Mona, and it was feared by the invading Roman armies who saw it as a stronghold of druidic resistance. The druids were renowned for their mystical powers and their ability to inspire fierce loyalty in their followers. Tacitus, considered one of the greatest historians of ancient Rome, described Mona as 'a place inhabited by a warlike people, and a common refuge for all the discontented Britons' (Tacitus. "Annals." Book 14, Chapter 29. Translated by John Jackson. Loeb Classical Library. Cambridge, MA: Harvard University Press, 1937. Pp. 233). I remember going to a bar like that in Bangor in 1975. The Romans general Suetonius Paulinus was so intimidated by the druids of Anglesey that he hesitated to attack them, fearing that their magic might turn the tide of battle against him. In the end, the Romans emerged victorious, with the Celtic tribes and druids suffering heavy casualties.

I'd forgotten how lovely Beaumaris is. In fact, I would rate it as one of the most attractive towns in Wales... although, (and I'll only whisper this), I've heard it described as an English town. Its picturesque setting on the Menai Strait, with wonderful views over to the mountains of Snowdonia, gives it a tremendous advantage but added to that, much of the town's well-preserved Georgian and Victorian architecture remains unspoiled. It's one of those rare places where, by design or accident, the planners seem to have got something right. Being designated a conservation area in 1966 will have undoubtedly helped. The town's name derives from the French for 'beautiful marsh.' It would have been named by the French-Norman invaders who arrived in the area, and everywhere else it seems, in the 11th century.

Sarah and I sat sipping coffee for a while at a pavement table where we could watch the world go by, and in the gaps when it wasn't going by, we could admire the castle at the end of the road. Beaumaris Castle is perhaps the greatest castle in Wales never built… famous because it still isn't finished. A shortage of funds and the distraction of the warlike and discontented Scots meant the last, and perhaps what would have been the most impressive of Edward I's castles, was never completed. It's more of a bungalow version really, though what remains of its unique design and its impressive fortifications, which were way ahead of their time in terms of military technology, is still very impressive and attractive. Today, Beaumaris Castle is a popular tourist attraction and a UNESCO World Heritage Site. Our coffee break gave us the chance to recap on our journey so far and look ahead to the rest of our day's ride. Next up was something I'd somehow got more excited about than I probably should have done – the birthplace of the Tudor dynasty.

It's something that got HV Morton animated as well. So much so that he used up seven pages writing about Plas Penmynydd and the Tudors of Anglesey (Morton, 1932). I can't compete with that, and I'm not going to try. I certainly wouldn't hold your attention for seven pages on the subject, so I'll keep it brief. Sarah and I turned off the B5420 road to Llangefni, onto a tiny track that leads to a small cluster of houses and farm buildings. Outside one of those houses, a sign reads, 'Cartref Y Tudoriaid,' which is Welsh for 'Home of the Tudors.' It was Plas Penmynydd, the ancestral home of the Tudor family and the birthplace of Owen Tudor, who was a Welsh courtier and soldier. Today's house, now a private home, sits where the Tudors lived during their peak. It was rebuilt in the 17th century and later renovated.

The next few lines warrant a soft violin background. The story of Owen Tudor and Catherine of Valois is a tragic one, but it is also a romantic one. It is a story of love, loss, and redemption. And it is a story that helped to shape the course of English history. Let's go back to Henry V of England, of Agincourt fame, who we met back in Monmouth at the beginning of this *Journey through Wales*. Aged thirty-three, Henry V married Catherine de Valois, the beautiful and intelligent teenage daughter of King Charles VI of France and his wife, Isabeau of Bavaria. It was in June 1420. Catherine produced an heir the following year, but only a year later, her husband was dead. 'Catherine the Fair' was a widow, and the infant son had become King Henry VI. Only being 9 months old, his abilities as a monarch were limited, so a regency council was established to rule on his behalf. Also on the royal court scene at that time was Owen Tudor from Plas Penmynydd, Anglesey. Through his bravery on the battlefield in the service of his king, he gets a gig as bodyguard and attendant to the queen. With Henry V dead, the handsome and dashing Owen catches the queen's eye, but surely, she wouldn't fall for such a rough and unpolished diamond? He was from such a poor background, had no royal blood, and – *Mon Dieu, il était Gallois*! Apart from anything else, it would have been against the law for her to marry a commoner, but it seems love found a way and they married in secret. He was promoted to Clerk of the Wardrobe, which I imagine was a lot more important than just ironing Catherine's frocks, and presumably he had access to the queen's chamber. As the expression goes, 'In for a centime, in for a franc,' and in time, Catherine bore the couple four children: Edmund, Jasper, another Owen (just to confuse us, but at least it wasn't another Henry), and Margaret. Catherine's last childbirth, in 1437, was so problematic that she became ill and died. With his mother dead, Henry VI took over full royal duties aged just sixteen. At about this time, the news of Catherine's marriage to Owen Tudor leaked out. He was arrested, placed in Newgate prison (twice), escaped (twice), and eventually made his way back to a much quieter life in Wales again.

Let's return briefly to the oldest of Owen Tudor and Catherine's four children, Edmund. In 1452, aged twenty-two,

Edmund Tudor was created Earl of Richmond by King Henry VI. Edmund had already established himself as a loyal and capable member of the royal court by then but his new title placed him among the upper ranks of the English nobility. He married the thirteen-year-old Margaret Beaufort, heiress to the house of Somerset, and just over a year later, she gave birth to Henry Tudor in Pembroke Castle. That son, grandson to Owen Tudor and Catherine of Valois, later became Henry VII, father of Henry VIII. We will return to the story when we reach Pembrokeshire but for the moment just ponder the irony of the situation: the Tudor dynasty, the Reformation, Mary I and Elizabeth I, the defeat of the Armada, and the discovery of the colonies are all part of what some people consider the greatest period of English history… and it all began with a country lad (and also a member of the Welsh gentry) from Anglesey.

Plas Penmynydd is now a private residence, so Sarah and I just looked at the historic place from a distance before continuing our tour of the island. We rode past Red Wharf Bay up to Amlwch (pronounced 'ahm-looch'). The name 'Amlwch' is derived from the Welsh words 'am' and 'llwch,' which together mean 'surrounding dust,' referring to the dust and debris that was generated during mining activity in the area, particularly from nearby Parys Mountain, where Sarah and I were heading. Parys Mountain is part of the Copper Kingdom UNESCO Global Geopark, one of six such parks in the UK, but the only one in Wales.

Parys Mountain is a huge hill covering an area of about 2.8 square miles, which has had the top sliced off by years of mining. The copper mine was in operation from the late 18th century to the early 20th century, and during its peak years, Parys Mountain produced around 3,000 tons of copper ore per year. The mine was so productive that it helped make Britain the world's leading producer of copper, and it played a significant role in the development of the country's economy and technology in the Industrial Revolution.

Sarah and I parked the bikes and took a circular walk around the site. It's free to visit what must be one of the most unusual landscapes in Britain. There are several well-marked trails that guide visitors around the old mining site and the surrounding area. Similar to the Monty Python arguments, you can choose from two options, a one-hour or two-hour version. It looks like a big open expanse of heathland at first, but you soon come across the remains of the mine workings, including huge open cast pits, spoil heaps, and underground tunnels. The exposed rock formations, rich in copper, iron, and other minerals, give the landscape a distinctive palette of red, brown, yellow, and orange colours. It's a quite striking, almost alien landscape, but you'll be fine if you're used to walking around the surface of Mars.

We skirted round the north coastline of Anglesey, past some stunning coves, beaches, and seascapes, before dropping down to the town of Holyhead. We drove around the centre and went straight back out again. It was good to get a view of the ferry port, but the town itself was completely jammed with visitors. A long line of lorries, on their way to Ireland, formed what looked like a 2-mile-long lorry park on the main entrance road to the port.

A glance at the OS map of Anglesey shows that, like Pembrokeshire and west Cornwall, the area is sprinkled with chambered cairns, standing stones, hill-forts, burial chambers, and other archaeological sites, and these are just the ones that have survived. Anglesey's rich history dates back to the Neolithic period, and the island has been settled by various groups throughout history, including the Celts, Romans, and Vikings. Its strategic location on the west coast of Britain (a sea lane superhighway in ancient times), at the mouth of the Menai Strait, made it a prime location for trade and commerce. That led to the construction of defensive structures such as hill-forts and castles. We are fortunate that the abundance of archaeological sites on the island has been relatively undisturbed because of the lack of development on the island.

Passing on our right, Anglesey Airport, the former Royal Air Force base and now a civilian airfield, Sarah and I rode south to look at Barclodiad y Gawres burial chamber. The site dates back to around 4,500 BC and is one of the most significant prehistoric monuments in Wales.

It's a lovely short walk from the car park on the A4080, out to the headland next to Porth Trecastell. Its Cornish-sounding name shows the common Brittonic language roots. I smiled and nodded in respect to its builders as I approached the ancient tomb, a neat grassy dome which lies serenely on the headland, bordered by water on three sides and with panoramic sea views. The guys who built this must have really taken their time and nailed the very best of the very best grand locations. The occupants were presumably extremely important people. A funky looking circular solar panel sits on top of the mound, presumably to power lights in the tunnels in the tomb below. The burial chamber is an awe-inspiring monument that marries both incredible engineering and breathtaking artwork. The construction is remarkable, featuring a stone passage leading to a cruciform-shaped inner burial chamber, all covered by a massive stone slab that weighs a whopping 25 tons… and heavy lifting cranes would have been scarce in the Neolithic period. But it's not just the civil engineering that's impressive, it's also the intricate artwork etched onto the large stone slab at the entrance, featuring mesmerising zigzags and spiral patterns. It's an intriguing combination of brute force and delicate artwork and the artists responsible seem to have known about similar creative designs in the tombs of the Boyne Valley in Ireland – more evidence of the maritime links between the western seaboard of Britain and Ireland.

From where we'd left the bikes, it was less than a 2-mile walk south along the coastal path to St Cwyfan's Church (Eglwys Cwyfan). Built in the Romanesque style, the small, 12th-century church, dedicated to St Cwyfan, a 6th-century Welsh saint, is on the small rocky island of Cwyfan, connected to the mainland by a causeway, and only accessible during low tide. The island is a quiet and secluded spot, surrounded by the Irish Sea, and a large population of seabirds. When you first see it, it's almost painfully beautiful. The tiny little whitewashed building, with a small bell tower at the western end, is surrounded by the sea and wide-open space. It provided the solitude sought by the 12th-century monks from nearby Aberconwy Abbey, who are believed to be the original builders.

St Cwyfan's Church

We returned to the motorcycles and continued to ride along the coast road, over the Aberffraw Estuary, and down to Newborough Beach. The sun beat down, the temperature rose, and when we got to the beach car park, we could see why the rest of Anglesey seemed so quiet – everyone was in Holyhead or at Newborough Beach. The car park was absolutely bursting at the seams. Not a problem with a couple of motorcycles, but we were quite taken aback at just how busy it was. At the top end of the beach, separating it from the car park, is a long mound of marram grass covered sand dunes. Approaching a gap in the dunes to get to the beach, the view beyond looked breathtaking. It must have been the constant news from Eastern Europe that made me see the view through the gap as a Ukrainian flag, but as well as jukebox issues, my brain has a geographical bias. The bottom half of that view was all yellow sand, and the top half was the azure blue of the sea and sky.

We didn't stay long. We had planned to see the Llanddwyn Island Lighthouse (Tŵr Mawr Llanddwyn), which we did at a distance, but to see it at its best, I think we'd have to go back on a quiet early morning or late evening, when there was no one around. Pictures of the iconic lighthouse and island have graced many a calendar and tourist brochure, and again the view is achingly beautiful. It was another place to file away and mark up for another visit, with more time. There's so much to see on Anglesey that allocating only one day was a bit of an insult… but it's difficult to stay anywhere too long when you're trying to see a whole country in one long journey.

Despite the hectic schedule already, we still had more to see on Anglesey before heading back to the mainland. First, to bring some added flavour to the trip, we were going to visit a sea salt factory (known as a saltcote) and after that, we were going to check out one of the finest prehistoric passage tombs in Wales. How's that for a varied agenda?

As part of my research for the trip, I'd read about an Anglesey based company that's made a name for itself by producing top quality sea salt. The story sounded fascinating, so I added the company's visitor centre to the list of places to visit. The name of the company is Halen Môn, which translates from Welsh to English as 'Anglesey Salt.' Their production facility and visitor centre are on the banks of the Menai Strait near the village of Brynsiencyn. It was about 5 miles from the Newborough Beach car park.

Sarah and I pulled into a garage on the way to Halen Môn to top up with petrol. Experience has taught me not to leave things until the last drips. It's not worth the anguish. I left Sarah with the motorcycles, and I entered the shop to pay, where the guy behind the till was chatting away in Welsh to the customer in front of me. They started speaking English as I came in, which was thoughtful, and the complete opposite of some stories I'd heard. When I came to pay, the guy told me I was a dead ringer for his brother-in-law. 'I hadn't heard that George Clooney had a relative working in a Welsh garage,' I said, pushing both incredulity, and my luck to the max. He humoured me with a chuckle and seemed keen to chat, as most Welsh people seem to be. I took advantage of the moment by asking what being Welsh meant to him. His reply was almost in the form of a song, such was the melody in his voice. After a brief pause for thought, he told me Welshness went through him like the writing on a stick of seaside rock and was embedded in every fibre of his DNA. Well, that was more colourful than some responses I'd had. He asked me where I was from, where I was heading for, and where I'd been on Anglesey. I told him about my book, and he immediately reeled off a top ten list of places I *had* to visit on the island. He seemed a great guy, and he was obviously very proud of where he lived.

Another customer came in and began speaking Welsh. The guy behind the counter introduced us and explained to the new customer how I was touring Wales and writing a book. Oh, and wasn't I a dead ringer for his brother-in-law? The new chap switched immediately to English, but with a *very* strong Welsh accent. He too was keen to chat, and while Sarah waited patiently outside in the shade, the guy gave me a 5-minute introductory course on the Welsh language, with several profanities included. They were the sort to make you blush, but he clearly felt it was important to get a smattering of words to describe sexual anatomy into my vocabulary ahead of more classic foreign language phrases like, 'How much for 2 kilos of apples?' or 'Where is the railway station?' I steered the conversation towards what I thought was the safer ground of my *Journey through Wales* and told him I was heading for the Halen Môn visitor centre.

'Oh, you must go to the see-saw,' he said. '

Right… er, is that something in the village?' I replied, as my mind conjured up an impressive item of playground equipment, in the form of a finely balanced red dragon.

'The see-saw,' he said again, waiting for me to respond. Seeing the blank expression on my face, he then repeated it for a third time, slightly louder, and more slowly. I sensed a verbal impasse, but the garage owner thankfully intervened to explain that the Halen Môn visitor centre was right next to an aquarium called the Sea Zoo. Ah yes, of course, I could see what happened there. Sea Zoo, not see-saw. The three of us then parted with smiles and back slaps, like the best of friends. I went back outside to Sarah and told her I'd just been given directions to the visitor centre and a see-saw. 'Don't ask,' I said, 'I'll explain later. Just follow me!'

I'm normally quite proud of my trip planning (Plas Newydd in Llangollen and Bangor aside) and like to think that I've left no stone unturned, but my military-like efficiency had a minor hiccup with the Halen Môn visitor centre. Although I'd corresponded with the owners weeks previously and received an invitation to visit, I hadn't followed up to agree the timing, and as we were only about 5 minutes away, I might have left it a bit late. Naively, I was just hoping we could turn up and everything would be alright. Sarah and I rode on, following the directions I'd been given, through gently undulating farmland, along more delightful country lanes. Before long, we came to a tiny seaside road that ran along the shoreline of the Menai Strait. We followed the signs and turned right, away from the sea, into a driveway that led to the Halen Môn visitor centre. Immediately to the left of that was another entrance which led to the Sea Zoo.

Leaving our motorcycles in the visitor centre car park, we went into the shop, hoping for a sympathetic reception. There was a handful of visitors queuing up at the till with arms full of candles, books, towels, condiments and… salt. The guy behind the counter saw us arrive and asked if he could help. I asked if there was any possibility of having a tour.

'I'm really sorry but we're not doing any more tours today,' he replied, 'and we'll have to close the shop in another 5 minutes or so – sorry.'

There was no need for me to fake a special deflated expression. I was genuinely despondent and also cross with myself for not thinking ahead. In response, I offered back an apologetic,

'Ah, OK, no problem. I should have called in advance. I'm the chap writing the book, but I forgot to organise a time and day to come.'

'Oh, you're Mark?' said the guy behind the till. 'I saw the emails a few weeks ago… I tell you what, I just need to close the shop after these visitors are finished, then I can give you about 10 minutes to tell you about the place. Would that be OK?'

When he'd seen the last customers out of the building and put the closed sign up, Rob Jardine introduced himself as the manager of the shop and apologised that he didn't have more time to give us the full tour. He showed Sarah and me to a room next to the shop where he sat us down at a table and put six small samples of salt (table, rock, European sea, pure, flavoured, and smoked) on paper mats in front of us. He then left us for 10 minutes on our own, watching a video about the company.

David Lea-Wilson and his wife, Alison, founded Halen Môn in 1997, but the story goes back to their student days at Bangor University. They earned money to supplement their student grants by growing oysters… not an obvious choice for most students, but it was inspired by their marine biology studies. Their knowledge and experience grew over the following 12 years as they added more fish and game to their business. Seeing how interested people were in fish, the couple expanded their business in 1983 by creating an aquarium by the seashore on Anglesey. They called it the Sea Zoo, and it's now the largest aquarium in Wales, with over 150 species. It's also an independent research and marine education centre. For me, all it lacks is a red dragon shaped see-saw.

Like most seasonal holiday businesses, the income from the aquarium was heavily skewed towards the summer months, so the couple sat down to brainstorm the options for something that could keep them and their handful of staff employed over the winter months. After leaving a saucepan of seawater to boil on the kitchen Aga for slightly longer than they intended to, David, and Alison saw the most wonderful salt crystals beginning to form. A light bulb came on somewhere. The couple thought about how they could turn that process into a commercial product. Because of the Sea Zoo, they already had a licence from the Crown Estate to draw 20,000 litres of seawater from the Menai Strait every day. David and Alison had their solution… and it was clean and salty. They knew the extracted water was exceptionally clean because the aquarium seahorses were happy with it and, as we all know, seahorses are notoriously picky about their seawater quality. Maybe the beautiful briny seas of the Menai Strait had the potential to produce the world's finest sea salt?

The company is now housed in a unique £1.25m bespoke building called Tŷ Halen. Staff numbers have risen to twenty-eight, supplemented at busy times by a Jack Russell called Bella and a chocolate labradoodle called Jolene. The company supplies Halen Môn salt to over a hundred of the best delicatessens and restaurants in the UK, as well as stores like Marks & Spencer, Waitrose, and Harvey Nichols. Just for good measure, ex-US president, Barack Obama, is one of their loyal customers.

Rob came back just as the video was ending. Sarah and I tested the samples of salt he'd brought in earlier and I surprised myself by tasting subtle differences between at least some of them. Rob even brought some Halen Môn gin into the session, although we had to politely decline the offer, as we had to keep our motorcycles upright when we left.

Rob was brimming with enthusiasm, and it was infectious. We'd already used up our 10 minutes, but Rob was more than happy to continue. Despite our protestations about him working overtime, he took us through to the production area of the building and meticulously took us through the process step by step: seawater being brought into huge holding tanks, the large trays being filled with brine under powerful lamps, the crystallised salt being removed, and the careful packaging. It was all done with hospital operating room cleanliness. In between descriptions of the process, Sarah and I slipped in a few questions, and Rob had an unending supply of amusing anecdotes, like the time he went to give a presentation at the Houses of Parliament and had to be security-checked to find out what those strange bags of white stuff were. From the stories you hear about MPs' parties, I'm surprised they even asked.

We ended up in the shop, of course, and Sarah and I loaded up with a few salty gifts to take home. We were hugely indebted to Rob for all the time he'd given us, and for being such a friendly host, especially as we had dropped in out of the blue. I always take great pleasure in seeing top experts in any field, whether it's sport, art, or business, who are also passionate about what they're doing… and Rob was such a person.

We had two more places to visit on Anglesey, one being an ancient burial site and the other a small village with the longest place name in Europe. The first, Bryn Celli Ddu, meaning 'the mound in the dark grove,' is near the village of Llanddaniel Fab, which sounds like somewhere renamed by the funk committee during the summer of love. It was a 4-mile ride from the Halen Môn saltcote. There's a danger of getting ancient site blindness after a while on Anglesey because they come so thick and fast, and you must remind yourself how special each one is in its own right. They were constructed with no sophisticated tools, just hard labour, so the motivation of their creators must have been immense. Bryn Celli Ddu is unusual because it is aligned with the rising sun on the longest day of the year. On the midsummer solstice, light from the rising sun (cue The Animals) illuminates the burial chamber, and people gather to witness the alignment of the passageway with the rising sun, in the same way they do at Stonehenge. The ancient site has many legends associated with it. There are stories of a fairy queen who lived in the mound, bringing fertility and prosperity to the surrounding area. Well, we all need one of those, and I had a quiet word in case she could come and work her magic on my recently acquired allotment.

Our final stop on the island was somewhere with the longest place name in Europe. Take a deep breath to say Llanfairpwllgwyngyllgogerychwyrndrobwllllantysiliogogogoch. I'll only write that once to save a few forests and to save the book from becoming several volumes long. Those fifty-eight letters are not so much a place name but more of a short story. And the story is this: St Mary's Church in the hollow of the white hazel near to the rapid whirlpool of Llantysilio of the red cave. The name was first used in the 1860s, when the local railway station was built. The station was originally called Llanfair Pwllgwyngyll, but the name was extended to its current length to see if they could attract a few more visitors. Tourists came from all over the world to see the village and its ridiculously long name. Sarah and I had to have our photos taken by such a ridiculously long name and it was a toss-up between the sign on the Co-op or the one at the station. We ended up going for the traditional version at the station. Assuming standard UK brick dimensions in millimetres of 215 x 102.5 x 65 with 10-millimetre mortar joint, the length of the sign must have been approximately 7.5 metres long. We took our photos and headed back to the mainland.

Caernarfon is another of those North Wales coastal towns which begins life with the unfair advantage of an incredibly beautiful location. The town is situated on the banks the Menai Strait about 3 miles from the open sea, to the south-west. The Halen Môn saltcote and the Sea Zoo are almost opposite on Anglesey. Bordering the town to the south and east is the Afon Seiont, a small river that rises in the mountains of Snowdonia. The town is dominated by its magnificent castle, the third (after Conwy and Beaumaris) of the UNESCO World Heritage Site 'Castles and Town Walls of King Edward in Gwynedd' that I'd seen on this trip. There was just Harlech to go, and we had that on our schedule for another day. We walked around the town and did a tour of the castle from the outside. HV Morton regarded the castle as the grandest in all of Britain. (Morton, 1932). He wasn't so taken with the drinking establishments of the town. What's remarkable about Caernarfon Castle, and the town walls, is how much of the original structures remain. While parts of the main shopping area of the town looked a little tired, like most towns, there were some lovely narrow streets and elegant houses in the part which was surrounded by the town walls. With a series of concentric walls and towers, a massive gatehouse and drawbridge, the castle is one of the most impressive examples of medieval military architecture in Britain. Just by the town's large open space (Y Maes), and in the shadow of the castle, we spotted a sign that drew us to the self-proclaimed smallest bar in Wales, the Bar Bach, or Tafarn Lleiaf Cymru. I suspect, like Arthur's Round Table, that there are quite a few contenders, but the sign did its job and we arrived at the bar... to find it closed due to staff shortages. Oh, well, next time. We noticed that there were a lot of pubs in the town and it turns out that the town is famous for its hostelries. In the late 19th and early 20th centuries, Caernarfon was a bustling port town, and the numerous pubs and inns that lined the streets were an important part of the social and cultural life of the community. At one point, it is said that there were over 400 licensed premises in the town, catering to sailors, dock workers, and other visitors. One that still survives today is the Black Boy, but the reason behind the name doesn't involve a chimney sweep, as with the Monmouth version. Although various theories exist, (I often seek out multiple explanations and try to keep an open mind), one of the most plausible goes back to the 17th century, at the time of the English Civil War. King Charles I of England was married to Henrietta Maria, who was the French daughter of King Henry IV of France and Marie de' Medici. Sorry to throw another Henry into the mix… and having a 'Henrietta' doesn't exactly help! She had a son named Charles who she called 'My beautiful black boy,' because of his dark complexion. People who supported the king would secretly meet up, but anxious that Oliver Cromwell's spies would overhear them talking about the king's son, who later became King Charles II, they would discreetly drink a toast to the 'Black Boy.' Our current King Charles popped in for a drink during his investiture as Prince of Wales in 1969. Many people of my generation will remember the event, which was a big thing at the time.

Sarah and I headed out of town, but we had one more stop to make before continuing our journey to the Llŷn Peninsula and our one-night stopover in a shepherd's hut. When the Romans bullied their way into Wales, they established a series of outposts in strategic positions to maintain control over the region. The fort of Segontium was built in the late 70s AD and the Romans occupied the site until the early 4th century. The fort was strategically located on a steep hill that rises out of Caernarfon, providing the garrison with great views of the Menai Strait, and all those weird druid guys on Anglesey. When the Romans went home to pasta like only mama could make, the fort was abandoned and fell into ruin, but some remains can still be seen, including the foundations of the various buildings. The ruins are easy to see as you ride out of Caernarfon, but to begin with, we couldn't see a way in; a sturdy-looking iron railing fence separated us from the site at the roadside. Perhaps it wasn't open to the public and had been fenced off? I could see Sarah wasn't over-excited about pursuing it any further, so she stayed with the motorcycles while I took matters into my own hands. An inelegant clamber over the railings and I was into the site. To be honest, there wasn't much to see. Visitors should not go there expecting a Disneyland experience with a 'Colosseum Drop' rollercoaster or a 'Pompeii Eruption' water ride. Expect instead the outlines of several rectangular buildings, and the remains of a few low walls. It was only when I was on my way out that I stumbled across the open gate that was the main way into the site, next to a small museum. Sarah was beginning to show signs of archaeological site fatigue, so it was time to end our day and ride the last 15 miles to Llithfaen.

On arrival, we were amazed by the stunning setting. Our luxury shepherd's hut was located in a private field, complete with its own garden area, offering breathtaking views of Cardigan Bay to the south and the hills further along the peninsula to the southwest. Caroline, our host, had the most delightful Welsh accent, which made everything she said sound like a poem or a gentle song. I could have listened to her talk all day. Caroline had many tips for us, including a must-visit place called Nant Gwrtheyrn, the Welsh Language Centre. Despite not being on our radar, Caroline insisted it was worth a visit and it was just a short distance away, 'over the crossroads and down the hill.' The next morning, it was the first place to see on my amended spreadsheet of visits.

8

LLITHFAEN TO TREGARON

From our shepherd's hut at Llithfaen, it was about 2 miles to the former quarrying village of Nant Gwrtheyrn. You approach it via a narrow road that zigzags down a steep coastal valley (Nant is Welsh for steep-sided valley) and as we started to descend, it seemed we were entering a secret world. The valley is surrounded by rugged hills and cliffs, part covered in coniferous trees, and the blue sea sparkled in the distance. As Sarah and I reached the bottom of the hill and approached the seashore, we found a couple of terraced rows of immaculately presented stone cottages and a cluster of equally neat, whitewashed buildings. The sea was like a mirror and when we parked and switched off our engines, the only sound was the rhythmic wash and backwash of the waves gently caressing the pebbles on the beach. Scanning the hills around, the outlines of the old quarry workings became apparent, whispering tantalising secrets about the village's past and the secluded valley.

Nant Gwrtheyrn was originally established as a quarrying village in the 19th century and was home to a community of quarry workers and their families. The hills surrounding the valley would have echoed to the sound of rock blasting, heavy machinery, and the miners' hammers and chisels.

There might even have been the odd expletive in Welsh if a hammer hit a miner's thumb. The village was largely abandoned in the mid-20th century when the quarry closed, and it stayed that way for several decades. However, in the 1970s, a group of Welsh language enthusiasts and activists set out to restore Nant Gwrtheyrn and create a centre for the promotion and preservation of the Welsh language and culture. Today, Nant Gwrtheyrn is a thriving cultural centre that offers Welsh language courses, arts and crafts workshops, and a range of other cultural events and activities. It has a café, a heritage centre, and a shop. With its own private beach, chapel, and accommodation, it has even branched out into weddings. A Billy Idol tribute band burst out of my brain jukebox, unannounced: 'It's a nice day for a… Welsh wedding.' My memories of Nant Gwrtheyrn are of the near silence, stillness, and those glorious views. I can imagine it's a great place to shut out the world and study – or even write a book. After a look around the heritage centre, we made our way back to the motorcycles. It was a nice day to start again, and we slowly climbed the steep hill back up to Llithfaen and hung a right to head south, working our way slowly down the Llŷn Peninsula.

We rode down little twisty country roads, going through tiny villages and settlements, many of them with white-painted cottages. The houses and buildings were mainly constructed from local stone, and the gardens and surrounding fields were full of colourful wildflowers. We rode along a spectacular coastline of rocky outcrops, sandy beaches, and secluded coves. The sun glinted off the deep blue-green waters of Caernarfon Bay, with the distant mountains of Snowdonia visible on the horizon, and we felt a gentle breeze blowing landward.

As we approached Aberdaron, the landscape became more rugged and hilly, with steep cliffs and rocky headlands rising from the sea. The village itself is nestled in a sheltered bay, surrounded by hills, and in its centre is a sprinkling of white-painted buildings. After a stroll around the village and a walk along the pebble beach, Sarah and I stopped at a café that was housed in a tiny black and white building in the heart of the village. Once again, we were able to watch the world go by, and it did so mainly over a little humpbacked bridge over the Afon Daron. Inside the café, an old sign hung on the thick, white-painted walls told us we were in Y Gegin Fawr (the big kitchen). The building went back to the 14th century and pilgrims stopped there to claim a meal before taking the 2.5-mile ferry ride over to the monastery on Bardsey Island (Ynys Enlli).

The island has been referred to as a 'Cradle of Celtic Christianity' and the 'Island of 20,000 saints,' because of the Celtic and Christian monasteries established there since the 6th century. That many buried saints would need about 12 acres of land, but that makes a lot of assumptions about the standard dimensions of a saint and ancient burial practices. The island has been a place of pilgrimage since medieval times, when three pilgrimages to Bardsey Island were thought to be equal to one pilgrimage to Rome, although HV Morton seemed to think they should have equal value. The island's latest claim to fame is its night sky. It has become the first site in Europe (there are sixteen other sites worldwide) to be awarded official International Dark Sky Sanctuary certification (that's something I'll come back to when we get to Pembrokeshire). With my geographer's hat on, it's all about location. The island is already remote, but the Mynydd Enlli mountain, on the mainland side of the island, forms a natural blackout blind. I have read reports claiming that the closest major light pollution might come from Dublin, which is over 75 miles to the west, across the Irish Sea.

Our ride back up the south side of the Llŷn Peninsula took us through Abersoch, Pwllheli, and Criccieth. Many of the narrow lanes were lined with steep-sided dry-stone walls topped with green gorse and ferns, sometimes supporting a line of drunken telegraph poles. We saw several 'For Sale' boards outside houses, with the name 'Tudor Estate Agents,' which set my imagination going for the next few miles... could the current Tudors trace their family back to all those Henrys and Owens? Could they one day raise the family flag, rally the faithful, and march on Westminster to claim back the throne for Wales and the House of Tudor? (which would be a four bedroom, immaculately presented one, with fine views in a popular rural village location, near to schools and other local amenities). As if to shock me back to reality, a pair of RAF typhoon fighter jets roared past us, directly overhead. Wherever they were going, they were in a hurry.

Sarah and I stopped for some lunch in Harlech and looked around the town. It was busy with tourists, not that we could complain because we were tourists as well. The visit gave me my full set of four UNESCO Castles and Town Walls of King Edward in Gwynedd. Conwy was the first I'd visited on this trip and I remember saying to myself, 'That's awesome; it's got to be the best one.' I had the same reaction at Caernarfon, Beaumaris, and now Harlech. Compared to the first three, Harlech Castle has a more compact design, with a narrow and elongated shape that reflects the shape of the rocky outcrop on which it is built. The castle's walls, towers, and gatehouses are still largely intact, and the remains of the Great Hall, the royal apartments, and the chapel can all be explored. But it's all about the location (again). None of King Edward I's other three coastal fortresses has a setting quite as dramatic as Harlech. It sits atop a sheer rocky crag overlooking the dunes and the sea far below. The views stretch for miles and the rugged peaks of Snowdonia form the most perfect backdrop. OK, I'm going to go with Harlech as my favourite.

The famous song, 'Men of Harlech,' was written about a long siege that happened during the War of the Roses. Dafydd ap Ieuen ap Einion defended Harlech Castle for an incredible 8 years on behalf of the Lancastrians, making it the longest siege in the history of the British Isles. Eventually, Dafydd and his troops surrendered because they were starving. Harlech Castle was the last castle to surrender to the Yorkists. The Lancastrian survivors must have been good negotiators because they were allowed to leave with their lives.

The National Library of Wales is a large research library located in Aberystwyth. It is a legal deposit library, which means it has the right to receive a copy of every book published in the UK and Ireland. It is home to the only remaining complete copy of the first book to be printed in Welsh in 1546. It has no title and is known only by its opening words: 'In this book.' It's how every good book about Wales should start.

Sarah and I rode to Aberystwyth to visit the library and also to see the Nanteos Cup that I'd read about at Strata Florida. We were also meeting up with Sarah's friend, Dan, who was riding up from Winchester on his Husqvarna Enduro 700 motorcycle, to join our adventure for a couple of days. Dan is a tall guy with smouldering Italian good looks, long dark hair, and tattoos. I sometimes feel I'm looking in the mirror when I see him. He's a barber to celebrities, wellness counsellor, and an all-round nice guy. The two of them were going to ride down to Pembrokeshire at the end of the weekend, leaving me to continue with my *Journey through Wales*.

Our visit to the National Library of Wales was our only brush with Aberystwyth, and as the library is on one of the main roads leading out of town, this meant that we didn't really see the place at all. That's another spot that will have to wait for proper visit. Sarah and I pulled into the car park of the library and looked up, as it towered over us. Its white Portland limestone cladding dazzled against a cloudless blue sky; it was time to get the shades on. The building sits on a hillside, near to the university, and looks down on Aberystwyth and the sea. The impressive building and its setting are quite a statement.

We were soon joined by Dan, and the three of us went inside the library to look around. I have nothing but praise for the place. It's free to enter, is kept immaculately clean and tidy, and the staff couldn't be more helpful. I felt like taking my boots off and walking around in my socks because the bright red carpets looked like they'd been laid the previous evening; they were spotless. It was a nice touch, and it made us feel very special, but how did they know we were coming? A few interesting facts: the library's collections include a copy of the first book ever printed in Welsh, which was back in 1546; they also have the personal papers and manuscripts of many prominent Welsh figures, such as Dylan Thomas and the politician Aneurin Bevan; the library is home to a resident colony of bats, which live in the building's attic and help to control insect populations; and, perhaps most importantly, the library has its own on-site café, which serves, amongst other things, traditional Welsh cakes.

When Sarah and Dan finally managed to drag me kicking and screaming out of the map room, we found our way to the Nanteos Cup. According to tradition, the cup, a fragile bowl of wood, was taken from the Strata Florida Abbey for safe-keeping by Cistercian monks at the time of the dissolution of the monasteries. The cup is said to be the Holy Grail, from which Christ and his disciples drank at the last supper. As I was reading this, I was thinking back to my visit to Chepstow; this is Dan Brown territory. The cup is said to have supernatural healing powers. That's still to be proven, but I waved my dodgy left knee as close as I could to it, just in case. I'll take any help I can get.

The three of us stopped off in the café and went over our plans for the next couple of days. From Aberystwyth, we were heading down to Llanrhystud for an appointment with a watermill. We were going to stay in the coastal village of Borth overnight, and then ride back up to Machynlleth the following day. With barely disguised glee, Sarah and Dan both confirmed that it sounded like a great plan.

Today, we can get food from all over the world delivered to our doors, a luxury unheard of 200 years ago when most relied on the local land. Every village had a mill, sometimes several, powered by wind, rivers, or tides. These were vital to rural life. Typically owned by manorial lords or monasteries, locals had to use them, giving up a portion of their grain. Rural Wales had hundreds of mills, including 400 in Ceredigion. Over time, many have disappeared or have been turned into homes, with only two still operating commercially in Ceredigion and North Pembrokeshire. We were on our way to visit one. We were in Llanrhystud, a short ride south from Aberystwyth, to meet Andrew and Anne Parry, who had kindly agreed to show us around their Felin Ganol watermill, the last mill standing of three watermills that once had their wheels spun by the Afon Wyre as it sped through Llanrhystud on its way to Cardigan Bay.

With immaculate timing, I'd scheduled our visit for the driest July in Wales since 1911. The Felin Ganol millpond was as calm as… well, a millpond. It was even more un-ruffled than usual because it was also as dry as a bone. The river level had dropped, the millpond had dried out, and the mill wheel had shuddered to a halt weeks ago. Like a pub with no beer, it was the watermill with no water. With great charm and enthusiasm, however, Anne and Andrew were still happy to show us around and to tell us their story.

The couple bought the mill in 2006, although at the time, they hadn't gone looking for one. With a bit of land, an attached cottage for Anne's mum, and a pleasant garden, the property ticked all the boxes, especially the garden, which is now delightful. Felin Ganol was just the place for a quiet retirement. Oh, and by the way, it was also once an old watermill. Almost by accident, the Parry's found themselves in a time capsule; they had become the owners of an astonishing piece of rural Welsh history.

When they looked into its background, they discovered the mill was associated with the Moelifor Estate, which dates back to the 12th century, and when Andrew and Anne moved in, it was as if the miller had moved out the previous day. Almost everything required for a working watermill was there, including several pairs of millers' nailed boots sat on a shelf, a little dusty but ready for use. This old-fashioned footwear is a source of much amusement to the school parties that Anne occasionally shows round.

Old boots and tools, ready for another day's work in the mill

It wasn't quite a question of flicking a switch on and milling flour, though. The old millpond was completely over-grown, and the waterwheel had sunk on its bearings and not turned for nearly 50 years. Andrew took early retirement shortly after moving in and found himself with a project. He may have given up his regular job, but his daily grind was just about to take on a whole new meaning. He dug out the millpond and several hundred metres of the leat back to the river (the leat is the mill's artificial watercourse), and by 2008 he had the water flowing again. The millpond filled. With help from an expert from St Fagan's Museum, they carefully repositioned the overshoot mill wheel on new bearings. Anne and Andrew went for a few crash courses on milling, joined The Traditional Cornmillers' Guild, and visited as many working mills as they could find. It was a task that separated the wheat from the chaff, and by February 2009, the mill's two 1850 French Burr millstones were turning again. Anne and Andrew had produced their first wholemeal flour!

The couple had come a long way in 3 years, after buying a nice house with a pleasant garden. They had become milling enthusiasts. Anne told us, 'We feel like custodians of the mill with a responsibility to look after the traditions and keep them alive.' They're certainly doing that. Having locally sourced two more French millstones, they now produce around 25 tons of flour per year, mainly to order. They supply a range of traditional flour types to local bakers, in Aberystwyth and Llanidloes, for example. With some grain coming from fields within sight of the mill, the food chain couldn't be much shorter.

After she'd given us the background story, Anne took us around the mill, the millpond, the leat, and the river to show us how everything worked (normally). It's difficult to overlook not having water with a watermill, although who would have thought that would be a problem in West Wales?

The couple's enthusiasm was obvious, and they were very generous with their time. We felt privileged to have a guided tour of such a special place. The watermill has come quite a way since they first moved into their pleasant house by the river for a quiet retirement! Before we left, we had to buy some flour to take with us. 'Sorry, we haven't got any,' Anne said, 'We're waiting for water!'

Sarah, Dan, and I backtracked on our route a few miles to stay overnight in a comfortable caravan at the seaside village of Borth. We couldn't stray further south because we had an exciting appointment the following day near Machynlleth.

In Wales, it doesn't rain stair rods or cats and dogs, it rains old ladies and walking sticks (bwrw hen wragedd a ffyn). After twenty-six rainless days on my *Journey through Wales*, the unstable female seniors turned up overnight. I awoke at about 2:00 am, to go for a wee walk. It was a pitch-black night. I couldn't see a thing, but I could hear the old ladies gently drumming their sticks on the caravan roof. It was a gentle, rhythmic sound, like a relaxing meditation app. My thoughts flashed back to the mill with no water. The sound of rain must have been music to the ears of Anne and Andy back in Llanrhystud. They could soon call Felin Ganol a watermill once again. I imagined the River Wyre filling its banks once more and surging to the sea, the sluice gate opening, and the Felin Ganol waterwheel creaking into action once again.

By 7:00 am I was creaking into action again myself. Those old ladies certainly had some stamina because they were still drumming their sticks on the caravan roof as a heavy drizzle set in. It might have been welcome for mill owners but didn't hold the same attraction for anyone about to get on a motorcycle. The forecast was promising, however; it was due to dry up by mid-morning.

It didn't. After a coffee at the beach café in Borth, Sarah, Dan and I rode a soggy 12 miles to the compact market town of Machynlleth, in the Dovey Estuary (Aber Dyfi). The town wasn't looking at its most attractive in the greyness of the damp morning, but I dare say the good people of Machynlleth were thinking the same about me. At least the town would return to looking good again on a sunny day.

Machynlleth, the ancient capital of Wales, is a town of great historical importance. It was here in 1404, in the presence of leaders from Scotland, Spain, and France, that Owain Glyndŵr was crowned Prince of Wales. He set up the first Welsh Parliament, in defiance of the English King Henry IV. The restored Parliament house, considered one of Wales's most important historic buildings, is now a National Heritage

Centre dedicated to the last native-born Welshman to hold the title, Prince of Wales.

The town sits at the mouth of the stunning Dovey Estuary in the heart of the UNESCO Dyfi Biosphere Reserve, an AONB and diversity, described by UNESCO as having some of the finest and most inspiring species in Europe. There are seven of these reserves in the UK. They aim to 'develop and promote solutions that reconcile the conservation of biodiversity with sustainable use of the areas' natural resources' (UNESCO, 2021).

I must admit, to my shame, that the landscapes of Mid Wales came as a revelation to me on my *Journey through Wales*. Like Southampton appearing in the Champions League Final or the sudden appearance of a group of cardinals from the Spanish Inquisition – I hadn't been expecting that! Somehow, dazzled by the rugged beauty of Snowdonia in the north and the splendour of the Bannau Brycheiniog, The Wye Valley, and Pembrokeshire in the south, this delightful middle part of Wales had gone under my radar for far too long.

Apart from the upland beauty of the Cambrian Mountains, the area boasts some superb coastal and estuarine landscapes. I remember visiting the nearby Centre for Alternative Technology back in the mid-1970s, when it was a ramshackle collection of wind turbines, hydro generators, and self-composting toilets. It has developed enormously since then as a research centre for ecological technology and sustainable development, and it plays an important role in lobbying for environmental policy both in the UK and internationally.

The rain eased as we rode out of Machynlleth. Instead, it just felt like we were riding through saturated air, a bit like riding through a cloud. We were heading for an appointment with Scott Roe. He and his wife, Ruth, own an 18th century stone cottage that squats on the mountainside, off the beaten track, just north of the town. As we climbed higher, the winding road we were following became gradually narrower and eventually became that beaten track. Fields dotted with sheep gave way to dense coniferous forest. How far the forest extended, over the hills and far away, was impossible to say. It was lost in the clouds.

Scott and Ruth's remote off-grid cottage, bought by Ruth's father in 1970, is called Bron Yr Aur. Scott is an ex-music producer and band manager, who is now an environmental science consultant and musician. Ruth is also a musician and a singer, and she teaches at a nearby school, not that anywhere is particularly nearby. We were very fortunate to have an appointment to meet them.

The Welsh name, Bron Yr Aur, translates into English as 'breast of the gold,' which can be interpreted as the hill of gold or golden hill. It's certainly a place of music gold, if not multiple platinum; some music critics have described Bron Yr Aur as the most significant location in the history and development of rock music. That's quite a claim... let's consider it further...

Back in the 1950s, the cottage was a holiday home used regularly by the family of a young lad called Robert Plant – the same Robert Plant who became the lead singer of the group Led Zeppelin. Between 1969 and 1979, Led Zeppelin sold over 200 million records, making them the most popular rock group in the world. They remain one of the most successful rock bands of their generation... and it was my generation. A powerful trio of exceptional musicians, guitarist Jimmy Page, bass player John Paul Baldwin/Jones, and drummer John Bonham, fronted by an equally powerful lead singer, Robert Plant, created a whole new sub-genre of rock music. And a whole lotta love. The style was blues based but included elements of mystical folk-rock, funky pop, a pinch of exotic Middle Eastern vibe, and levels of rock heaviness rarely heard before. Robert Plant's vocals ranged from face-melting demonic to touchingly sensitive.

When it comes to off-the-scale outrageous rock lifestyles, Led Zeppelin wrote the book. At the end of their fifth American tour, towards the end of 1969, the band members were close to burnout and needed to recuperate after several years of life on the road that had pushed their bodies way beyond their design limits. You can only go so long without proper sleep, on a diet of little more than drugs, sex and rock and roll… or at least, that's been my experience.

Robert Plant remembered his old Welsh holiday cottage and in 1970 he and lead guitarist Jimmy Page retreated to Bron Yr Aur to rest, chill, and re-set their lives. When they felt ready, they wrote and recorded music for the band's third album, Led Zeppelin III. The simplicity of life in the cottage, the quietness of the hills, and the beauty of their surroundings gave them the chance to slow down and put things back into perspective. A new day had dawned – and it inspired musical greatness. It marked a change of direction for the band that put more emphasis on the acoustic and folk elements of their existing heavy rock formula. It must have been something in the Welsh mountain air – or the whispering wind. The boys kept an old cassette recorder to capture promising riffs and lyrics and, according to Jimmy Page, it was from bits and pieces of taped music on that recorder that the idea for Stairway to Heaven was born. Imagine that – perhaps the greatest rock song of all time, beginning life on that Welsh mountainside. Maybe the forests above the cottage echoed with laughter.

The weather dashed the plans that Sarah, Dan, and I had to help Scott with some jobs around his garden and vegetable plot. Instead, we spent a few hours sitting under a tarpaulin in the rain discussing music, careers, philosophy, and generally putting the world to rights. As the grey clouds draped themselves over the surrounding hills and a light drizzle settled in, we heard about Scott's background in the music industry and his passion for environmental projects, and about Ruth's experiences as a teacher and as a singer.

Over the last year or so, Scott has used his contacts in the music industry to put together an album, which may have been released by the time you read this. As he describes it, the album combines rock royalty, indie stars, folk heroes, strangers, old band mates, and international rock legends. They come together in one super-group to deliver the album of a lifetime. The names tripped off his tongue like the contents page from a book of musical excellence – big stars, leading session musicians, and lesser known but talented artists. Scott described it all in a matter-of-fact and modest way. The album is music produced for all the right creative reasons, not to satisfy a music label's marketing plan. Scott told us how he would phone up some musical legend and just say, 'It's in the key of D, just put eight bars out man.' I'm not sure what that means, but it sounds pretty cool.

While Ruth served up a fabulous salad, Scott described his passion for the World Land Project (WLP), an international conservation charity that protects the world's most biologically significant and threatened habitats. Scott's new album is raising money for the WLP. His crazy stories of music making over the years at Bron Yr Aur, delivered with dry Midlands humour, had us either open-mouthed in disbelief or falling about with laughter. There was the one about the guy lost in the forest with a piano, the one about the woman who couldn't talk (also lost in the forest), and the one about Jimmy Page's priceless plectrum that Scott recently found – and then lost again. I mustn't forget the one about the pianist with a bottle of wine in each hand, the one about the fan who rambled on, walking all the way from Germany, and the one about the shaman owl song. It all sounded very rock and roll… and those were the stories he *could* tell us.

After a while, Scott declared that 'Coming here, you have to make music, you've got no choice,' and so off we went, inside the cottage to create something which had notes in it. When I told the story to my neighbour, Karen, back home she said, 'Well, there is nothing quite like the sound of good live music.' I had to break it to her that what we produced in that half hour of musical mayhem was *nothing* like the sound of good live music. With a mixture of drums, bass guitar, rhythm guitar, and percussion, our hastily formed super-group created a unique blend that fused soulful blues and heavy rock with psychedelic medleys, driving rhythms, and a lot of tambourine bashing. Sarah was smashing it out on various items of percussion, and I think Scott and his daughter's friend were both playing something musical on their guitars. With his experience in a heavy rock band, at least Dan didn't look out of place on the drums. Our creation leaned heavily on the Morecambe and Wise musical playbook – we were playing all the right notes but not necessarily in the right order. In my case, I wasn't even playing the right notes, although I felt my ability to reach musical fulfilment might have been constrained by only having a rain stick and a pair of castanets. It was one of those surreal moments in life when you know you're experiencing something extraordinary, but it's so far from your normal that you think it might be a dream. Let's just say we created something unquestionably unique. It was enormous fun, and we felt incredibly privileged. As Scott put it, 'Even Bonham didn't play drums here!'

Sadly, our super-group rose rapidly to greatness, peaked, and fell apart again all too soon. Our band had split before we'd even named it… something about royalty percentages and irreconcilable musical differences. I think Scott's daughter's teenage friend wanted to pursue a solo career, and who can blame her? The world will never hear the likes of that session again, and perhaps we should all be grateful for that. The remains of the band retired to the calmness of the lounge for coffee and Ruth's delicious cake. By late afternoon, the cloud base had moved to the contour immediately above us, and the rain had stopped. We said our farewells, headed back down the mountain, and eventually found the main road again. Scott and Ruth had been incredibly hospitable and given us an unforgettable experience. And as we wound on down the road, one philosophical phrase among so many that Scott had said during the day kept coming back to me and has stuck with me ever since: 'Sometimes you gotta take a chance in art and life.'

Well, it makes you wonder. The three of us rode south for a while before splitting to go our separate ways. While I went to look for my B&B in the village of Llanon, south of Aberystwyth, Sarah, and Dan headed further south to Pembrokeshire. Dan had been great company for a couple of days and I felt sad to be losing my girl, but it had been fantastic to be with her for so many days; a memory to treasure.

As I continued south on the A487, still thinking about our incredible experience at Bron Yr Aur, I was brought back to Earth by the sight of an immaculately presented horse-drawn carriage emerging onto the main road next to the Llanon chip shop, just as I approached it. Good; things aren't quite back to normal just yet then, I pondered. I popped into the chip shop for a bag of Welsh fries and got directions to my accommodation for the night. Luckily, it was less than a mile away because by then, the old ladies had returned with their sticks, and they hung around overnight and into the next day – normal West Wales weather had returned.

I was in no hurry to leave my B&B on Sunday 31st July. The view from my bedroom window, which had extended a mile to the sea when I'd arrived the previous evening, now stretched to a maximum of 50 very misty metres. Light grey curtains of fine rain were being drawn sideway across sodden fields. My excitement for the day ahead could not be dampened, however. I would shortly be on my way to my first National Eisteddfod! While the weather outside did its best to be very Welsh, I took considerable consolation from a superb, cooked breakfast. I spent an hour writing up some notes from the previous day, in the forlorn hope that the rain would lift before I had to face it. I eventually gave in to the inevitable, after a second cafetière of coffee, and got my wet-weather gear on.

In my slow 10-mile ride from the B&B in Llanon to the Eisteddfod site at Tregaron, I went through at least four climate zones. I set off in a 'grey-out' downpour worthy of a West African rainforest, but within minutes it had eased to mere monsoon. Those aren't the most enjoyable riding conditions. As I headed inland, however, the rain eased rapidly and then stopped. Before long, there were a few breaks in the cloud, and then the odd burst of sunshine. Steam rose from the tarmac on the road ahead as it warmed, and I suddenly felt very overdressed. By the time I arrived in Tregaron, it was a summer's day.

Having never been to a National Eisteddfod before, I wasn't sure what to expect. I'd been to the International Eisteddfod at Llangollen twice and really enjoyed it, so while I was expecting more of the same, I had a feeling there could be something extra involved at Tregaron – and I was right. HV Morton clearly enjoyed the National Eisteddfod. He devotes over sixteen pages to describing the one he attended in Bangor in 1931. I'll spare you that many pages, but if you're interested in the details of the event, its history, and traditions, I recommend the author's enthusiastic account in his book *In Search of Wales.* I love the way he weaves his description of the Welsh, their Celtic roots, and the traditions of oratory, poetry, and singing into his account of the events he observes.

So, for the non-Welsh people reading this, what is an Eisteddfod? Well, it's a competitive festival and celebration of the culture and language of Wales… and it is very Welsh. The National Eisteddfod takes place each year, alternating between locations in the north and south of Wales. They held the 2022 Eisteddfod in Tregaron in Ceredigion, where around 160,000 visitors enjoyed a week of music, poetry, singing, dancing, eating, drinking, and generally hanging out with their mates.

'Eistedd' translates to 'sit' in English, and 'fod' means 'to be, to dwell.' The combined meaning of 'being sat together' seems to sum up what the Eisteddfod is all about, or at least that's how I saw it. It seems to be annual occasion, where Welsh people can come together to enjoy a few days with *their* people. The music and other cultural events are a treasured tradition, but it is equally important to get together with old friends, to relax, and enjoy life with people of your tribe. It was good to see.

The earliest event we know of, which bears any sort of resemblance to an Eisteddfod, was held in 1176, when Lord Rhys invited poets and musicians from all over Wales to his castle in Cardigan and awarded a chair to the best poet and musician. By that I mean, literally, a chair to sit on. The word for poet in Welsh is 'bardd,' which has been translated back into English as bard. You can find references to named Welsh bards from the 6th century onwards, and similar roles can be seen as far back as ancient Greece.

Being a bard in medieval Wales was an interesting job. A patron such as a king, nobleman, or tribal chief would have employed one as a kind of musical spin doctor. The job description of a bard seems to have involved maintaining an oral archive of historical facts, fiction, folklore, and idle gossip, and using it to tell stories, create poems, and make music. Some of the poetry was composed in complex metrical systems, so it was no easy gig. Job security depended on bigging up your patron and their ancestors. It was all about enhancing the bosses' standing in the royal court or among influencers in the tribe or community. Victory on the battle-field would be in the face of impossible odds, by men of immense bravery, led by the most courageous leader, while a loss – if, and when acknowledged – might be interpreted as a brilliant tactical realignment of forces. Only the bard's patron could bring peace and prosperity to the beautiful lands over which they ruled.

Although, by being a poet these days, you are *ipso facto* a bard because that's what the word means, there is a more formal definition that involves an association called until recently Gorsedd Beirdd Ynys Prydain (the Gorsedd of the Bards of the Island of Britain), but now known as Gorsedd Cymru. Its aim is to maintain the old traditions and to develop, promote, and enrich poetry, literature, music, and art in Wales. The Chairing of the Bard at the annual National Eisteddfod is for many people the highlight of the festival, and there is also a Crowning of the Bard ceremony. The Gorsedd was founded in the 18th century to celebrate Welsh culture and the links to its Celtic heritage. Modern-day members are poets, writers, musicians, artists, sportsmen, sportswomen, and others who have contributed significantly to the Welsh nation, its language, and its culture in general. The First Minister of Wales, Mark Drakeford, and the TV presenter, Huw Edwards, were both inducted into the Gorsedd at the 2022 Eisteddfod. There is a story that says if you sleep on the summit of Cadair Idris overnight, you'll wake either a bard or a madman – that's always an option, but at 50-50 it's high risk.

In lavish ceremonies held at the beginning and end of the Eisteddfod week, the winners of two main poetry competitions are announced. The Archdruid, head of the Gorsedd, invites the winning bard onto the stage to sit in a specially-made carved bardic chair. A sword is partly unsheathed, and the Archdruid asks the gathered crowd, 'A oes heddwch?' meaning 'Is there peace?' The crowd responds, 'Heddwch!' ('Peace!'). The sword is sheathed, and the crowd roars its approval.

The traditions of poetry and music are very important, but the week-long festival has a packed programme that also includes performances and competitions in writing, story-telling, comedy sketches, recitation, folk dancing and modern dance, art, and science. In the stands and booths that form a small village around the performance venues, every aspect of life in Wales seems to be represented. Political parties, agricultural bodies, universities, media outlets, and language centres all have stands alongside the food and drink vendors, and people selling books and arts and crafts.

I only had one day to look around, but I could have stayed all week. Two things hit me as soon as I walked past the line of ticket booths and into the Maes (the Eisteddfod field). First, just about everyone was speaking Welsh. That's fair enough, they're Welsh, and this was a Welsh festival. Second, just about everyone looked insanely happy – like they'd been given happy pills as they walked in. People were going around with huge smiles on their faces and there was lots of laughter. I'm sure it wasn't the case, but it felt like everyone else there knew each other.

I began by taking what I thought was a systematic meander through all the stalls in the main show-ground. Among the stands I visited on my first circuit were the Books Council of Wales, The Welsh Language Commissioner, several historical societies, and the Senedd (Welsh Parliament). I stopped off to talk to people at Welsh Water ... 'would you like a free water bottle?' and the Cambrian Mountains Society ... 'would you like a free pen?' They were all extremely welcoming and wanted to tell me all about their organisations – thankfully, in English. I asked them all, 'Why are you at the Eisteddfod? The Senedd representative said they were there to engage with the Welsh public '...Oh, and would you like a cup of tea?'

Before long, I'd wandered into another part of the Maes and entered a huge temporary building that turned out to be the main Eisteddfod Pavilion. I settled into the terraced seating, along with perhaps a hundred or so other people, and listened to some brass bands. I wouldn't say I was normally a brass band fan, but these guys were seriously good. They were all smartly dressed in red jackets and black trousers, and they sounded very professional.

I'm sure I didn't make too much of a performance myself as I removed my damp boots and peeled off my still soaking over-trousers during the changeover between bands. As I was doing so, I noticed in the centre of the seating area, a desk where two people sat scribbling notes. I guessed they were the adjudicators, so while the next band was setting up, I went to ask them what was going on, who I'd just been listening to, and who was on next.

I was told by the timekeeper, not an adjudicator, that the next brass band was The Northop Band, and by the time I'd got back to my seat, they'd started their 20-minute set. Their funked-up version of 'Men of Harlech' was boldly different, and it was good of them to include it – almost as if someone had told them about my recent visit. They followed it with a very moving version of 'Anfonaf Angel.' It did not surprise me to find out later that I had watched a winning performance.

As I came out of the Pavilion, I heard a choir nearby. The sound was coming from a small marquee, the competitors' lounge, about 15 metres away. I felt like a wall of sound knocked me back as I entered two open doors. A choir of about forty-five mainly young people (of course, to me, most people seem young) was rehearsing in front of a handful of friends and family. As the music swirled around me, butterflies began swirling somewhere inside me, and I felt my throat tightening. I did not know what the choir was singing because it was all in Welsh, but there were multiple layers of interlocking harmonies, at times booming, and then transitioning into something gentler. It was visceral, and it really touched me. I apologise now to anyone in Côr Dyffryn Dyfi who noticed a damp overdressed elderly gentleman blubbing away in the doorway; I hope it didn't affect your rehearsal. Being a very manly guy in motorcycle gear, I had to step outside to gather myself before going back in to enjoy the rest of the rehearsal. What a state to get into.

Hearing something that resembled a mixture of an acoustic Bob Dylan and the Orkney band, Saltfishforty (which is a good thing), I was drawn as if in the grip of a *Star Wars* tractor beam into a yurt-like tent marked 'Tŷ Gwerin.' It's the place where they perform traditional and experimental folk music, dance, song, and story. I listened to a few songs by Osian Morris, aka the Dolgellau Bluesman. Supported by a bass, drum, and fiddle, it was lovely melodic folk music and he had the audience enthralled. Conscious of the time, I moved on and found myself in a tent in Maes B – described as the Eisteddfod's rebellious younger brother. A singer-comedian was being young and rebellious. Announcing that not everyone in the audience would understand the Welsh lyrics to his songs (correct), he said, 'I'm sorry, I'm not very good at speaking Englishly.' There were chuckles of Welsh appreciation. He told his audience that for his next song he'd translated the Welsh words into English using Google translate – more giggles. I wasn't in on the joke, of course, but it seemed his lyrics were based on humorous English mis-interpretations of Welsh phrases, which went down very well. The chorus of 'In the eye of your face' was a guaranteed winner and had the audience in peals of laughter every time it came around.

All too soon, my day at the Eisteddfod ended, and it left me wishing I'd planned to stay longer, especially to see the Crowning of the Bard on the Monday, and the Chairing of the Bard later in the week. I made a mental note, similar to one I'd made about 12 months earlier, to plan better for next year. I summoned up my best Arnold Schwarzenegger impression and prepared to move onwards through the rest of Wales.

The Eisteddfod reminded me of that feeling when you go to the cinema or the pub on a Saturday night, and for a few hours, you leave behind, in another world, the credit card bills, the household chores, concerns about donor control of the political agenda, and worries over the Southampton FC centre back partnership. For a short while, you enjoy life in a parallel universe – one that you want to be in. My day in Tregaron had exceeded my expectations, although I'm not really sure what they were. Even though I'm not Welsh, I totally get the Eisteddfod. Apart from maintaining important traditions and keeping a year-long focus on Welsh culture, it's a collective homecoming to people of the Welsh tribe. It's a celebration of being Welsh, with your friends and family, and it has no equal among the other nations of the UK. I discovered a lovely Welsh word, cwtch (it rhymes with butch), which has now found its way into the *Oxford English Dictionary*. It means being held in somebody's arms, in an affectionate cuddle or hug. When Welsh people walk past the ticket office and into the Eisteddfod, as well as a week-long festival of music and culture, they receive a huge collective cwtch from their extended family. No wonder everyone was smiling.

9

TREGARON TO ST DAVIDS

The phrase 'west is best' kept coming into my head during the next leg of my *Journey through Wales*. It was something we used to say as surveyors when working for OS's Western Region, and the west of Britain is undoubtedly where you find some of its most dramatic scenery. My wife, Jan, was going to be joining me again for another section of the journey and I was looking forward to sharing some time with her in Pembrokeshire. She drove up from Dorset and we met in Cardigan. The plan was for us to meander down the coast to St Davids and stay in a shepherd's hut on a farm there for a couple of nights while we explored the area. Jan's arrival meant we had a car for a few days, and we began our mini-journey around Pembrokeshire by taking the A487 south out of Cardigan towards the Preseli Mountains (Mynydd Preseli)… or Hills.

You see them referred to as either, but when we were in the area, we heard the locals call them mountains, so I'll go with that. They rise to 600 metres high, but although they may only seem like hills on the map, they look more like mountains when you're there and see them emerging dramatically out of their surrounding landscape. In terms of Welsh mountains, they are a remote western outlier, less visited than their better-known counterparts in Snowdonia, The Cambrian Mountains and the Bannau Brycheiniog. Somehow, they look slightly out of place – like someone has taken a massive block of igneous rock, approximately 7 miles by 3, and dropped it into rural north Pembrokeshire. The Preseli Mountains couldn't have been more benign on the day we were there. It was the perfect summer's day and warm rather than hot – an ideal day for walking. If we had more time (oops, not again), we could have walked the 'Golden Road' trail that traverses the high-level ridge across the tops of the Preseli Mountains. It's relatively unknown, but one of the finest walks in Wales.

You can find signs of prehistoric activity all around Pembrokeshire. Names and map symbols of standing stones, stone circles, settlements, forts, hut circles, and burial cairns jump out at you as you scan the OS 1:50,000 map of the area. The archaeology goes back to the late Neolithic period (circa 5,000 years ago) and one of those many prehistoric monuments was first on our list of places to visit when we turned south off the A487 shortly before Newport.

Pentre Ifan is one of the most recognisable of our prehistoric monuments. Made of the same bluestone rock used to construct Stonehenge, I've seen it described as the largest and best-preserved Neolithic dolmen in Wales… and even the finest in Britain. Dolmens are those megalithic tombs with three or more vertical stones which support a large flat horizontal capstone. You reach Pentre Ifan via some very narrow lanes, so I was hoping we wouldn't meet something coming the other way. There's a tiny parking area from which the monument is a 5-minute walk. We met a young woman at Pentre Ifan with her 12-month-old son, Harry, strapped to her chest and a lively collie, called Angus, by her side. She lived nearby and just loved to visit the monument to enjoy the fresh air and the special atmosphere of the place.

Although the original structure of Pentre Ifan would have originally been much grander, the surviving stones are still impressive. On a bare grassy hilltop, a 5-metre-long capstone (estimated to weigh 16 tons) sits precariously atop three tapered stones, 2.5 metres off the ground. Whether intentional or coincidental, the angle of the capstone reflects the Carn Ingli ridge 2 miles to the west. The choice of location for the Pentre Ifan monument is exceptional, as it usually is with ancient burial sites. With the Preseli Mountains guarding its back, the monument stands on a prominent ridge with far-reaching views overlooking the Nevern Valley and beyond to Fishguard Bay. Its honoured guests were treated to the finest of outlooks for their extended stay. Once again, hats off to the original design team!

When we'd finished looking around the site, Jan and I wound our way along another mile of high-banked, narrow Pembrokeshire back lanes to reach the quarry at Craig Rhos-y-felin. If that name rings a bell, it's because it's one of two sites (the other being Carn Goedog), which many archaeologists believe to be the source of the bluestones used to construct Stonehenge in Wiltshire. I choose my words carefully because the accepted truth behind the Stonehenge bluestones changes periodically. It seems to depend on how the latest evidence is interpreted and who's doing the interpreting. I'll describe what I've come across at the time of writing, but by the time you read this, it might all be different (I imagine some eminent professor has already thrown this book down in disgust). I'll keep it brief, but there are plenty of information sources out there on this subject, if you want to explore the topic more.

The enormous standing stones that form the main circle of Stonehenge are sandstone blocks known as sarsens. Archaeologists have pinpointed their source to a quarry about 15 miles from Stonehenge, near Marlborough. So far so good and that seems to make sense – we all know the phrase 'Think global, quarry local.' The smaller stones, known as 'bluestones,' are the ones that come from the Preseli Mountains. There are eighty of them at Stonehenge. They are a mixture of volcanic and igneous rocks, the most common of which are dolerite and rhyolite. Carn Goedog, up on the Preseli ridge, is the source of the dolerite bluestones, a blue-green igneous rock with white spots. Craig Rhos-y-felin, the quarry that Jan and I were standing next to, produced the rhyolite bluestones.

When I use the word, quarry, you're probably thinking of a big hole in the ground which gets gradually bigger as more stone is removed. The Preseli bluestone quarries aren't like that. Think instead of an enormous block of grey rock sticking out of the ground – like a petrified dragon's body. I would guess the exposed block at Craig Rhos-y-felin is approximately 70 metres by 30 metres on the ground and up to 20 metres high. Now imagine the outcrop already fractured into large blocks, which are falling away at the sides. We saw several coffin-sized pieces lying on the ground. It's easy to think of 2-ton slabs being prized away 4,000 years ago, or even take-away samples lying on the ground, ready to collect. It's more difficult to imagine prehistoric man deciding they'd make excellent building materials – and wouldn't it be a great idea to transport the blocks 185 miles away to Wiltshire. This is what the geological evidence suggests, but how could it be done? Large teams of people, maybe with animals such as oxen, could have transported the blocks, and there are modern-day examples in places like India that prove it is possible. It would take a lot of project management, considerable labour, and a long time. Some researchers argue that in ancient times most of the route would have been covered in forest, and if it wasn't, it would have been impassable because of rivers and swamps. It's fair to say the jury is still out.

Radiocarbon-dating has been used to estimate the age of evidence left at Craig Rhos-y-felin by the quarry workers, for example the age of burnt hazelnuts and charcoal from their campfires. The dates produce a bit of a conundrum because they suggest a 500-year gap between the stones being quarried and being used at Stonehenge. You might say it would take them that long to get them there, but another theory emerged in 2021, which suggested the stones were first used to make a Welsh stone circle near to the two quarries. They then moved the monument at a later date, let's say about 500 years later, to Stonehenge. Think of it as a take-away stone circle flatpack from a Neolithic version of Ikea. If that was the case, (and there are plenty of other theories saying it wasn't), it's anyone's guess whether local tribes migrating to what is now Wiltshire took their sacred monument with them, whether a tribe from Wiltshire muscled in and removed the stones by force, or even if some sort of deal was struck. I tried to imagine what could have inspired our ancestors to move those large stones so far. It must have been an incredibly powerful belief, or fear, of something. Maybe those labourers from prehistory were installing stone circles as part of a combined bloody ritual / crop management system. It might have been a ceremonial site for honouring their super-celebs or somewhere to acclaim their leaders before they checked out for the next world? We'll never know.

Jan and I made our way another 4 miles further down the B4329 to a hill called Waun Mawn. The open moorland rises to 339 metres on the northern flank of the Preseli upland ridge, a mile southwest of the village of Brynberian. We went there to look at a site which some archaeologists believe to be that of the prototype Stonehenge – the 'Ikea' one later taken to Wiltshire. With the car parked, we set off up a well-marked footpath over short grass and moorland, skirting around two frisky Welsh cobs, one jealously guarding a new foal. We soon found the site of the old stone circle and its one remaining standing stone. Well, it's a cracking location for a monument and it's easy to believe it was the site of something special. The Preseli hills form a backdrop to the south, and the views to the north are stunning, probably stretching for over 20 miles towards Cardigan. It felt atmospheric and significant, but that might have been me reading more into it than was really there. Jan saw it as a stone on some moorland, but I think that was just her way of getting back at my schoolboy comment of 'Pull over and look at Cardigan.' Was it the site of the Stonehenge bluestones 500 years before someone upcycled them into an even greater monument 185 miles to the east? Who knows? The Waun Mawn theory sounds plausible – but there is plenty of scepticism about it and the mystery continues. The Stonehenge controversy is in some ways a distraction from a landscape that is awesome in its own right. Our visit to it was all too brief, and I really want to return to the area in the future to walk that Golden Road across the Preseli ridge.

I'd seen the Tafarn Sinc described as quirky, full of character, and the highest licensed pub in Pembrokeshire. That's enough to grab my attention. As luck – or moderately competent journey planning – would have it, the pub was in the small village of Rosebush, a short drive from Waun Mawn. We were there in less than 15 minutes. Rosebush is an anglicised version of the Welsh name of Rhos-y-bwlch, which means a gap, col, or pass on the moors. It's a satisfyingly simple, and geographically correct, description of its location just south of two passes that lie between the peaks of Foel Eryr and Foel Cwmcerwyn, at the western end of the Preseli Mountains.

Jan and I arrived in the village, parked up, and headed for the pub, walking past an old railway line in front of the pub's entrance. They opened the Maenclochog Railway in 1876 to serve the old slate quarry at Rosebush, but you'd wait a long time for a train now. The station closed in 1937 and when it did, the former Precelly Hotel remained in business and in 2017 it became the community-owned Tafarn Sinc pub. A footpath behind the pub takes you northwards past the old quarries to link up with the Golden Road trail… unless you stop off on the way for some wild swimming (what we used to call swimming) in the clear waters of the old Rosebush quarry.

I guess a pink corrugated iron pub, with sawdust on the floor, and walls decorated with agricultural implements, flannel shirts, and old newspaper cuttings, counts as quirky and full of character. And it's not every pub that has sides of ham hanging down from low wooden ceilings. The atmosphere was good and the staff were friendly. It felt a bit like stepping back in time. Although most of the people in the bar were visitors like us, the woman behind the bar told us how the pub was very much the centre of community life and it was quite common to hear the pub ringing to the sound of old Welsh songs. It felt like the sort of place where you'd want to end up after a long day walking in the mountains. We enjoyed our stay, but I soon felt that familiar and uncomfortable need to move on, to see more of the places on my list before time ran away with us.

Our plan was to head back northwards to the Gwaun Valley, and then follow the Afon Gwaun to the Pembrokeshire Coast at Fishguard. And that's what we did… eventually. Almost as soon as we'd left the pub, we sniffed out an opportunity for a bit of Welsh cheese tasting. As if under a Derren Brown spell, we were drawn into the Cheese Shed, just a few hundred metres from the Tafarn Sinc. It's the premises of a family-run company called Pant Mawr Farmhouse Cheeses. I saw the sign, and I'm sure the car turned into the drive all by itself. The friendly, and I suspect well-rehearsed sales banter of owners, David and Cynthia, charmed and amused us as they described their handmade artisan cheeses. They also told us a bit about their fascinating background and how they ended up making cheese in Rosebush, a story that included sub-chapters on Libya, North Yemen, and supplying products for Concorde and British Airways flights. Back down to Earth, and several samples later, Jan and I emerged with a mixture of hard, soft, and smoked cheeses that probably had our names on them as soon as we'd walked in. As we left, David told us to look out for the word, 'CAWS' (Welsh for cheese) written into a tree plantation to the right of the path that leads from the village up to the old quarries. He explained how the land is on a bit of a slope, and because it was difficult for commercial planting, the family went for some creative tree positioning instead. It's easy to spot their handiwork as you head west and look back towards the village. Their clever bit of dairy product marketing even shows up on the Google Maps aerial image.

After retracing our route 4 miles up the B4329, back past Waun Mawn, some nifty cross-country navigation by Jan got us through more tiny lanes to the head of the Gwaun Valley (Cwm Gwaun), a glacial meltwater valley that has been described as 'One of the great surprises of Pembrokeshire' (Parker and Whitfield, 2003).

We followed the Afon Gwaun for most of its 10-mile cameo appearance down to Fishguard. The narrow road winds one way then the other, clinging to the base of the valley's steep wooded slopes as it picks its way along the edge of the river's narrow flood plain. With the sun shining, entering the valley felt like wandering into an enchanted world. Strobe lights of flickering sunbeams pierced the wood-land canopy wherever it covered the road, filtering through shady tunnels of oak, beech, hazel, and ash trees. It was slightly ethereal. If you overlook the addition of a strip of tarmac road, the verdant valley feels completely natural and unspoiled… somewhere time has forgotten. In some ways, the Gwaun Valley *is* in its own time capsule. When the rest of us adopted the Gregorian calendar in 1752, the people in the Cwm Gwaun hamlets of Pontfaen and Llanychaer continued on their merry way with their tried and trusted Julian calen-dar. They still maintain a local tradition of Hen Galen, in which they celebrate New Year's Day on 13th January… as it should be, according to the old calendar. Children go from house to house bearing fruit and singing traditional Welsh rhymes, and are rewarded with treats, such as sweets or money.

Jan and I were heading down the valley to the hamlet of Pontfaen, to visit somewhere else trapped in time. The pastel blue coloured Dyffryn Arms, also affectionately known as

Bessie's goes back to 1840 and has the reputation of being the time-warp pub from yesteryear – a no-nonsense country pub like they used to be, with a bar in the front room and beer taken from the cask by a glass jug before being decanted into the customer's glass.

Dyffryn Arms, known by many as Bessie's

Owner Bessie Davies served her first pint in the pub over 70 years ago. Now in her nineties, she has become something of a living legend who runs an authentic pub, where you get a good pint of beer with no frills, the way it's supposed to be served. Walking in, it feels like you've entered one of the buildings in St Fagans National History Museum... the 1950s traditional parlour pub. To the right of the narrow passageway as you enter is the owner's private living room. Turn left and you enter the bar. A portrait of the late Queen Elizabeth II at her coronation and a limited-edition print of Bessie standing outside her pub hang from the picture rail that runs around the walls decorated with flowery wallpaper. The dark wooden furniture, including some old church pews, is functional and sits on a black-and-terracotta-tiled floor. There's nothing gastro (unless you include a bag of crisps), fruit machine, or skinny latte going on here. The room has an old-world charm that visitors travel from far and wide to see, but Jan and I had the place to ourselves. We rang the bell by the serving hatch and a man arrived to serve us. I broke a slightly uncomfortable silence by saying what a lovely pub it was and asking what beers they had. 'Bass' came the briefest but undeniably accurate reply. We decided – on balance – to go for the Bass – and anyway, it was the beer for which the pub is famous. It lived up to expectations; I'm sure Bessie would have been proud to have poured it herself. When we left, Jan and I had a brief chat with Bessie, who was sitting in her living room and looking a little frail. She was keen to chat though – that eagerness to engage with customers and pass the time of day still burning brightly. We felt privileged to have met the grand lady and to enjoy the living history that is her unique pub.

We had one more call to make before we left the Gwaun Valley area. A mile from Bessie's is the Guan Valley Brewery, the next stop on another hectic day of varied visits. The micro-brewery is housed in a converted granary building on Kilkiffeth Farm, just off the B4313 that runs between Narberth and Fishguard. As we entered the brewery building, we were smothered by the onrushing aroma of malted barley and hops. It was lovely. A wooden serving bar stretched across the stone floor, dividing the room into two. On our side of the bar, the room was relatively empty apart from some tables and chairs, and casks of beer stacked high in one corner, ready for delivery. The owner had papered one wall with a huge mosaic of 1:25,000 scale OS maps covering the whole of Pembrokeshire. It felt like my kind of place. On the other side of the bar, the brewing process was underway, an impressive and mainly shiny installation of stainless-steel tanks and pipes, all in full view. Also on the other side of the bar, and leaning against it, was the brewery owner Nigel. Behind him were two massive hi-fi speakers. Nigel likes his music while he's brewing and it sounded like he had good taste in music as well as beer. He took over the micro-brewery business in 2018, after previously milking cows for a living and being a keen home brewer for many years. While telling us about his personal background and the Gwaun Valley Brewery, he gave us a few samples of his hand-crafted real ales – 'Try this one, it's full of oats, with lots of banana flavour going on.' The list of ingredients in his Vienna Lager was as simple as you could ask for – spring water, barley, wheat, yeast, and hops. Nigel's enthusiasm for his work and his understanding of the process required for a quality brew were clear. He had a genuine passion for his work and we were pleased to hear that his skills had been rewarded with several awards. The brewery arranges regular live acoustic music sessions and has its own one-acre campsite with superb views of the surrounding hills. It sounded like a perfect combination – live music in a brewery with a campsite in which to crash out afterwards. Jan and I waddled out of the brewery with a varied selection of bottled beers… it would have been rude not to buy some, and the samples were superb. We had one more stop before visiting Fishguard, after which our plan was to go to Carregwastad Point near Llanwnda, then down the coast to Porthgain, before driving on to St Davids for our appointment that evening with a shepherd's hut.

Seizing goods illegally at sea has been a popular pastime for as long as people have taken goods to sea, but the Golden Age of Piracy lasted from the late 17th and into the early 18th century. During that period, countries like Britain, France, Spain, Portugal, and the Netherlands were busy robbing overseas colonies of their valuable resources and exploiting their people. That involved shipping valuable cargoes across the Atlantic between the Americas, Africa, and Europe. Had those same colonial asset strippers not been too busy waging war against each other in Europe, they might have had enough ships and men to govern their overseas interests properly and look after their precious transatlantic shipments. High value cargoes and unprotected trade routes provided a perfect scenario for a spot of piracy. The favourable geography of the Caribbean turns that serendipitous mix into a perfect tropical storm. Tiny islands, secluded coves, and rocky shallows were the perfect place for nimble pirate ships to out-manoeuvre the British men-of-war and Spanish galleons that were much larger, less agile, and had deeper draughts.

You are probably wondering what all this has got to do with a road trip around Wales. Well, the Welsh seem to have been disproportionately represented in the business of piracy. Wales provided some of the most notorious pirates of all time and my timbers were gently shivered when I read claims that almost half the pirates of the Golden Age were Welsh or had Welsh family connections. I'm not sure how statistically sound those figures are. I don't suppose pirates were keen on census forms or demographic profiling questionnaires. Pedantic accuracy aside, however, it seems the high seas were awash with grogged up Welsh hearties, and a top-ten list of infamous pirates would probably include the Welsh trio of Henry Morgan, Howell Davis, and Black Bart Roberts.

Apart from the hard drinking, womanising, feasting, looting, and eccentric dressing, it's hard to see the attraction of being a pirate. Life on the maritime robbery circuit wasn't all glamour, though. A pirate's career was wildly excessive and very brief.

Henry Morgan was arguably the greatest pirate who ever lived. They even named a brand of dark rum after him. He was born in Llanrumney, between Cardiff and Newport, and his height of fame came in the late 17th century, when he did very nicely thank you as a privateer or buccaneer. In effect, he was a legalised pirate. While England was at war with Spain, mercenaries like him were encouraged by the English crown to attack Spanish ships and ports. As a reward, they could keep most of the loot. As well as gaining a handy stash of gold doubloons, Henry was rewarded with a knighthood and given the post of lieutenant-governor of Jamaica for his long-term service in degrading Spanish overseas assets. Although he died three sheets to the wind, a rum-addicted alcoholic, he was at least one of the few pirates not to lose his life at sea. Howell Davis, born in Milford Haven, didn't even manage the usual 3 years life expectancy of a pirate, but in his brief career he earned a reputation for being one of the most cunning and clever pirates around. Unfortunately for him, he wasn't cunning and clever enough to spot the soldiers that were sent to ambush and kill him on the Portuguese island of Principe, off the west coast of Africa. Even though he died less than a year into his career as a pirate, he'd already captured at least fifteen ships. Perhaps his greatest legacy, though, was developing the pirating skills of Bartholomew Roberts – the infamous Black Bart. He was born in the tiny village of Little Newcastle or Casnewydd Bach, and that was the next place that Jan and I were heading for. We set a compass bearing of 254 degrees. It was just over 6 nautical miles from Nigel's brewery.

When they watched the quiet 13-year-old John Roberts (the original name of Black Bart) leave school to join the Royal Navy back in 1695, little did the villagers of Little Newcastle realise that he would become one of the most famous pirates that ever lived. By 1719, he'd worked his way up to second mate on the slave ship, Princess. Apparently, he wasn't particularly enthusiastic about joining the pirates who captured his ship off the coast of West Africa, but when the alternative option of death was explained to him, he began to see the advantages of life under the black flag. As a skilled navigator and fellow Welsh speaker, Roberts soon became the right-hand man of Howell Davis, and took over from his boss 6 weeks later, following his captain's unfortunate ambush incident. Changing his name to a more pirate-like Bartholomew Roberts, and later to the even more badass Black Bart, he earned a reputation as a charismatic leader, who treated his men well. He was also brutal and dispassionately ruthless, however, in capturing over 400 ships during his 3-year career as a pirate. His legacy was his black flag – depicting a pirate and a skeleton holding an hourglass between them, which was a forerunner to the famous skull and cross-bones. He is also credited with introducing the pirate code – a set of rules by which his crew had to live. They included sensible and business focused principles like having equal shares of the spoils, keeping their cutlasses clean, and not letting women onboard.

There is a standing stone on the village green close to where we dropped anchor in Little Newcastle. On it was a small plaque with the words; 'BARTI DDU – In this village, the famous pirate, Black Bart, was born' (along with more words in Welsh). It's a lovely quiet village with a pretty 19th century church, a nice-looking pub, and a large green. Before we went any further, I told Jan that I wasn't sure I should really have a woman aboard. She pointed out that I was about 40 years too late to be thinking about that. It seemed a fair point, so we weighed anchor, and set sail for Fishguard.

Abergwaun, meaning 'mouth of the River Gwaun,' is the Welsh name for Fishguard (population approximately 5,000). A glance at the map shows how well Fishguard was blessed when the geographical features were being dished out. With its next-door twin town of Goodwick, it has a sheltered harbour and lies at the end of the enchanted Gwaun Valley, surrounded by beautiful rolling Pembrokeshire farmland in the shadow of the magnificent Preseli Mountains. If anyone wanted a base for a fishing fleet, or possibly a ferry port for nearby Ireland, the combined harbours of Fishguard and Goodwick would do the job nicely.

That relatively short distance to Ireland, about 62 miles as the Bleriot XI monoplane flies, was the reason behind pilot Denys Corbett Wilson's one hundred minutes of fame. It was from Goodwick on 22nd April 1912, that he flew to Crane, near Wexford, to record the first ever flight between Britain and Ireland. I'm surprised Denys Corbett Wilson's name is not one we're more familiar with. I'd never heard of it before this trip, but he sounds quite a character, and I'm sure there's quite a story behind that record. There's a commemorative plaque in a field above Goodwick to mark the spot from where the flight took off.

Fishguard is thought to have been established sometime around AD 1000, possibly the result of a Scandinavian raid. Vikings introduced their aggressive overseas resource accumulation tactics all along the Welsh coastline, wherever they spotted something worth nicking and there was room to land a longship. How much of their intervention was bloody mayhem committed by savage heathens and how much was more civilised trading by a bunch of Nordic softies is difficult to know after so many years. Archaeologists now point to evidence of Vikings being cultured people with highly developed metalworking traditions and a love of storytelling. Disappointingly, they probably didn't even wear horned helmets. Traditionally, however, they have been portrayed as ruthless marauding raiders, raping, murdering, and pillaging their way through Britain's undefended settlements and monasteries. Maybe the reputation comes from stories recorded by the unfortunate occupants of those monasteries. The truth might lie somewhere in the middle of those two extreme characterisations, and/or it could include a bit of each. Vikings' raids were probably just a blond-haired, ABBA-singing version of the lawless inter-tribal violence that was day-to-day life throughout much of European history… the winner takes it all. Anyway, the name Fishguard is an anglicised version of the Old Norse 'fiskigarðr,' meaning fish catching enclosure, suggesting that at some stage the Viking incomers established a trading post supported by the local fishing resources.

Catching fish led to the town's development as a herring port during the Middle Ages and beyond, peaking in the late 18th century. Oats were the other big export during much of that time. Between 1909 and the beginning of World War I, Fishguard had the distinction of being the first port-of-call for Cunard transatlantic liners arriving from the US. The breakwater built to help with the development of the service caused unexpected silting up of its formerly deep harbour, however, and the liners didn't return after the war. Instead, the harbour has become an important ferry terminal, taking freight, vehicles, and passengers to Rosslare in Ireland.

We can divide the twin towns of Fishguard and Goodwick into two parts; it's a town of two halves. The first being Fishguard's old lower town, and the second being the rest of Fishguard (Main Town) and Goodwick. The former is quaint and pretty, the latter isn't; it contains the more modern development, including the ferry port.

Jan and I made our way to the quaint and pretty part. The old quay has enjoyed a starring role in several films, including the 1971 version of Dylan Thomas's Under Milk Wood, starring Richard Burton and Elizabeth Taylor. We saw a bronze statue of a shoal of fish on the quayside, a reminder of the lower town's historic herring industry, when locals had the nickname 'Sgadan Abergwaun,' or 'Fishguard herrings.'

We took the short drive north out of Fishguard town on the A487 to a parking spot that overlooks the harbour. A 5-minute walk from there takes you out to Castle Point, the site of the town's 18th century fort. The fort became a ruin after they deserted it at the end of the Napoleonic Wars in 1815 but it's well worth the short stroll to see what's left: four cannons have been set up to provide an impression of what the fort would have been like in its heyday, and the view is superb.

HV Morton's book, *In Search of Wales*, doesn't dwell long on Fishguard, and poor old Goodwick doesn't even get a mention. The author thought that Fishguard (he was referring to the lower town) has one of the most beautiful harbours... but only when the sun is shining (Morton, 1932). According to the locals I spoke to, that's not very often. HV Morton then turns his attentions to the bizarre incidents surrounding the last hostile invasion of British soil. The story prompted Jan and me to head for Carregwastad Point, a rocky promontory about 2 mile west of Fishguard.

We drove out to the hamlet of Llanwnda and parked next to St Gwyndaf's Church. The low stone building appears to be crouching down, sheltering from the winds that howl across from the nearby clifftops for much of the year. We looked around inside and saw a rare copy of a 1620 Welsh Bible on display. A short walk across the road from the church is the Llanwnda Holy Well. A dense screen of bushes and trees ensures it is well protected. They say that pilgrims travelling from the north on their way to St Davids have used it for centuries.

From Llanwnda, it was a walk of about a mile across fields, occupied by inquisitive sheep, to Carregwastad Point, where a small plaque commemorates the unusual events of 1797. Back then, this marked the opening scene of something that sounds more like Blackadder than like true-life events. Some parts of the story are established as fact, while other parts may have been added to or changed over time to become more of a myth. I apologise in advance if in telling the story I omit some important details, distort the story further, or appear to make light of events which were tragic for some of those involved. Anyway, there we were: Jan and I were standing on the clifftops looking down at the bay where the strange happenings began.

For the prologue to the story, we have to go back to post-revolution France. Not content with fighting Austria, Prussia, and Russia on the continental mainland of Europe, les bleus also wanted a scrap with Britain. The French Government plotted with the Society of United Irishmen to support an uprising against British rule in Ireland. A force of 15,000 soldiers would be sent to Ireland to support the rebellion there, and a cunning plan was hatched. As a distraction, and to prevent British reinforcements being sent to Ireland, two smaller forces left France, one to northeast England and one to the southwest. Colonel William Tate, an American who had fought against the Brits during the War of Independence, set off from France with a motley bunch in the southern distraction force and headed for the Bristol Channel. The original plan was to sail into Bristol, England's second largest city at the time. They'd land the invasion force and smash the place up. Having destroyed Bristol, the invaders would cross into Wales and head north to take Chester and Liverpool. What could go wrong?

'This is the shipping forecast issued by the Met Office, on behalf of the Maritime and Coastguard Agency, at 11:30 pm on Tuesday 21st February 1797: 'Portland, Plymouth, Fastnet, Lundy, Irish Sea. South to South-westerly, 8 to 10 becoming violent storm 11. Rain. Very rough. Poor.'

The French strategy depended upon sauntering down La Manche in benign weather to the West Country. As things turned out, more typical winter conditions prevailed in the English Channel... and the cunning plan went the way of most cunning plans. The ships got nowhere near Bristol and were blown north towards Pembrokeshire. An even more cunning Plan B was required and one was quickly hatched; land the boys anywhere possible. The people of Fishguard weren't to know anything about what was coming their way on 22nd February 1797, but this is how it played out...

Four French men-o-war sailing ships, flying British flags, appeared from the west. The dastardly foreigners thought they could slip in disguised. This initially caused much excitement and there was loud cheering amongst the locals. One old, retired sailor wasn't so impressed. He recognised the vessels as French warships and he raised the alarm. The French *mal garcons* aborted their attempt to enter Fishguard Harbour, turned around, and headed out to a nearby cove next to Carregwastad Point.

Excitement amongst the locals turned to panic when they realised that they had no military defenders to fend off the invaders. Lord Cawdor, the acting lieutenant of the county, was the man responsible for rustling up the town's defence, but he was 30 miles away. What were the people of Fishguard to do?

The French fleet dropped anchor and deposited an invasion force of 600 infantrymen and 800 convicts, who quickly went about setting up camp. Remember, this was February – most of the invaders would have been cold, suffering from *mal de mer*, and wishing they were somewhere else. The land-lubber ex-prisoners were probably just glad to be on dry land. They immediately began pillaging local properties, looking for food and anything they could use to keep warm. They smashed up the pews in St Gwyndaf's Church in Llanwnda to make a fire, and tore pages from its 17th century Welsh Bible to use as kindling. Some reports describe how a Portuguese trading vessel had gone aground nearby a few months earlier, and the local Welsh villagers had liberated fine wines, spirits, and other agreeable consumables from its cargo hold. The French rabble looted its way round the nearby villages and drank all the fortified wine they could get their hands on – any port in a storm. Before long, they would have been in no state to fight anyone. Some of the ex-convicts either conveniently forgot to return to base or were too hammered to find their way back.

On the afternoon after the landing, what remained of the French force scanned the hills surrounding their position in the cove. They saw what they believed to be terrifying and overwhelming forces lined up against them. Their commanding officers must have wondered what they'd signed up for. Those of their force who hadn't already run away were off their faces with stolen booze. Outnumbered and outgunned, things didn't look good. As if that wasn't bad enough, their only escape route had just vanished – their naval support had up-anchored and set sail for home. Their job was done… *au revoir mes amis*. The position of the invaders looked hopeless.

While the French had been busy plundering and desperately trying to keep warm, Lord Cawdor had been trying to scrape up enough of a defence force to see them off. By noon on the day after the invasion, he had assembled 750 mainly yeomanry soldiers. They were the Dad's Army of its time, a home guard of mainly farmers and farm workers. A few hundred more civilians had also turned up for the fight, armed with little more than a handful of muskets and whatever farm implements they could lay their hands on. One volunteer, who distinguished herself was 47-year-old Jemima Nicholas, the wife of a Fishguard cobbler. She fearlessly marched out to meet the invaders, armed only with a pitchfork. She rounded up twelve of them, marched them back to Fishguard, and locked them inside St Mary's Church. You can still see a memorial stone to this brave lady outside the church.

Back at the standoff, Captain Davies, a professional soldier who had at least seen some active service, set about positioning the Welsh defence forces rustled up by Lord Cawdor. His tactics (and the questionable state of the French invasion force) were to prove decisive. Captain Davies distributed his men in groups on the hills surrounding the cove. To the French, the numbers may have seemed more than they really were. Several hundred Welsh women, dressed in their traditional red coats and tall black felt hats, came to witness the unfolding drama and support their men. Can you imagine the sight? Captain Davies got the women to walk up and down the hills for several hours. Through eyes blurred by an all-nighter on Portuguese brandy, the French thought the womenfolk were a detachment of British grenadiers – and that the handful of yeoman darting back and forth on horseback must be cavalry officers organising an overwhelming force of infantrymen. *Sacré bleu!*

The officers in charge of the French presumably thought they had done their job by distracting such vast numbers of British soldiers. There was no point being slaughtered by an overwhelmingly superior force, so by evening, they raised a flag of truce. A council of war took place in the Royal Oak pub in Fishguard, where the French were told to surrender unconditionally or face the shock and awe of 20,000 elite troops lined up against them. The bluff worked, and they surrendered. For them… *la guerre était finie.* They were relieved of their firearms, marched into Fishguard, and distributed around the local prisons, churches, and gaols for safekeeping, before being processed and sent off to England. It was all over; the French party had been spoiled by English gales, Portuguese wines, and Welsh spirit.

The reports make the failed invasion sound like a farce, but there was a serious side to it. There were at least six deaths and many locals would have been traumatised. You can only imagine their intense relief, and the wild celebrations in the pubs of Pembrokeshire on the night of the surrender.

There is a final chapter to the story, in which two Welsh girls on guard duty fall in love with two of their French captives. They provide their lovers with a piece of bone to dig their way to freedom and the escapees even steal Lord Cawdor's yacht to sail away to France. Apparently, years later, after peace had broken out, the two girls returned to Pembrokeshire with their new husbands, and were given a rousing welcome. I can see the story of the last invasion of Britain being made into a comic / tragic opera… or maybe it's more suited to a pantomime. In Fishguard Town Hall, you can view an impressive tapestry, which tells the tale of the failed invasion. The tapestry, which took seventy-seven local people over 4 years to make, is over 30 metres long and similar in style to the famous one in Bayeux.

From Fishguard to our overnight stop in a shepherd's hut near St Davids was a drive of about 20 miles, but before we could put our feet up for the day, we had an evening appointment in the port of Porthgain, a small coastal hamlet on the north Pembrokeshire Coast. There's a picturesque route from Fishguard that picks its way along the country lanes, passing a myriad of prehistoric forts, standing stones, and burial chambers. We didn't go that way. We had a deadline to keep, so to get to Porthgain on time, we drove down the main A487.

That route also took us through pretty scenery, but a lot faster than the winding coastal road. Jan and I were heading for an 8:00 pm dinner reservation at The Shed Fish & Chip Bistro, recommended to us by Lisa, our Welsh born yoga teacher back home in Dorset. I'm so glad we got there on time; I didn't want to be late and find ourselves in a difficult position. We arrived with just enough time for a stroll around the harbour. By the time we arrived, it was a perfect evening. The sun was soon to disappear behind the massive brick wall of a large harbourside building, but before it said farewell for the day, it cast a golden light over a handful of fishing boats that were lazily bobbing up and down on their moorings. Porthgain was formerly a commercial port that processed and exported stone from the local granite and slate quarries. Many of the buildings and a lot of the old machinery still survive, leaving a strange mixture of industrial heritage and natural beauty. Nowadays, its position in the Pembrokeshire Coast National Park, its pub, bistro, coastal walks, and a handful of art galleries make Porthgain a popular tourist spot. Jan and I enjoyed a relaxing meal together after another hectic day with so much to take in. My brain was in overload, which doesn't take much these days, and I needed to get my notebook out in the restaurant to get some thoughts down, before everything tumbled out of my head. Who said romance was dead? Oh… and the fish was fresh, and the meal was superb.

Our shepherd's hut was on a farm less than a mile from the city of St Davids and about the same distance from Treginnis, the most westerly settlement in Wales. That's further west than Newquay in Cornwall or Oban in Scotland. We were just a few hundred metres from a coastline rated by *National Geographic* magazine experts as the second best in the world.

Shepherds' huts go back a few hundred years. They were originally used to provide their sheep-minding occupants with shelter from the weather and somewhere to rest. Inclement weather is not unknown in Wales during the lambing season, in the first few months of the year. While keeping snug, the shepherd could also keep an eye on the flock, which would have been a valuable asset to the farm. By early Victorian times, the basic hut design became standardised (a shed with a bed, on wheels) and they were manufactured commercially. Shepherds from hundreds of years ago could never have imagined the luxury of the hut that Jan and I were in. It had a comfortable double bed, a gas cooker, double-glazed windows, a log burning fire, hot water and a shower... and there wasn't a single sheep in sight. What was in sight out of one window was the tower of St Davids Cathedral, and out of the window on the opposite side we could look over the sea. Next stop was Ireland or North America, depending on which tack your ship was on.

Our hut sat on the edge of a working farm with wonderful views for almost 360 degrees. Jan and I had enjoyed just another day of prehistory, brewing, cheese, and piracy. Time to wind down and we were in the right place for that. Within 5 minutes of arriving, we had our feet up and a glass of wine in hand. It was so quiet and peaceful. A wonderful location. We could have happily stayed there for the rest of the summer.

10

ST DAVIDS TO TENBY

You know what it's like when you look up at the dark sky at night and wonder in awe at the billions of stars above you? That's what I was doing at 2:15 am one early August night, on a farm in south Pembrokeshire. I was lying flat on my back, outdoors on a wooden picnic bench, in my t-shirt, and pyjama shorts. Twenty metres to my left was a farmhouse. A few metres away to my right was our shepherd's hut, and in front of me, about 79.7 light-years away, was the constellation Ursa Major. It was a cool but not cold night, and the soft sound of breaking waves in the distance was the only thing that interrupted complete silence.

A clear view of the Milky Way is something I can add to the long list of things that were *obviously* much better in my day… like the size of Mars bars, observance of the highway code, and the destructive power of fireworks. A few decades ago, everyone could see the sky full of stars on a cloud-free night, but as the world has become increasingly industrialised, we've added more and more urban development. As a result, there's now more artificial light around at night. Approximately 99% of the population of Europe and the US live under skies polluted by artificial light, which makes it impressive that approximately 18% of Wales lies under protected dark skies. The need to protect dark skies isn't just about being able to observe the stars – although that's good enough reason; diminishing dark skies affect human well-being and the health of nocturnal wildlife. Fortunately, someone's doing something about it. Through its International Dark Sky Places (DSP) initiative, the International Dark Sky Association (IDA) monitors, preserves, and protects the world's dark places. Wales has a network of DSPs of various categories, and in Snowdonia and Bannau Brycheiniog (which we used to know as the Brecon Beacons), it has two of only eighteen International Dark Sky Reserves (the largest geographic category of DSP) in the world. And then there's the Dark Sky Sanctuary of Bardsey Island. But it's not all about those officially designated reserves and places; there are hundreds of places to go in Wales where light pollution is minimal and the night skies go on forever – and on that early-August night, I was in one of them.

None of these statistics were going through my mind as I lay on that picnic table, gazing into deep space. The sight above me was mesmerising. I traced the faint band of light that the Romans called *via lacteal* or milky road, as it stretched from horizon to horizon. I thought back to previous times when I'd seen the night skies so crystal clear – once in Latvia, another time in Zanzibar, and a few times in Hampshire, when I was a child.

But something else has changed over the years... I watched little pinpricks of light as they slowly tracked in straight lines across the enormous dark sky in silence. Looking up from my improvised table-top observatory, there was always at least one satellite in view. As it disappeared, another one came into view – at times I could see three or four simultaneously. When I was born, the number of satellites orbiting the Earth would have been precisely zero, but by 2022 there were 9,000 of them in low Earth orbit (up to 1,200 miles from Earth). They are an indispensable part of modern living. A multitude of telecommunication, navigation, and military applications now depend upon them. We depend on them when we're driving somewhere new, doing our online shopping, or zapping that all important selfie around the world for our friends to like.

If you stare into space for a while, your mind can soon wander into some deep philosophical thoughts. I imagined someone looking up at those same stars 4,000 years ago, trying to make sense of everything after a hard day shifting bluestones. Questions kept coming into my head. What's out there? Is ours one of an infinite number of parallel universes? Am I even here, or just part of a sophisticated computer simulation? Or should I just concentrate on painting my palette blue and grey? I didn't ask it to happen. Don McLean's classic 1971 hit had auto-cued in my head and there was no going back. I stayed for another 10 minutes on that starry starry night reflecting on sad lyrics about an insane world. I eventually synched back into the real world, my joints creaking in harmony with those of the wooden bench, as I heaved myself from it and back to the hut for what was left of the night.

My little nocturnal adventure seemed like a hazily remembered dream by the time the sun's rays came pouring through the window a few hours later to kick-start a new day. I wanted to get out and enjoy the morning, so I left Jan to have a lie-in, and took a 10-minute walk down to the beach. The owner of the farm had told us to help ourselves to their kayaks any time we liked – so I did. A footpath took me around a couple of fields of potatoes, and when I arrived at an empty beach, I had the little cove of Porthlysgi Bay all to myself. Well, just me, and a few oystercatchers and gulls that were out searching for their breakfast, their cries piercing the stillness of the morning air.

It was a glorious summer's morning. The temperature must have been in the mid-teens, there wasn't a cloud in the sky, and the sea was flat. Low, grassy coastal cliffs drop down to sea level at the cove, where the beach is mainly shingle, with a few rocky outcrops and rock pools. When I arrived, there was a lovely sandy patch about halfway down the beach that stretched out to the water's edge. With the tide halfway out, I had to drag my bright yellow kayak quite a way across the sand to the mirror-like blue sea before jumping in, or more precisely, on… it was one of those ride-on polyethylene kayaks. I spent an hour very slowly pottering around shallows of crystal-clear water, being gently lifted, and then lowered again by the long rhythmic swell of the Atlantic. From time to time I took a few extra deep breaths while I drifted along, and the salty air filled my lungs. It was so calming. When I thought I should be getting back, I pulled the kayak out of the water and hauled it to the top of the beach before popping back into the water to swim for a few minutes in the calm (but cold) waters. It was so quiet that I felt guilty disturbing the peace by splashing around. I savoured a few more moments before heading back to the hut to make Jan a cup of tea, have breakfast, and burst into another busy day of visiting places on my list. I made a mental note to show Jan the beach and the cove later.

Our agenda for the day was to visit the city of St Davids, the cathedral, and the nearby Chapel of St Non, where St David was born. It was all within a few miles of our shepherd's hut. After that, we'd drive down through Pembrokeshire, stopping off at a few towns along the way, and then come back to our hut after visiting the county's most southerly point, St Govan's Head.

St Davids is the smallest city in Britain, but with a population of less than 2,000, it feels more like a village. It sits peacefully in gently undulating farmland on this most westerly tip of Wales. The settlement developed on the site of a monastery founded by St David (Dewi Sant) in the 6th century. His shrine lies within the cathedral, which is also named after him. The city centre (it seems odd to call it a city, but that's what it's been since 1995) is a collection of small streets around a war memorial, with a couple of pubs and a few shops. You'll find local produce for sale, including St Davids Seaweed Gin, some of which Jan and I took home for evaluation. A sizeable supermarket and a sixty-three-bed hotel seem incongruous at first sight, but hint at the number of tourists and pilgrims the city must attract.

The hollow in which St Davids Cathedral stands beside the River Alun (Afon Alun), has been a sacred place for centuries. St David founded his monastery less than 100 years after the Romans had left. They'd got fed up with this far-flung outpost, got Brexit done, and went home to their Mediterranean diets and sunshine. They left behind a population with a blend of Celtic, Roman, and Christian traditions. Roman authority had provided control over competing tribes for nearly four centuries and discouraged anyone else from invading Britain, but their exit signalled a free for all and the end of Christian worship in many communities. Anglo-Saxons and Jutes arrived in southeast England, with new pagan beliefs and rituals, and gradually spread north and west. The Brittonic speaking people were pressed westwards towards Wales, Cornwall, northwest England, and Ireland, taking Roman Christianity with them. The Age of Saints lasted through the 5th and 6th centuries. Believers sought secluded places and monastic life, holding onto belief systems, worship, and culture led by the example set by Celtic saints… of whom St David is the most famous. Language, religion, and traditions from that period have survived the ages to underpin Welsh identity today.

Since Norman times, the religious site at St Davids has enjoyed the endorsement of a series of celebrity supporters. William the Conqueror prayed there in 1081. Thirty-four years later, King Henry I ordered the building of a church dedicated to the Welsh saint and soon after, in 1123, Pope Calixtus II created the pilgrimage to St Davids, which made the site even more popular. The Pope famously declared that two pilgrimages to St Davids were equal to one to Rome, whilst three pilgrimages were equal to one to Jerusalem (we're back to the Bardsey equation). The pedant in me couldn't shake this off for a while when I first read it – where does your pilgrimage start? Could someone from nearby Fishguard pop 15 miles down the A487 three times in a day and claim a Jerusalem pilgrimage? However, that might be missing the point. I suspect real pilgrims are concerned more with spiritual fulfilment than technical conformance to the qualification criteria.

The current cathedral building began life back in 1181 and is one of the oldest cathedrals in Britain, founded almost 50 years before Pope Gregory dispatched St Augustine to these isles to convert the population to Christianity. The cathedral is built of local fine-grained Cambrian sandstone, which normally looks a sombre grey but, in some light can take on an episcopal hue. It has a slightly modular look, with several rectangular blocks of various heights stacked around a long rectangular base and a central square tower. The rural setting is something else that sets it apart from most of its ecclesiastical peers; from some viewpoints, the background is entirely trees and rolling Pembrokeshire hills.

Jan and I were about to become two of the 300,000 visitors who visit the cathedral, a UNESCO World Heritage Site, each year. As we entered the cathedral, we were greeted by soothing organ music, a standard cathedral smell, and a big space that quietly echoed the hushed whispers of respectful visitors. The scale and historical significance of the building immediately impresses you, in the way every cathedral does – they're meant to do that. I felt there was something extra going on here though, perhaps reflecting the cathedral's place in Welsh history and national identity. My take-away memories relate to the building itself and to the people resting there. On the structural side, the wooden ceiling is unusual and impressive, and the floor must be unique, sloping almost 4 metres from one end to the other. The restored shrine of St David, patron Saint of Wales, is, of course, deeply significant. Two of the many tombs in the cathedral are also hugely significant and thought provoking: the Welsh Prince, Lord

Rhys (Lord Rhys ap Gruffydd, Arglwydd Rhys), and Edmund Tudor, the father of King Henry VII, founder of the Tudor dynasty.

Jan and I left the cathedral feeling good. It's an impressive place by any measure, and I can't imagine anyone leaving without being touched by its religious, historical, and cultural significance. After our visit and some lunch, we took the short drive down a narrow county lane to visit the Chapel of St Non and its holy well. The chapel is where St Non gave birth to St David, and the well is one of the most sacred in Wales.

Along the lanes of the St Davids peninsula you see trees bent into right angles, their tops swept eastwards, sculpted by the regular westerlies that rush over the ancient landscape from the Atlantic. On this day, though, a gentle easterly breeze was blowing the opposite way, over the green fields that fell away towards the clifftops above St Non's Bay. The bright azure sea was almost flat, and you could just make out the swell from long rollers lazily making their way to land from far out in the Atlantic. Just before the road reaches a 1930s style building called The Retreat, it ends at a car park with space for half a dozen cars. Next to the car park, in one of those grassy fields, are the ruined remains of the old chapel and the Holy Well of St Non.

Hard facts about St Non and St David are hard to find. Most written records didn't appear until the Middle Ages, so most of what we know about the 6th century comes from tales handed down orally through the generations, and mythology... symbolic narratives of unknown origin but often with some seeds in actual events. Most accounts refer to St Non giving birth to St David in a chapel on the Pembrokeshire clifftops, bathed in golden light while a thunderstorm raged outside. That's a night she wouldn't forget in a hurry. No one is sure about the date, but it was around AD 500.

I'm sure it would be different when a westerly gale was blowing, and the rain was arriving horizontally from the Atlantic, but on the day Jan and I visited, things couldn't have been more idyllic. The location was glorious, and the view exceptional. There was a serenity to the place. Getting out of a car next to us was a young woman about to take her little Jack Russell Terrier for its regular clifftop walk. Angus scampered over and looked very pleased to see us. He gave us a single affectionate lick each and then hastened back to his owner. Trying not to be offended by the brevity of the dog's attention, I joked, 'Well, that was nice while it lasted.' The owner laughed and told us how Angus had been doing the same walk almost daily for every one of his 14 years. She explained, 'Usually he gets a little treat from the Sisters of Mercy, but he's a bit confused now they've gone.'

I have to say Angus wasn't the only one confused. I didn't realise the 1980s Gothic rock band had moved to West Wales and was providing daily titbits for passing dogs. As we walked with Angus's owner along a footpath towards the chapel and the clifftop, she provided a bit more background and the situation became clearer. The Sisters of Mercy is a Catholic institution originally founded in Ireland in the early 19th century. Nuns from the order had managed The Retreat (the building next to the car park) since it was built in 1934. It was a resting place for pilgrims visiting the Chapel of St Non and the Holy Well of St Non. But not anymore. Jan and I were told that the building had become economically unsustainable during the COVID pandemic and was facing a change of use, which was still to be decided. We were told that three elderly Sisters of Mercy, now in their seventies, had to move out. One had moved to Bristol and two to London. That seemed a heavy burden to bear after living for so long on the idyllic Pembrokeshire Coast.

The footpath we were following took us past both the old chapel and the holy well on its way to the clifftops and the coastal path. A few crumbling walls are all that now remain of the small, rectangular Chapel of St Non. There might not be much to see, but the setting overlooking rocky St Non's Bay is breathtaking, and its spiritual significance is the important thing. The holy well, which is said to have appeared during that fateful thunderstorm, lies next to the footpath, between the old chapel, and the car park. The water from the well is considered to have healing and miraculous powers. I thought I'd put it to the test by splashing some on my dodgy left knee. I had a slight headache as well, so I slapped a few drops on my forehead for good measure. I'm not sure if my result is statistically significant, but within an hour, it had completely disappeared (the headache, not my knee).

Conscious of the heavy schedule we had planned for our second day in the area, Jan and I were up early and heading down the A487 to Haverfordwest. It was frustrating to be missing St Bride's Bay and Skomer Island, but we only had limited time for another busy day of visits, so those other beautiful places would have to wait for another time. Our plan for the day, which reads like a train timetable, included visits to Haverfordwest, Milford Haven, Lamphey, Manorbier, and Tenby… all change. There was a 5th century chapel at St Govan's Head and a medieval castle in the village of Carew to throw into the mix as well – so no time to hang around.

Haverfordwest is the ancient county town of Pembrokeshire and has a population of just over 10,000. The Western Cleddau river runs through the middle of the town and the Norman castle towers above it. The town developed in Elizabethan times, when it was the second largest port in Wales. When HV Morton arrived in Haverfordwest in the 1930s, it struck him how English it was; he thought he'd left Wales and returned to Somerset. He suggested you could divide Pembrokeshire into two parts. The northern half had all the difficult to pronounce Welsh names, but the southern part was full of English sounding names, like those ending with the Anglo-Saxon 'ton'… places such as Johnston, Jameston, Milton, and Hundleton, for example. The author considered the county to be an example of colonisation, being to Wales what Ulster is to Ireland (Morton, 1932).

He was right, and the origins of the partition go back to Norman times. On the European mainland, Flanders had become overpopulated after a series of disastrous floods. Many of the population quit and moved to nearby England. Henry I decided to take back control of The Borders and came up with an elegant solution – relocate the Flemish incomers to Wales. It's a strategy revisited in recent times by the UK Government, but whereas they encountered strong moral and human rights objections when they tried to send migrants to Rwanda, Henry had no such constraints when sending Flemish immigrants to south Pembrokeshire. English people were also encouraged to settle in the area, and they were further attracted by favourable farming conditions. The incomers slowly displaced the locals and the Welsh language from the area. Flemish gradually gave way to English, but with a distinctive dialect and accent. An invisible boundary called the Landsker Line joined over fifty castles and strong-holds built by Normans and Flemish immigrants across Pembrokeshire to protect themselves from the indigenous Welsh. There is still some evidence of an anglicised culture and sense of separation, and the area has been called, 'Little England beyond Wales.'

It's about 10 miles from Haverfordwest to the watery expanse of Milford Haven (Aberdaugleddau), which is a ria, or drowned river valley, flooded at the end of the last Ice Age. It is one of the top ten natural harbours in the world, and one of the deepest. The natural harbour of Milford Haven has always been hard to resist for invaders. Vikings used it exten-sively, and its name has Scandinavian origins. The name, Melrfjordr, is anglicised from the old Norse 'Melr' (sandbank) and 'fjord' (inlet). The French landed in Milford Haven in 1405 and if the winds of fortune and the English Navy hadn't intervened, a Spanish Armada may have arrived in 1597.

Jan and I made our way down to the coastal village of

Dale, near the mouth of Milford Haven, and then out towards St Anne's Head, where we took a short walk to Mill Bay. The shoreline was rocky and uninviting, but this was another Plas Penmynydd moment – one of those occasions when you know you're looking at somewhere historically deeply significant. By far the most important moment in Milford Haven's history, and one of the most significant in the history of Britain and even Europe, was on 7th August 1485, when a 28-year-old man called Henry Tudor (the one with the grandad from Anglesey) stepped ashore at Mill Bay under the flag of the Welsh red dragon. He had with him a band of around 2,000 French mercenaries, and the expectations of the Welsh people. Before the month was out, that young Welshman would be standing in a muddy field in Leicestershire, having become Henry VII, King of England. It was one of the turning points in British history. The Middle Ages were over, and the modern period of history was about to begin. Henry VII's descendants transformed religion in Britain, changing the face of the country (largely by destroying its monasteries) and the balance of power. Britain's powerful army and navy allowed it to create an empire that spanned the globe and established the country as a world power. For the parties involved, that was better for some than others.

Before we move on, a few more words on Henry VII because his success story is remarkable. We somehow seem to prefer a romantic loser to a success story, and if he'd only worn a kilt and been less successful, he'd be the subject of countless ballads, adorn a million tea-towels, and have a leek named after him. When you consider the formidable historical legacy of the Tudor dynasty, I find it fascinating how much it depended on a series of very lucky breaks. His chances of becoming king were about as likely as your chances nowadays of spotting a postman in long trousers, but somehow, he did it. His claim to the throne was very flimsy, at best. And that's probably being generous. While his claim to the English throne by bloodline was weak, he knew that beating a king in battle was another way of taking over the top spot.

Henry Tudor was born in Pembroke Castle on 28th January 1457. It wasn't the best of starts; his father was already dead, and his mother was only 13 years old. When he was only 5 years old, his grandfather was captured and executed. As events unfolded (it gets very complicated), Henry Tudor found himself the sole surviving male with any ancestral claim to the House of Lancaster. At fourteen, with the House of York in the ascendency, he had to flee to the continent. Having tried unsuccessfully 2 years earlier, Henry gathered support for one more roll of the dice – another attempt to land in England and claim the throne. I can see him now staring out across the English Channel saying, 'It's a long shot but, do you know what, by my troth I'm going to give it one more try.' Henry was either very confident, feeling the burden of expectations, or just a compulsive gambler. After landing in Mill Bay, he marched his men up through Wales, rallying support along the way. By the time he crossed the border at Shrewsbury, his army had doubled to around 4,000. King Richard III's royal army was more like 10,000 strong as the two armies converged on Bosworth, Leicestershire. How the two sides would finally match up depended upon Henry's stepfather, Thomas, Lord Stanley. He brought his own private army of several thousand men to the battle, but no one knew who they were going to fight for. It seems Lord Stanley was waiting to see how things panned out before committing his men to the side most likely to win. This is where Henry got lucky. After 2 hours of bloody mayhem, King Richard spotted his challenger and dived into the battle to attack him. Richard was knocked off his horse as it struggled in the mud, but continued courageously on foot, famously offering his kingdom for a replacement mount. Canny Lord Stanley saw that the battle was going Henry's way and charged in to let him know he'd been right behind him all along. King Richard was struck down and killed. As the Yorkist army retreated to the sound of groans and clanking armour, Richard's crown was taken to Henry, and they made him, a Welshman, King of England on Crown Hill.

Back to my *Journey through Wales* – it was Sir William Hamilton who founded the town of Milford Haven in 1793. He invited Quaker whalers from Nantucket to live and work there, and then, a few years later, he persuaded the Royal Navy to create a dockyard for building warships. Sir William's good friend, Admiral Horatio Nelson, presumably helped to swing that decision for him. The admiral was a frequent guest of the Hamiltons,' especially after he found that Sir William's wife, the beautiful young Emma, could float his boat even better than the deep waters of Milford Haven. Nelson described Emma as 'A woman of remarkable talents'… I'm just going to leave that there. She was indeed a glamorous woman who captivated the hearts of many of Europe's most powerful men, but the story of her life is like the plot from a tragic opera. A woman of immense wit, beauty, and sexuality, she became an artist's model, a friend of royals, and a high society trend-setter. A husband 34 years her senior and a whole sub-cast of predatory male partners accompanied her on a rollercoaster of fluctuating fortunes. Finding true love with a national hero, only for him to then be shot dead, preceded poverty and imprisonment in the penultimate act. Her final demise came through a tragic ending, as required of all operatic heroines.

In the 19th century, Milford Haven became one of the UKs biggest fishing ports. As the fishing industry declined in the 1960s, the port became important for storing and refining oil. Having grown up associating the name Milford Haven with images of oil tankers and terminals (and the oil spill from the Sea Empress in 1996; Britain's worst environmental disaster), I think I prefer the Welsh name for the town, Aberdaugleddau, which means 'Mouth of the two Rivers Cleddau.' It's also quite satisfying to pronounce (Aber-dye-gle-thai). Nowadays, the port is one of the biggest Liquid Natural Gas (LNG) terminals in Europe. Because it acts as a gateway for gas to enter the European pipeline network, the LNG facility has become increasingly important in recent times, as countries move away from their dependence on Russian gas.

Jan and I made our way down through the towns of Pembroke Dock and Pembroke, heading towards the county's most southerly point, St Govan's Head. Pembroke Dock used to be known as Paterchurch, a small Pembrokeshire fishing village. It became the town of Pembroke Dock and expanded rapidly after the construction of the Royal Navy Dockyard in 1814. Over its 112-year life, the dockyards built 263 naval vessels and five royal yachts, before closing in 1925. Running east-west, parallel to the High Street and closer to the docks, is Bush Street. It was there on 10th September 1893 that William Henry Ormoad Probert was born. He later became Private 120 590 Army Service Corps, and his son eventually became my dad.

A mile further south, the small town of Pembroke (Penfro), and its almost complete Norman castle, stand on a limestone ridge alongside the Pembroke River (Afon Penfro). The walled town of around 8,000 people dates back over 900 years and in the main street, you can still see many Georgian and Tudor houses. Jan and I drove through the little village of Bosherston, about 4 miles south of Pembroke, and continued southwards towards the sea. We meandered down more high banked narrow Pembrokeshire lanes, flanked by green fields decorated with fluffy white sheep. Shortly before we got to the coast, we had to drive through a Ministry of Defence firing range – but it, and the road, were closed. Most sensible people would check if the road was open *before* driving there. On this occasion, we were lucky with our timing. We only had a 20-minute wait before the road was re-opened. We waited patiently in the car for the 20 minutes to pass, with the windows open in the heat of the afternoon. Listening to the not-so-distant pounding of artillery, we felt very thankful we weren't on the wrong end of it. At precisely 4:30 pm, bang on time, a guard popped out of his hut, gave us a nod that said, 'OK, on your way,' and lifted the barrier. We just hoped everyone on the range also knew the rules and had accurate watches.

Jan and I parked in an enormous car park at the end of the road, near the top of the cliffs. We were the first to arrive there after the range opened. The car park was enormous; a sign of how popular the headland must be for walkers and people like us, going to visit St Govan's Chapel. A van pulled up next to us, despite all those other empty spaces, and a group of dishevelled millennial lads emerged, talking excitedly about the rock climb they were about to attempt. The boys assembled their gear, double checked they'd got everything, and set off at a brisk pace over the Trevallen Downs towards the cliffs. They didn't want to hang around. Or rather, they did; those guys must have been desperate to get dangling from ropes. I've never had a head for heights and despite it being far from perfect, I've grown accustomed to my body being in its current configuration. There are usually perfectly acceptable paths to get you to where you want to go, and if not, it's obviously too dangerous to go there. Like horse racing and fishing, rock climbing is a sport I just don't get!

St Govan's Chapel, a Grade I listed building, was just a couple of minutes' walk from the car park. Legend says it is impossible to count the steps that lead to the holy site; something to do with the mysterious transition between our 21st-century world and that of St Govan. I'm going with fifty-two steps… or at least a number somewhere between forty and sixty.

The tiny chapel clings tightly to the rugged limestone rocks halfway down the cliff. The amazing medieval relic is one of the most recognisable images of Pembrokeshire and must adorn thousands of tourism leaflets, calendars, and posters. St Govan (or Gowen, Govern, Gofan or Gobin) was another of the Celtic Christian monks, who lived in seclusion in the southwest area of what is now Wales during the age of the saints in the 5th and 6th centuries.

St Govan's Chapel

The folklore of the site has many variations, but one story that is often repeated goes like this. As St Govan was on the run from marauding pirates from Lundy, the rocks of the cliffs opened up and closed around him for protection. The pirates eventually moved on and St Govan decided to make a chapel in his handy new hideaway to avoid similar confrontations in the future. As luck would have it, a well appeared, and provided him with water. With that and a diet of fish, he had all he needed for a secluded life of contemplation and worship. Mindful of the physical risks and mental issues brought upon by the pirates, he kept a bell to warn others in case the marauding maritime miscreants appeared again. The pirates weren't happy with him cramping their style and stole the bell from him, only to get their comeuppance later when a storm blew up and sank their ships. The angels responsible for the sudden storm retrieved the bell and encased it in rock on the cliff side to prevent it being stolen again.

The location of the chapel isn't clear as you pick your way

down the steps, but suddenly you climb through a small opening in the wall and you're there, inside it! Descend a few paces from the chapel and you will find St Govan's Well, one of over 700 holy wells in Wales. It felt like I'd seen most of them on my trip already. The current version has a small well-house covering it, like the one at St Non's Well, but probably dating to the 19th century. Many tales of cures were told about the well during the 17th to 19th centuries. The well's water was said to be particularly efficacious in curing lameness, eye problems, and rheumatism. Those cured would leave their crutches and walking sticks at the altar of the chapel. We saw none of these. These days, the water or its healing powers have either dried up, those cured are less trusting in where they leave their unwanted medical supports, or they are more aware of the need to re-cycle wherever possible.

It's worth the climb down to the chapel and back, for the view, the setting, and to be in another of those special places. As a place for holy men (and women) and devout pilgrims to visit over the centuries, the chapel and its well are now curiosities for secular tourists like us to tick off their list of Pembrokeshire beauty spots. At one time somewhere for the selfless, it is now somewhere for a selfie. I wonder how many visitors stop to think about the sacred ancient landscape they're in and, like the constant tides that wash the shore below, the steady flow of visitors who have come and gone over the centuries.

We returned to the car, headed back to Pembroke, and then east the short distance to the village of Lamphey. While we were at lunch in a pub in St Davids earlier, we were tipped off about the ruined palace in Lamphey. It wasn't on my original list, but it turned out to be a real bonus. Lamphey Palace was a medieval bishop's palace built in the 13th century as the residence for the Bishops of St Davids. It was essentially where they hung out for some peaceful R&R in rural luxury, and they didn't do things by halves. Over the centuries, it became a grand complex of buildings with a palace, chapel, and a great hall. With a massive corn barn to bring in the finances, a dovecote, deer park, four ponds, and three orchards, the bishops weren't exactly slumming it... the clue is in the word 'Palace.' Their palace was an important centre of power and influence during the medieval period, with the bishops hosting influential guests and holding important meetings and events. After the Reformation in the 16th century, the buildings were dismantled, and the stones were re-purposed through numerous alternative building projects in the area. Today, only the ruins remain, but they are still impressive and provide a glimpse into the grandeur of the palace in its heyday. For me, they are even better than the bishop's palace next to the cathedral in St Davids. We had Lamphey Palace completely to ourselves, and it was free to visit.

We were well overdue another castle visit and luckily, Carew Castle was just a few miles up the road from Lamphey. A castle in Wales is never far away, but their availability shouldn't undermine how wonderful each one is. Carew Castle is another treasure, with the bonus of having the only intact tidal mill in Wales a short walk away. The castle was built in the 13th century by the Normans. It was significantly upgraded during the time of Edward I, but came to prominence in the Elizabethan period when Queen Elizabeth I granted it to Sir John Perrot in recognition of his military achievements in Ireland. He was also rumoured to be the illegitimate son of Henry VIII, which may have had something to do with things. Sir John's military achievements were mainly concerned with keeping disgruntled Irish people under control in their home country. He was also respected for his diplomatic skills in negotiating with the Irish nobility. That CV gave him the ideal credentials for the job of Lord President of the Council of Wales and the Marches, a position that gave him broad powers over the region. His duties included maintaining law and order in this corner of Wales and The Borders, and defending England against potential threats from the Welsh. Part of his job description was keeping pirates and smugglers under control, but it seems he interpreted his brief ambiguously and some of Sir John's considerable fortune came from a mutually beneficial working partnership with the local maritime entrepreneurs. It didn't end well for him, though; he ended up dying in the Tower of London, accused of treason by his political enemies, who alleged that he had plotted with his old Catholic noble friends in Ireland to overthrow Queen Elizabeth I. The three coats of arms on display (Prince Arthur, Henry VII, and Catherine of Aragon) linked nicely to the Tudor story I kept bumping into along my *Journey through Wales.*

The Carew tidal mill, located on the eastern side of the castle, was built in the early 19th century. It was designed to harness the power of the tidal waters of the nearby Carew River to grind corn and wheat into flour. The mill was in use for almost 100 years, and its story is told to visitors on a series of information boards. Looking around, it reminded me of my recent visit to Felin Ganol in Llanrhystud, and it re-enforced how crucially important mills must have been to communities in their day.

Just like the proverbial wait for a bus, a second castle came along almost immediately. Less than 20 minutes after leaving Carew, Jan and I were approaching the gates of Manorbier Castle, on the Pembrokeshire Coast. We were stopped in our tracks by a sign telling us the castle was closed but due to open shortly. I'm not sure that would have cut much ice with 12th century attackers. It's another fabulous castle. Again, there are so many in Wales you can get blasé about it, but here was another cracker – largely intact and with plenty to see, when it opened, not least of which are the stunning views across Manorbier Bay. The castle was originally built in the 11th century by the Anglo-Norman de Barry family, one of the first Norman invaders to settle in Wales. Built on a promontory overlooking the Bristol Channel, it was designed to defend against potential attacks from the sea. Its Great Hall is just that, and there are claims it's the earliest stone building in Wales. Information boards tell visitors just how great the hall was. Diners could be treated to a meal of heron, swan, or even dolphin, washed down with ale, mead, or imported wines… much safer to get off your face with alcoholic beverages than risk drinking unclean water. Gerald of Wales was born in Manorbier Castle in 1140 and it's from his 12th century chronicles that we know much about medieval life in Wales.

In case you're wondering why I've not mentioned HV Morton for a while, he by-passed south Pembrokeshire on his 1930s trip around Wales, but we will catch up with him again at Carmarthen. Coming towards the end of another hectic day, Jan, and I were homing in on Tenby, our next stopover. We were going to look around the town and stay for a couple of nights. After that Jan was going home again and I'd be joined for the last leg of my Welsh adventure with my old pal, Nick. Before Jan and I could rest for the evening, we had one last visit to make, Penally.

If you zoom in on an aerial image of the coast at Penally, about 2 miles west of Tenby, you'll see a bewildering pattern of wavy lines and zigzags cut into the grassy fields that slope back from the clifftops. The area extends over 250 metres from east to west and is about 100 metres wide. At first sight they resemble the Nazca Lines – the strange geoglyphs, or line drawings, etched into the southern Peruvian desert, one of the driest places on Earth. That's a label you'd never associate with Wales, even after the summer of 2022. The nearby Penally Camp, used for military training gives you a clue… the curious lines are the remains of trench systems dug at the time of the World War I. Jan and I parked the car outside the army base and walked a short distance over the fields to look at the trenches. To get to them, you have to cross a railway line, but fortunately there is a tunnel underneath it. Two adjacent signs provided mixed messages as we emerged from the tunnel. The big one said, 'This path will remain open during times of firing.' Next to it, the smaller one included the potentially important additional information, 'Keep out! Military firing range.'

It seems you're OK if the red flag isn't flying, so we pressed on, taking care to follow the public right of way up to the top of the hill. Standing there, next to the information board, the view of the trenches stretches out below you. It's a grim reminder of our past, and the poor guys who quickly had to learn how to build trenches on the clifftops of Wales before being sent to France between 1914 and 1918.

The pretty seaside town of Tenby is probably at its very busiest in August, and it's not a time I'd normally choose to be there. My journey schedule was constrained by some fixed dates, however, such as the National Eisteddfod and the World Bog Snorkelling Championships. No one in their right mind would want to miss either of those.

Tenby is situated on a promontory, bordered by the sea on three sides, and is famous for its stunning beaches, colourful houses, and rich history. The town's centre is enclosed by medieval stone walls, which were built in the 13th century to protect the town from invading armies. It's a familiar story in Wales. Jan and I passed through the walls at The Five Arches Gate, mandatory ice creams in hand, and explored the town's maze of narrow streets and alleyways that are lined with shops, restaurants, and pubs. Shops selling the obligatory beach accessories, such as buckets and spades, crabbing nets, sun hats, and flip-flops, were selling plastic inflatable rugby balls instead of the conventional colourful round balls you might expect if you weren't in Wales. On our way to look at the harbour, we walked past East Rock House, a tall, elegant Georgian house. There was a sign on its blue-painted front wall telling us that Admiral Lord Nelson stayed there in 1802 with his pals Sir William and Lady Hamilton.

While at the town's museum (I don't think there can be another one in the UK with such a magnificent view), we were told about some old tunnels that are rumoured to be under the town. No one has found them yet, but the rumours are numerous. One says they are secret escape routes in case of invasion, and then there's the old tourists' favourite – smugglers. Another theory suggests the tunnels lead from St Mary's Church, underneath Boots the Chemist, to houses near the harbour, providing a getaway passageway for priests during times of persecution. The conversation led us to discuss St Mary's Church, and Jan and I set off to look around. The church, with its striking Gothic architecture, intricate stained-glass windows, and towering spire, dominates the centre of the town. It mostly dates to the 12th century, but some parts are even older. It was already on my list of places to visit because of its memorial stone to a man called Robert Recorde.

I'd always thought that mathematical symbols had their origins in ancient civilisations such as the Egyptians, Persians, and Arabs, but apparently it was a Welshman who invented the equals sign! Robert Recorde was a physician, mathematician, and astronomer, who was born in Tenby in 1510. He is known for many contributions to mathematics and is said to have introduced the world to the equals sign in his 1557 book, *The Whetstone of Witte*. Prior to this, mathematical equations were written out in words or abbreviated phrases. According to legend, Recorde was inspired to create the equals sign while in debtor's prison, where he became frustrated with the tedious process of writing out equations. We've all been there. After falling on hard times, Recorde died in a debtors' jail in London, having been sued for defamation by a rival. In death, all men are equal, and it's something Robert Recorde would have been able to express more succinctly than most. This slightly sombre train of thought seemed to block the usual prompts that make the jukebox in my brain come up with a song for the moment. Instead, it dragged out an old Bob Dylan quote, 'All this talk about equality. The only thing people really have in common is that they are all going to die.'

I was cheered up again by the sight of an OS benchmark

on the outside of the church. That, and another ice cream, and I was good to go again. Jan and I had a nice meal out that evening and looked back on what was undoubtedly a hectic and varied few days for her. She kindly pretended she'd really enjoyed it, and I promised her a more relaxing holiday next year.

11

TENBY TO PORT-EYNON

I should introduce you to Dr Nick Lindsay, my travelling companion for the last section of my *Journey through Wales*. Nick made a cameo appearance on the pages of Chapter Six when I described a visit we both made to Bangor back in the 1970s. Anyone who has read my *Journey through India* (profuse thanks to both of you) will be well acquainted with Nick… but please continue reading the rest of this book anyway. Nick's highland estate is in Brora, on the northeast coast of Scotland and like me, he's a senior person who hasn't admitted it yet. At the beginning of 2022, I asked Nick if he'd like to join me for a shot at the World Bog Snorkelling Championship. The event was due to take place in Llanwrtyd Wells in August. I can't repeat his two-word reply in full, but it ended in 'off' and roughly translates to 'no.' On the other hand, he was more than happy to come along and support me with my attempt, which he interpreted as meaning he would drive around his country of birth for a few weeks, going to interesting places, and drinking beer.

I thought it might take Nick a while to adjust to the new west coast time zone, and as he'd driven all the way down from near John o'Groats, I gave him the luxury of a morning off in Tenby to get over his road lag. Sarah and Jan had both somehow survived a few weeks with me, and I knew Nick would soon get up to speed. His legendary ability to adapt and thrive in challenging circumstances has been well proven over the years, as his fan base would be quick to confirm. It turns out we both have family connections with the south Pembrokeshire area: his father lived in Kilgetty when he retired, and my dad was stationed at Tenby with the RAF in the 1940s.

Given the time pressure on my agenda, I couldn't be too lenient with the old chap, so we set off by late morning for Saundersfoot, just a few minutes' drive along the coast. We were both feeling excited to hit the open road again on our first adventure together since India in 2020. Saundersfoot is a charming coastal village, famous for its sandy beaches, picturesque harbour, and scenic coastal walks. Legend has it that the village got its name from the arrival of St Issels, a 6th-century Irish saint, who sailed across the Irish Sea in a coracle. She was welcomed on the beach by a local chieftain and his people, who presented her with a sandal, or 'saint's foot' as a gift. With her sandal firmly in the door, the village was subsequently named after the famous foot-related event.

When we arrived in Saundersfoot, we just about squeezed Nick's car into the very busy public car park and headed to the beach for a look around. Sensing the chance to get more feedback on what it meant to be Welsh, we dived into a beach café, ordered a couple of coffees, and chatted with the woman behind the counter. Annie, from London, had lived in the village for just over 2 years; she's another person who came for a holiday and stayed. She absolutely loved the area and said she'd already been accepted completely as one of the locals, although I had to question that when I found out she hadn't yet been presented with a pair of flip-flops by the local chieftain.

I was keen to find out about a gentleman called Bill Frost, whose story was so nearly the opening pages of the history of flight. Bill is said to have flown an aeroplane from the village in 1904, several years before the Wright Brothers' first powered flight. He was a poor and humble carpenter, but legend has it that in the winter of 1876, a gale was blowing so strongly that it lifted Bill several yards through the air while he was carrying a long plank of wood. You see plenty of kite-surfers copying Bill's pioneering technique to this day. The experience sparked an obsession with flying for Bill Frost, who felt he was onto something that could really take off. With little formal training, he built a flying machine using bamboo, canvas, and wire, in the workshop of his house on St Bride's Hill in Saundersfoot. He achieved several successful flights, reaching heights of up to 15 metres. Crucially, for his chances of historic immortality, he lacked independent witnesses to those first flights, and most importantly, he had no photographic evidence. It would never happen nowadays; he'd have posted a selfie within seconds of landing. In 1894, he applied for a patent for his flying machine, which has been described as a cross between a glider and an airship, equipped with two reversible fans designed to raise the machine into the air. Sensing he was on the verge of some-thing extraordinary, but too poor to continue development, he applied to the government for funding. He was brought down to Earth and left disappointed… fiscal constraints in challenging economic circumstances, competing budgetary priorities, lack of proven application market etc. With an ironic twist that is almost too painful to contemplate, he was told the government had no intention of using aircraft either for navigation or for warfare. They usually know best.

Nick and I asked around to see if there was a monument to Bill Frost, or perhaps an information board, but we found nothing. Maybe we were looking in the wrong place, but no one we met seemed to know about the man who could have been Saundersfoot's most famous resident.

We cruised down to Amroth, another picturesque coastal village with another long sandy beach. The village has a rich industrial past because of its coal and iron ore deposits, but it's the beach and quiet countryside that attract visitors today. The weather was balmy, and the sun high in the sky. We rendezvoused with my sister-in-law Lesley and her husband Arthur, holidaying in the village. Over a leisurely lunch in the grassy garden of the New Inn, we relaxed and enjoyed the stunning sea views. We met a young couple who'd just completed the Pembrokeshire Coast Path, all 186 miles of it from St Dogmaels in the north of the county. They looked ready for a pint. It would have been *so* good to stay for the rest of the afternoon, maybe with a short stroll along a section of that coastal path, but we had a journey to continue. We headed inland towards Whitland, a small town with a big part in Welsh history.

I must admit that before the visit, I hadn't heard of the Laws of Hywel Dda, but I came away thinking it was one of the most important things I'd discovered on my *Journey through Wales*. After a bit of a struggle, Nick and I found the amazing Hywel Dda Centre, built by local subscription, with its interactive exhibits, a reconstructed courtroom, a medieval herb garden, and a 'Boston copy' of the original laws. Hywel Dda, or Hywel ap Cadell, was King of Deheubarth in southwest Wales during the early 10th century. The Laws of Hywel Dda are based on traditional Welsh laws and customs, which King Hywel Dda brought together, reformed, and consolidated into a unified legal code for his kingdom. They remained in use until the 16th century. That's quite boring, I hear some of you say – but no, it's really not!

What made the Laws of Hywel Dda so radical and important was how they established a level of social and legal equality that was unheard of in Europe at the time. The laws applied to all free men and women, regardless of their status, and placed a strong emphasis on individual rights and responsibilities. The laws allowed women to own property and to inherit from their husbands (that still doesn't happen in many counties to this day) and they provided protection for widows and unmarried women. They also established clear rules around marriage and divorce, and provided for the protection of children and the elderly. The laws set out specific penalties for crimes such as theft and murder, and placed limits on the use of capital punishment. The Laws of Hywel Dda were based on the Welsh concept of 'cynghordy' or consensus, in which disputes were settled through mediation and negotiation rather than by force or trial. In contrast, English laws relied heavily on adversity, combat, oaths, and judicial proceedings. The Welsh laws were particularly notable for their emphasis on the principle of equality before the law, regardless of social status or gender. English law was heavily influenced by feudalism and placed greater emphasis on the rights of the nobility. I came away thinking how much better things might have been if the rest of Britain had adopted the Welsh laws instead of Wales having to follow the English ones.

We visited the remains of Whitland Abbey, where monks had once lived in silence and contemplation, and where the Laws of Hywel Dda had been drawn up. Back home in Scotland, Nick is the chairman of a local heritage society, and he was keen to explore every nook and cranny of the ruins. He loves that stuff. I was content to sit back and bask in the eerie atmosphere, imagining the ghostly shadows of long-dead scholars and holy men.

Our next stop was the charming town of Laugharne (Talacharn), a place famed for its association with the poet Dylan Thomas. The town's name is pronounced 'Larn.' It was another undiscovered jewel (for me at least) – the river views and castle are incredible, especially if you're as lucky as we were with the weather. Nick and I followed the Laugharne Heritage Walk along the banks of the River Taf (Afon Taf), which winds its way through the town, on its way to Dylan Thomas's boathouse and writing shed, where the writer wrote some of his most famous works. It was in Laugharne in 1953 that the poet wrote his famous play, *Under Milk Wood*. It features a fictional village called 'Llareggub,' thought by many to be inspired by the writer's time in Laugharne. In the book, Llareggub (try reading it backwards) is a place full of eccentric characters and weird happenings.

A footpath takes visitors past Laugharne Castle and alongside the River Taff

Our circular walk took us alongside some lovely woods to St Martin's Churchyard, where we visited the writer's grave, and then back through the town. Dylan Thomas's grave is located on a hill overlooking the estuary of the River Taf, a peaceful, and tranquil spot surrounded by trees and greenery. The headstone of the grave is a simple, unassuming slab of white marble, inscribed with his name, dates of birth and death, and the epitaph: 'And death shall have no dominion,' a statement of the eternal nature of life and the resilience of the human spirit in the face of mortality. Nick and I made our way to Brown's Hotel, a pub where Thomas was a regular and which is said to have inspired his play, *Under Milk Wood*. Passing a house called Elton Cottage, Nick nodded in its direction and said, 'That's still standing.' Nice! I looked around in desperation for something to inspire a witty riposte.

You don't see many of those old General Post Office

(GPO) red telephone boxes these days. Maybe there's no call for them. They must assume everyone has mobile phones these days, which could be a problem in places where mobile phone ownership is low. I was glad to see a rare example of an old GPO phone box in the middle of Laugharne, but as we walked past, I could see it had no phone; the box now housed a defibrillator. 'Anyone dashing in there to make an emergency call is going to get a bit of a shock,' I said to Nick, determined to even things up after his Elton Cottage wisecrack.

Just before we'd completed our circular tour and arrived back at Nick's car, we got chatting to a lovely old local guy (he was probably younger than us) called Barry. We were reading one of the information boards in the village and he came over to tell us more about the place. It turned out he was a local alderman and former portreeve. In case you're wondering, because I certainly was, a portreeve is a member of a group (a corporation) elected to look after a town and its lands according to the town's ancient charter. Once he'd briefed us on the town's history and his role in its current administration, Barry went on to say, 'Mind you, now I mainly just sell junk.' I think he meant the upcycled, formerly owned trinkets, distributed randomly on the pavement, on the other side of the road. I took advantage of having someone else to quiz about 'Welshness.' 'Well,' he said, pausing to get our full attention, 'the most avid Welshmen in this town are the incomers.'

The road took us next to Carmarthen, one of the oldest towns in Wales. It has a mish-mash of old and new architecture, with many historical buildings dating back to the 18th and 19th centuries. One of the town's most notable landmarks is its 13th-century castle, which was yet another important stronghold for our old friends, the Normans. I felt I was fighting early symptoms of castle fatigue. The town also has a regular market, which has been operating since Roman times. Although I can't put my finger on anything particular, I didn't warm to the town. Fortunately for Carmarthen though, we were back on the route taken by HV Morton, and he loved it. He describes a town full of character – the most lively market town he'd seen on his travels around Wales (Morton, 1932). We owed the town more time really, but after an hour or so looking around, we continued on our way to Burry Port (Porth Tywyn).

The small coastal town of Burry Port looks out over Burry Inlet (Aber Tywyn), where the River Loughor (Afon Llwchwr) reaches the sea, towards the north coastline of the Gower Peninsula (Penrhyn Gŵyr). It played a key role in the development of the coal trade in South Wales and was a major centre for the production and shipment of tinplate, with exports from the port reaching their peak in the early 1890s, when Wales was producing 80% of the world's supply of the material. Today, it is quieter, and much less tinny, but still boasts a picturesque harbour and a pleasant town centre. Nick and I drove down to the harbour to find out more about the tin trade. One of the interpretation boards there told us about the Ashburnham Tinplate Works. It was a large manufacturing plant that operated from the late 19th century until the early 20th century, employing over a thousand people, making it one of the largest employers in the town. The plant was known for producing high-quality tinplate that was used in a wide range of products, including food cans, gas canisters, and other metal containers. The plant began to decline in the early 20th century, as competition from other tinplate manufacturers increased and demand for tinplate products decreased.

Continuing the flying theme from Saundersfoot, Nick and I had come to Burry Port to see a monument that celebrates a piece of aviation history. As the sun reached its apex on the 18th of June in 1928, the people of the town were treated to a sound unlike anything they had heard before. The low hum of engines grew louder and louder until it was impossible to ignore. Their gazes turned skyward to see a bright orange aeroplane approaching from the west, with the word 'Friendship' emblazoned across its fuselage. It was a Fokker F.VII Tri-Motor monoplane, fitted with floats for water landings. Where on Earth had that come from? Well, it had taken off from Newfoundland only 20 hours earlier – not that an Atlantic crossing mostly in fog would have seemed like 'only' 20 hours to those onboard. The plane made a circuit around the town, dipping low enough to give the onlookers a good view, before slowly descending towards Burry Inlet. And with that touchdown on water, history had been made.

You're not likely to recall the names of the American pilot, Wilmer Stultz, and his co-pilot/mechanic, Lou Gordon. That's because all the headlines were taken with the name of their passenger, Amelia Earhart, who had just become the first woman to cross the Atlantic by aeroplane. She went on to achieve great things in the world of aviation, including, in 1932, being the first woman to fly solo across the Atlantic, landing in Ireland.

But back to that historic day in South Wales in 1928. Where exactly did the plane touch down? Two villages lay claim to the honour, Burry Port and its neighbour, Pwll. Both have monuments to the record-breaking crossing. According to some sources, when Amelia Earhart opened the window of the aircraft and asked where she was, the reply from the locals was 'Pwll inlet!' The plane was then towed into the harbour at Burry Port, so when the crew of three stepped ashore, they had 'landed' at Burry Port. That explanation seems to satisfy the honour of both parties, so let's go with that.

Inspired by Amelia Earhart, Nick and I flew up the A484 towards Llanelli, exchanging a string of awful and predictable schoolboy puns about making a splash, tidy landings, and fast Fokkers. Nick and I were heading for Port-Eynon, on the Gower Peninsula, to stay overnight in the youth hostel there. We still had at least two stops to make before then, one at

Felinfoel, and another at Penclawdd, a village on the Gower Peninsula that is famed for its cockles.

HV Morton stopped at Llanelli in 1932, when the town was still known by the anglicised version of its name – Llanelly (it changed in 1966). Several hot and sweaty pages of his book, *In Search of Wales*, are devoted to his visit to a steel foundry which was a typical sight in the town (Morton, 1932). They are no longer a typical sight. Although there's still a tinplate rolling and coating facility in Trostre, Llanelli, the last foundry shut down in 2015. We had no option; without a steel foundry to visit, we'd have to find a brewery instead. Luckily, we were homing in on the small village of Felinfoel, just north of Llanelli. It has a big claim to fame: it is home to the oldest brewery in Wales – The Felinfoel Brewery.

There are a few exceptions, as I was to find out later, but I normally seem to be unusually lucky on my adventures, and so it proved to be with our visit to the brewery. Nick and I popped into the office and asked, using our most pathetic pensioners' expressions, if there was any chance of a tour around the brewery. Unfortunately, the brewery didn't do that sort of thing. The very friendly woman on reception, Wendy, told us how they used to have a museum, but that it was now closed. I mentioned my trip around Wales and my book, and brought up the subject of the first ever beer cans. In 1935, The Felinfoel Brewery was the first brewery in the UK and the second in the world to sell beer in cans. Wendy told us they still had one of those original cans in the brewery, but it wasn't on public display. Nick and I consoled ourselves with a look around the shop. While we were working out what to buy, Wendy slipped out of her office. She came back a minute or so later and said, 'I've had a word with the boss; follow me.' She led Nick and me through to meet Captain Beryn Charles Martin Lewis, Director of Felinfoel Brewery, representing the 5th generation of his family in the company. Captain Beryn told us how the family business was in good hands with a 6th generation also working in the brewery and a 7th generation recently born. The captain only had a few minutes to spare, but he was very generous with his time and spent much longer with us than he first planned. He came across as quite a character, a former Welsh guardsman who was proud of his former military duties, which had included guarding Queen Elizabeth II. He showed us the famous original tin can and explained how it came about.

The brewery dates from 1878. John Lewis, its founder, had worked at the Dafyn Tin Works before he started the brewery. The Lewis family continued to be involved in the tinplate industry in the area and by the early 20th century, the Dafyn factory exported tin all over the world, even becoming known as 'roofers to Australia.' When the market crashed with the 1930s depression, they had to think of some alternatives. The combination of a brewery and a tin business in the family led to what now seems inevitable – tin cans for beer! It's quite something to think of all those cans of beer you see in the shops and on the supermarket shelves today, and how it all started in that brewery in Felinfoel. Think of that next time you pull the ring on your can of beer. It was a very content couple of visitors who left the brewery with arms full of gift packs and Felinfoel pint glasses. Wendy and Captain Beryn had come up trumps for us and made us very welcome – another lovely example of Welsh generosity and hospitality.

It's a drive of about 15 miles from Felinfoel to the Gower Peninsula, another beautiful part of Wales and, in 1956, the first place in the UK to be awarded the status of AONB. Its vast, sandy beaches, dramatically rocky coastline, and unspoiled countryside make it a perfect destination for walkers and nature enthusiasts. The numerous walking and cycling trails that crisscross the peninsula include the 35-mile Gower Way. You can find some lovely villages and towns on the peninsula, such as Mumbles, Oxwich, and Llangennith. Rhossili Bay has breathtaking beauty and has been described as one of the best beaches in the world. If its rich cultural heritage you're after, there are plenty of historic sites and landmarks dating back to the prehistoric period, include King Arthur's Stone, the medieval Oxwich Castle, and St Mary's Church in Rhossili. A notable event from prehistory was the main reason Nick and I were on the Gower.

To begin with, we were heading for the village of Penclawdd, on the edge of the Burry Inlet. When the tide is out, the 6 square mile area is a flat, fairly desolate expanse of wet sand. The village was on my 'must do' list of places to visit because of the fantastic description of the cockle women of Penclawdd in HV Morton's book. I wanted to see if there was any trace of the industry left today. He tells how he saw an army of about 200 women of all ages, sheltering by a stone wall as they waited for the tide to drop low enough for them to dash out and begin their work. With their shawls over their heads, they looked like a ragged Bedouin tribe as they perched on the hindquarters of their donkeys to ride up to 3 miles out to the cockle beds. The donkeys trotted as fast as their loads would allow, and then waited, catching their breath, before making the much slower walk back, after the women had scratched around in the sands using hand-rakes and sieves for a few baskets of little seafood delicacies. They may well be delicacies, but on the only occasion I'd tried them in the past, they seemed like little gritty school erasers pickled in salt water. Maybe I should try them again.

The village of Penclawdd has a long history of cockle picking, going back to the Roman period. Traditionally, the cockles were hand-picked by women and children, and taken to Swansea and other nearby towns to be sold. By the 20th century, there were up to a thousand pickers in the village. Nick and I pulled into a place selling seafood to see if we could find out more. We got chatting to a guy who was just tidying up after returning from the sands on his tractor. He told us how the number of people digging for cockles has dropped enormously in recent years, since licensing was brought in to protect the area from over-harvesting. Just a few dozen licensed pickers take about 1000 tons per year from the

Burry Inlet nowadays. The cockle beds are carefully managed to ensure they don't get overcrowded or over-harvested, but if you're really keen, we were told that members of the public can take up to 8 kilos of cockles a day for their personal consumption. Who needs that many you may well ask, in a slightly nauseous tone. Anyway, I felt I was getting a bit closer to that Welsh breakfast I'd first attempted to buy back in Chepstow.

Our final destination that day was Port-Eynon, a lovely little village with a blue flag beach, on the southern tip of the Gower Peninsula. After checking in to the youth hostel (what a location), Nick and I took a stroll along the beach where we found, much to Nick's delight, the remains of an old salt house. We were in Port-Eynon because the youth hostel was there, but the following day we were going to see, about a mile up the coast, one of the places I'd been most looking forward to on the whole trip – Paviland Cave.

12

PORT-EYNON TO CARDIFF

When I was researching my *Journey through Wales*, I kept coming across the story of the Paviland Cave on the Gower Peninsula. After reading numerous accounts and watching several videos, I had to go there. And because he was with me, so did Nick.

Sometimes referred to as 'Goat's Hole,' Paviland Cave is one of the most famous archaeological sites in Europe. The cave is formed in near vertical limestone sea cliffs, high above the water level. Measuring approximately 10 metres long by 4 metres wide, and up to 3 metres high, it looks out across the Bristol Channel, and has maintained that lonely vigil for thousands of years. It's difficult to get to. You either have to approach it with climbing gear, dropping 20 metres on a rope from the clifftops, or approach it from sea level, which requires precise timing to be there at low tide. I've already explained my views on dangling from ropes.

What's so special about the Paviland Cave? When William Buckland, a theologian and distinguished geologist, explored the cave in 1823, he thought he'd found a Roman burial site. It contained the partial remains of a skeleton, which had been stained with red ochre powder. The remains were surrounded by ivory objects and perforated periwinkle shells, all similarly stained. It was clearly someone special who had been buried there, and with some ceremony. Buckland thought he was looking at the bones of a woman, and the find became known as the Red Lady of Paviland. You can see what he did there, and it made perfect sense at the time. Apart from getting the sex and age of the skeleton wrong, Buckland was spot on. Much later investigations in 2008, using radio-carbon dating, confirmed the remains were those of a man in his early twenties, and they would have been there for around 31,000 years before the Romans arrived, making them the earliest evidence of a ceremonial burial in Europe. It's likely that the Red Man of Paviland belonged to a small group of hunters who came from lands we now call France. They would have followed the herds of game that roamed the tundra, which covered the areas left behind by melting glaciers. The bones are now on display in the Oxford University Museum of Natural History.

Nick drove us around the coast from Port-Eynon and we parked at the side of the B4247 near Pilton Green. The coastal cliffs of Paviland were half a mile away. We followed a footpath that skirted around the edge of some recently ploughed and very dusty fields. The last part of the approach to the sea is down a steep-sided, rocky ravine that requires a bit of scrambling. Although I say it myself, our journey had been timed to perfection. We sat in the sun on a rocky outcrop near the base of the cliffs and enjoyed the cool, salty sea breeze on our faces as we watched the mesmerising rhythm of the waves and waited for the tide to reach its lowest point. Only then can you cross a short stretch of sandy beach to get to the opposite side of the ravine and work your way along the base of the cliffs before scrambling up to the cave. It was just 15 minutes before low tide – good job!

It was such a delightful day to be there; the sea was a beautiful deep blue, seabirds wheeled overhead, and apart from us, there wasn't a soul in sight. After about half an hour of patient wave watching, and a brief, slightly one-sided conversation with a seal, we began to suspect something wasn't right. The tide didn't seem to be going out. I checked the tide tables again, and then made sure that the low water time stated was BST, not GMT. I checked the tide tables again. Eventually, it became clear that the tide was coming in. We trudged wearily back to the car, a little deflated. To be honest, a lot deflated. We weren't going to see what should have been one of the highlights of our trip. A sweet feast of juicy black-berries from the hedgerow helped to counter the bitter taste of disappointment and allowed us to re-focus on our mission.

What had gone wrong? Well, it seems not all low tides are created equal. People used to living by the sea, previous boat owners, and qualified RYA Coastal Yacht Masters (no names mentioned) should know the difference between a spring low tide and a neap low tide. Spring tides occur when the gravita-tional pull of the sun and moon are in alignment, which causes the highest high tides and lowest low tides. Neap tides occur when the gravitational pull of the sun and moon are at right angles to each other. That causes the lowest high tides and highest low tides. That might sound like something from the Donald Rumsfeld book of lunar influence, but in short, we'd arrived at low tide, but it wasn't low enough. You need a spring low tide, the lowest of lows, to get across to Paviland Cave. I hadn't seen any mention of that.

A Welsh breakfast would put us back on track, so we headed for Swansea. Nick was confident we'd find the tradi-tional variety in the market there and his confidence turned out to be well founded. But before we searched out the market, we went to the museum. In fact, we went very briefly to two of them. The excellent Swansea Museum is the oldest museum in Wales and in it we found everything from an Egyptian mummy to a replica set of Red Lady of Paviland bones. It raises an obvious question – why weren't the real bones there? We didn't have time to do the National Water-front Museum justice, of course, but the quality of the content we did have time to see was matched by the impressive nature of the building – a 1901 dockside warehouse which was once used to store goods arriving at Swansea's busy port.

Swansea Market is a bustling indoor market located in the heart of the city centre, with stalls selling everything from fresh groceries and meat to clothing and souvenirs. There was plenty of local produce on view, which was fare enough. It didn't take long for us to home in on the seafood section, next to which was a salon offering a range of waxing and grooming services. The list of treatments looked like a smorgasbord of potentially excruciating experiences and not for the squeamish. I suspect you'd be lucky to have a 'back and crack,' without considerable discomfort, and even a 'speedo line' might be a close shave. Nick said he had cash available if I was tempted, but I quickly changed the subject. I told him I was on a mission to find a breakfast – the only cockles I wanted to think about were the sort that come with a greasy fry-up and a big mug of tea.

I found a café that offered a proper Welsh breakfast. It resembled a super-sized full English breakfast with the addition of cockles and laverbread (bara lafwr or bara lawr). The latter is a slimy green seaweed that has been described as 'Welshman's caviar.' I suspect my meal would have fed everyone who was in the market that day. It became a challenge, and in hindsight, I don't know why I persevered with it to the bitter end. The cockles were fine, but the laver bread was quite disgusting – to my taste at least. Thinking back, I should have suspected something when Nick said he was just going to have a cup of tea. He chuckled at my discomfort like a true pal as we left the café. I waddled uncomfortably over to the seafood stalls to speak to a woman behind the counter. She told me the cockles on her stall were fresh from Penclawdd that morning, but her Welshman's caviar had been brought by lorry from Scotland.

When we got back to the car, I was still feeling a bloated discomfort in the gastric department, and wondered what the rest of the day could possibly throw up. I needed a change of scene.

One of the most impressive sections of the National Waterfront Museum tells the story of the main industries of Wales, highlighting the crucial role that Wales played in the Industrial Revolution. While we immediately think of coal, iron, and steel, the role copper played was also important, but it never seems to get the same headlines. It was crucial in applications such as electrical wiring, plumbing, machinery, and cladding for ships. In the early 18th century, Swansea was a small market town with a population of around 2,000 people, but over the following 150 years, it became the centre of the world's copper industry.

The first copper works in Swansea were established in Landore in 1720 by Dr Lane and Mr Pollard, who had owned copper mines in Cornwall. The availability of copper from Cornwall and South Wales, coupled with the development of new smelting techniques, led to a rapid expansion of the industry in Swansea. Local coal mines provided the fuel needed to power the furnaces, keeping transport costs down. The River Tawe (Afon Tawe) provided a natural water source. Waterwheels powered huge bellows, which blew air into the copper smelting furnaces. Forced air was necessary to keep the fire burning at high temperatures to remove impurities from the copper ore. The river also provided a source of power for other industries in the Swansea Valley, including the tinplate and steel industries. Boats and barges were used to transport raw materials and finished goods to and from the smelting works, and the nearby Bristol Channel provided easy access to international markets for the finished copper products. The peak of Swansea's copper trade occurred in the mid-19th century, when tens of thousands of workers employed in over sixty copper works produced around 90% of the world's smelted copper. They called it Copperopolis!

As demand for copper began to decline in the early 20th century, many of the copper works closed, leaving a legacy of environmental damage and social upheaval. As mines were demolished, a new landscape emerged but a few traces of the old one can still be seen today. Nick and I stopped off on the banks of the River Tawe just south of the city's football stadium, at the site of the old Hafod-Morfa Copperworks. When it first opened in 1810, it was the largest industrial works in Europe. While most of the original site has been demolished, there are still a few surviving buildings and structures in various states of repair. There's a trail that takes visitors around what remains of the site, and some interpretation boards, but from what we saw, there's a lot of work still to be done. That should now be taking place because the city was awarded funds under the government's 'levelling up' programme to continue the renovations and to create better links to the city centre. Nick and I found the old rolling mill and counting house. At the rolling mill, copper ingots would have been heated and passed through rollers to produce the different thicknesses of copper sheets. The counting house was where they kept tabs on the company's money. One of the most recognisable features of the old site is the 50-metre-tall Hafod-Morfa chimney. Being a geologist, Nick couldn't stop himself from scratching around in the dirt and undergrowth around the remains of the old melting house, which was used to melt the copper ore and cast it into ingots. He uncovered what I called a few lumps of rock with green stains, but he called it copper ore… he was holding a piece of Copperopolis.

We're both mapping nerds, so Nick and I later looked up the Hafod-Morfa site on the old large-scale maps of the Swansea Valley. Using the excellent National Library of Scotland website (https://maps.nls.uk/), we viewed the OS 25-Inch map of the area (1892–1914), side by side with a modern aerial image. We could see that Nick had parked us right in the middle of what was the Hafod Copper Works, just across from the Swansea football club stadium, which is where the old Landore Alkali Works used to be.

We left Swansea behind us and headed towards Cardiff. Passing by the built-up areas of Port Talbot and Bridgend, Nick drove us along the pretty country lanes of the Vale of Glamorgan, in sunny rural loveliness. I was very impressed with the area, and now I might have to add Llantwit Major to my shortlist of favourite Welsh towns, along with Beaumaris, Conwy, St Davids, and Laugharne.

Llantwit Major is famous for being the site of St Illtud's Church, so Nick, and I made a beeline for it as soon as we arrived in the town. The current day building was constructed by the Normans in the 11th century and rebuilt in the 13th and 15th centuries. The Grade I listed building is one of the most renowned ancient parish churches in Wales and is sometimes referred to as the 'Westminster Abbey of Wales.'

The church is beautiful, and has its own rich history, but what lies underneath it makes Llantwit Major very special, and enormously significant in the history of Christian Britain. Somewhere beneath the current day church are the remnants of a college for priests that dates to around AD 395. There seems to be some debate among scholars and historians regarding its exact nature. According to some sources, it was a Roman school called the College of Theodosius, named after the Emperor Flavius Theodosius. Other sources suggest it was called Côr Tewdws (Bangor Tewdws) and part of a Celtic monastery. Whichever it was, the site is considered by many to be the first school in Britain and possibly the world's first university. That would mean it was teaching students before the famous universities of Oxford, Paris, Cairo, Bologna, and even Nalanda in India. Being near the coast, it almost goes without saying that the place was trashed by pirates and had to be rebuilt. In the early 6th century, the college was re-established by St Illtud, after which it became known as Bangor Illtud, or Illtud's College. With over 2000 students at its height, including members of the nobility and prominent religious leaders, Illtud's College sounds like a training academy for saints. Its impressive list of alumni includes St Patrick of

Ireland, St Baglan, St Tudwal, St Gildas, and St David of Wales. Its influence on the intellectual and spiritual life of its era cannot be overstated, making it a hugely significant part of Welsh and European history.

When we'd looked around the church and its grounds, Nick and I took a mid-afternoon break. We sat in the sunshine by the war memorial in the centre of the town, although Llantwit Major felt more like a village somehow. It seemed to have everything – it was set in lovely countryside, had a nice beach, a nearby castle, enormous historical significance, and was a short drive to Bannau Brycheiniog or Cardiff. There was no shortage of hostelries – we were sat opposite the Tudor Tavern and The Old Swan Inn. To our left was the White Hart pub and the road running alongside us was Wine Street. We feasted on Glamorgan sausage rolls and raspberry Danish pastries from the *Windy Wick Bakery*, washed down with delicious coffee from the *Café Vélo*. The café was keeping a steady stream of lycra clad road cyclists topped up as they stopped off for a breather on their tours around the Glamorgan countryside. It looked like the peloton had just dropped in at the end of a Tour de France stage. There were a few millennial riders, but most were in the MAMIL category (Middle-Aged Men in Lycra). Not that I can talk; I've long since passed into the OGIL category myself (Old Geezers in Lycra). Sarah from the bakery was a great advocate for the town and she reeled off a long list of things to do and places to see. Like many people growing up in rural Wales, she had longed for the bright lights of the city as a teenager. She later realişed just how great her hometown was and returned as soon as she could. I mentioned my book and she insisted we check out two things: the nearby beaches and St Donat's (Sain Dunwyd) Castle. A friend of Sarah's, who was an archaeologist, had told her about two leg bones that had been found in the cliffs at nearby Monknash beach in 2014. After the gruesome discovery had been reported, the police cordoned off the area and began their investigations. Fortunately, there had been no foul play. The bones turned out to be the 800-year-old femurs that once held a Cistercian monk off the ground. Monknash was the site of a grange in the Middle Ages, a farm run by monks to provide food for the monastery at Neath. The burial ground of the monks was near to the sea and over the years, coastal erosion had exposed the poor man's legs to the light of day once more. When we'd downed the last of our coffee, Nick and I headed for the beach at Col-huw Point before going in search of St Donat's Castle.

It was less than a mile to the beach, winding along the steep-sided valley of the Afon Col-huw. Thick deciduous woodland covers the steep sides of the picturesque valley, and there is a nature reserve at the end, near to the sea. When we arrived at the beach car park, the tide was out. Wide horizontal beds of rock stretched out to the shimmering sea, which sparkled in the afternoon sun. We were looking across the Bristol Channel to the hills of Exmoor, about 18 miles to the south. Cyclists must be regular visitors because there was a public tyre pump and set of tools available in the car park. We spent a few minutes walking along the beach, which seemed very quiet. I speculated on how different the scene would be if we were in Devon or Cornwall, while Nick scratched around at bits of rock in the cliffs. There was no harm in it, and fortunately no legs either.

Fair winds of optimism and curiosity filled our sails as we headed a short distance west again to find St Donat's Castle. After following a quiet country lane for about a mile, the satnav voice directed us onto what turned out to be a private road. A no entry sign and a metal barrier across the road brought a sudden halt to our progress, rapidly taking those fair winds out of our sails. I went into the reception building. In front of me, a couple of very well-dressed teenage Chinese girls were politely asking the security man about taxis to Cardiff. When they'd finished, I asked him if we could please visit St Donat's Castle. The good news was that we were on the right road to the castle. The bad news was that it wasn't open to the public. These days, the castle is now part of something called the Atlantic College. There was no way we would be allowed to visit unless there was a special event taking place – and there wasn't.

I went back to the car to give Nick the bad news. Neither of us had heard of Atlantic College, so we looked it up on the Internet. It's a residential school founded in 1962, the first of eighteen United World Colleges (UWC) around the world. The campus is spread over 122 acres of parkland, with stunning views of the Bristol Channel and Welsh coastline. Based around the 12th-century St Donat's Castle, the school has been dubbed 'Hogwarts for hippies.'

The castle was purchased in 1925 by the American newspaper magnate, William Randolph Hearst, who used it as a summer home. He made extensive renovations to the castle, including the addition of a 25-metre indoor swimming pool, Italian marble floors, French tapestries, and an impressive art collection including paintings by famous artists such as Rembrandt and Rubens. It reminded me a lot of Nick's house, but without the cats. Hearst's lifestyle at the castle was just as extravagant as the decor. He hired a private orchestra to play music during his lavish parties, which included guests such as Winston Churchill, George Bernard Shaw, and Charlie Chaplin.

Hearst may have been eccentric, but he was also a philanthropist. He donated St Donat's Castle to the National Catholic Community Service in 1956, and it was later used as a conference and retreat centre before becoming the home of Atlantic College in 1962. The current school has a diverse student body made up of around 360 students from over 155 countries. Aged between sixteen and nineteen, the students study the International Baccalaureate Diploma Programme, and the college places a strong emphasis on community service, intercultural understanding, and environmental sustainability. Half the places are available for eye-watering fees, while the other half are awarded based on bursaries that allow students from disadvantaged backgrounds to attend. The school attracts an impressive roll call of European royalty. From what we could see from the entrance, the campus buildings and the grounds of the college seem immaculate, and on such a lovely day in such a beautiful corner of Wales, it looked idyllic. Nick and I wondered if those students knew how lucky they were.

As far as our chances of seeing the castle were concerned, that was that then. Or was it? We checked the map (no surprise there) and came up with a Plan B. As well as being Sustrans Cycle Route 88, the road outside the college was part of the Valeways Millennium Heritage Trail. By continuing along the road towards Monknash and then following the Heritage Trail down a public right of way towards the sea, we could skirt around the outside of the Atlantic College campus and visit St Donat's Church, which was right next to the castle.

St Donat's Castle and St Donat's Church

The footpath led us down a wooded valley that contained a dried-up stream. Nick and I temporarily left the bright sunny day behind as we walked through the dappled light created by an overhead canopy of sycamore, alder, and elder trees. A scurry of grey squirrels bustled and fidgeted among the trees and along the path, as if curious to see who the new visitors were. We were soon at the church, tucked away in a clearing in the woods. Next to it rose the high stone walls of the 12th century St Donat's Castle, described by the writer Bernard Shaw as 'What God would have built if he had had the money.' The medieval church is worth a visit in its own right and Nick and I spent a very contented half an hour enjoying its architecture, beauty, and calm sense of timelessness. Heading up the footpath back to the country lane where we'd left the car, we looked across to the college campus to see a few students chatting and giggling as they ambled along in the warm summer sunshine, and into the castle. Some of them might even have been princesses.

Our next stop was St Cadoc's Church, in the small village of Llancarfan, near to Barry, and about 12 miles southwest of Cardiff. Built on the site of a 7th century monastery and founded around AD 1200, it looks from the outside to be just another beautiful, small Welsh village church. But inside, you will find what has been described as 'One of the finest paintings of its kind anywhere in Christendom.' During maintenance work in 2005/06, some lime-wash was knocked off one of the walls inside the church to reveal a curious red line. It took 12 years of patient and careful work by conservationists to remove twenty-one coats of lime-wash, distemper, and emulsion, flake by flake. Eventually, a beautiful, floor-to-ceiling, 15th century painting of George and the Dragon was revealed. It didn't stop there – the more they looked, the more they found, and eventually they uncovered paintings known as Death and the Gallant, the Seven Deadly Sins, and The Acts of Mercy. The works of art had been covered up at the time of the Reformation, when Protestants rejected excessive church decoration to create more austere places of worship. The paintings cover several walls and are awe-inspiring. It's well worth taking your time to soak up the atmosphere and put yourself back in the late 1400s. In their day, the paintings were the equivalent of today's newspapers, and websites – designed to depict biblical scenes, stories, and medieval folk-lore, making them accessible to those who couldn't read or write. They reinforced Christian teachings and morals, reminding the faithful of the rewards of virtue and the deadly consequences of sin. As a cautionary heads-up, fire breathing serpents seem to await you if you get led astray by any little horned devils and don't behave properly.

Behaving properly, we continued towards Cardiff, with two more places to visit on the way. Our penultimate stop was going to be Lavernock Point (Penmynydd Lavernock), but on the way there we dropped into a field between the villages of St Lythans (Llywneliddon) and Dyffryn to see what is charmingly known by the locals as 'The kennel of the greyhound bitch.' The field where it is found also has a local name, 'The accursed field' because nothing will grow in it. Nick and I tramped across the ill-fated rural enclosure, nego-tiating a minefield of cow pats, to see the St Lythans cham-bered tomb. What we found were the rocky leftovers of a once great Neolithic burial site. Similar in design to the dolmen at Pentre Ifan, the St Lythans remains were just three huge blocks of sandstone, arranged like three sides of a rectangle, with a massive conglomerate rock capstone (4 metres by 3 metres by 0.7 metres) on top. That would weigh about 35 tons and take a bit of shifting in Neolithic times. There is no sign of the 12-metre wide by 30-metre-long mound which once covered the stones, but a lot can happen in 6,000 years. This house of the rising sun (here we go again, cue The Animals) was aligned to face the east, presumably to give the dead occupants a warming sight to begin each new day, but we'll never really know what was in the mind of the architects all those sunrises ago. Their thoughts and reasons have been lost in time, the gaps filled by legends and folklore. The kennel name derives from a story about King Arthur leading an epic chase for a monstrous wild boar… presumably accompanied by a female dog that needed housing overnight. Like its nearby neighbour at Tinkinswood, the full story of the burial chamber will remain a mystery, but these places inspire wonder when you visit them – at both at the structural engineering required for their construction and at the beliefs and motivation that resulted in such awesome and long-lasting structures.

Fighting the temptation to dive into *Gavin and Stacey's* hometown of Barry to see what was occurring at the amusement park, we drove down to Lavernock Point, just south of Cardiff. I won't lie to you, it was tidy, bordering on lush. The headland is situated at the mouth of the River Severn and is popular with fossil hunters, drawn to the numerous finds that regularly crop up in the alternating layers of limestone and shale. It's the sort of place I could lose Nick for hours, possibly days, but I had to reel him in and focus on why we'd gone there. On a wall, in front of an achingly beautiful little church, there is an understated little plaque that tells its readers: 'Near this spot the first radio messages were exchanged across water by Guglielmo Marconi and George Kemp.' In 1897, Marconi chose Lavernock Point to build a wireless transmission station. When he sent the first message 6 miles across the Bristol Channel, from Lavernock to Flat Holm Island, it paved the way for modern wireless communications technology. In 1901, Marconi upped the distance significantly when he used the same signal station to send the first transatlantic radio signal. It must have been mind-blowing at the time, but is something we take for granted now, especially now everywhere in the world is connected via satellites. Places like Lavernock Point bring to life how different things were only a few generations ago.

We continued to Cardiff, the capital of Wales, since 1955. As I'd conned Nick to drive me around South Wales for a couple of weeks, I had to allow the lad a misty-eyed tour around his old haunts of Peterston-super-Ely and Roath Park. I would relate the story of him rowing his school sweetheart around the lake there, but it's too painfully emotional for me to go there again.

Although obviously not to the same degree as Nick, HV Morton was also sentimental about Cardiff. He considered it to be the only attractive city to have come out of the Industrial Revolution, and that Cathays Park was a remarkable collection of public buildings (HV Morton, 1932). Morton's detailed description of Cardiff in the 1930s includes a paragraph on the Chinese quarter, down by the docks. At the end of the 19th century, poorly paid Chinese sailors were used by the East India Company to transport goods like tea and silk to the UK. When new labour laws were introduced in the early 1900s, Chinese sailors found it hard to be employed on ships, so many turned to running laundries and restaurants instead.

A detailed discussion on the relative merits of chicken satay versus beef chow mein somehow led Nick and me to a Chinese meal that evening. According to our sources (which were also sweet and sour, and black bean) there's not much left of Cardiff's historical Chinese community to be seen today. In the Cardiff Bay area, once the centre of the city's Chinatown, there are a few buildings and landmarks, and they also have an annual Chinese New Year celebration, which includes a parade, dragon and lion dances, and other cultural activities.

HV Morton's description of the city is fascinating, and it would be great to spend a week or so to see what's left of the place he saw. Like most of the stopovers on the road trip, however, this one was frustratingly brief; it's just how it must be in order to see a whole country in a few months. We had the following day to look around Nick's home city, but then we had to move on. Cardiff was the gateway to explore the long fingers of the South Wales valleys that radiate northwards, towards the hills of the Bannau Brycheiniog.

13

CARDIFF TO LLANWRTYD WELLS

A look around the Cardiff Bay area was a great way to start the day. Ours was going to be a busy one, so we were up early on a very quiet Sunday morning to see as much as we could. Judging by the amount of fast-food debris around the water-front car park, the Saturday night crowd were very enthusiastic about vehicle interior cleanliness. I guess it's the same in any big city. Nick and I seemed to be the only two people about as we approached the impressive Welsh National Assembly Building, also known as the Senedd, home of the Welsh Parliament. We walked up a set of wide grey steps to the entrance and looked out across the bay, over a mirror-like surface of blue water on another glorious, and almost silent, summer morning. The Senedd is a bit of an architectural statement – a striking modernist building designed by Richard Rogers and completed in 2006. Its enormous rectangular flat roof, propped up on thin metal posts, hovers over a massive block of glass and steel. Very impressive. Just around the corner from the Senedd, Nick showed me The Millennium Centre. It's another striking modernist building, topped with an amazing copper-coloured dome, inscribed in both Welsh and English with the words, 'In These Stones Horizons Sing.' Nick will never read this, so it's safe for me to write that I was very impressed by the Cardiff Bay area. It was nice to have it all to ourselves… apart from a few seagulls looking for leftover kebab wrappers.

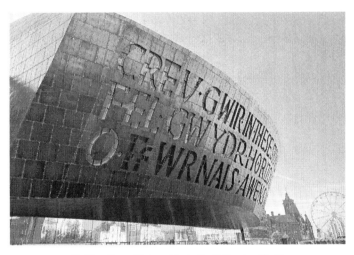

'In These Stones Horizons Sing' - The Millennium Centre

The car park where we parked was next to the city's famous Norwegian church, a beautiful example of Victorian Gothic architecture, with its distinctive tower and spire. The little white timber building was originally constructed in 1868 as a place of worship for Norwegian sailors who were visiting the busy port. After it was decommissioned in the mid-20th century, the building fell into disrepair and was eventually abandoned. In the 1990s, a group of Welsh and Norwegian volunteers came together to restore the building and turn it into a stylish arts centre and community space. Near to the building, there's a statue that looks like a mosaic of cracked white ice. It commemorates, 'The heroic Age of Arctic Exploration, and in particular Captain Robert Falcon Scott's expedition of 1910–13.' It was from Cardiff Bay, in 1910, that Scott's ship the SS Terra Nova set off on its ill-fated expedition to the South Pole.

As a proud Welshman, Nick pointed out what he saw as a

major flaw in my journey planning. I hadn't included the Millennium Stadium. It's a key symbol of Welsh pride and identity, as well as one of the city's major landmarks. I believe the correct name is now the Principality Stadium, because of a sponsorship agreement, but sometimes the original name sticks – I still think of the Hampshire County Cricket ground as 'The Rose Bowl.' Nick had a good point; with a seating capacity of around 74,500, the Millennium Stadium is the largest stadium in Wales and one of the largest in the UK. Located on the riverside right in the city centre, it's hard to miss it. I reminded Nick that midsummer isn't the best time to be visiting rugby grounds and I cunningly distracted him by raising the subject of the football World Cup. Only a few weeks earlier, Welsh football fans had left the Cardiff City Stadium in raptures, singing joyfully in the rain, and dreaming of sunny days in Qatar. A free kick from Gareth Bale (ex-Southampton) in a 1–0 win over Ukraine meant that Wales had qualified for the World Cup for the first time in 64 years. It turns out Wales is now a nation of football fans, as well as rugby fanatics. That seemed to do the trick. We drove off in search of Llanrumney Hall, with Nick dreaming of his World Cup heroes returning in triumph from Doha, riding around Cardiff in an open-topped bus. Gareth Bale and Michael Sheen were both holding the FIFA World Cup Trophy aloft, red ribbons streaming in the breeze as the huge crowd roared out a deafening version of Yma o Hyd.

Before Nick had time to come back to reality, we were in Llanrumney, on the northeast outskirts of Cardiff. We were parked opposite, and looking at, Llanrumney Hall. Back in Chapter Nine we came across Captain Henry Morgan, arguably the greatest of the 'brethren of the coast' who ever lived. Some sources say he was born in that very same Llanrumney Hall, in 1635, although I couldn't find a definitive record to confirm it. We couldn't look round the place and there was no one to ask, so the search for pirate gold or even an early morning glass of dark rum ended there and then. We

drove off to the opposite side of the city, on a new search...
for a late breakfast. By now Nick had returned to Earth and
he was reminding me of all the other Cardiff landmarks we
weren't visiting. Cardiff Castle, The National Museum, and
Llandaff Cathedral were all fair points, but the last place on
his list was St Fagans National Museum of History, and we
were on our way there. He thought we might even add a visit
to Castle Coch (Red Castle) on the outskirts of the city when
we headed for the Taff Vale (Cwm Taf) later in the day.

St Fagans National Museum of History is an open-air
museum in the grounds of St Fagans Castle, about 5 miles
from Cardiff city centre. The museum's mission is to promote
and preserve the culture and heritage of Wales, which it
achieves admirably by showcasing over forty historic buildings that have been moved to the site from different parts of
the country. Nick and I wandered around, looking at everything from an Iron Age roundhouse, via a 16th-century farmhouse, to a 1980s council flat. It's like stepping back into
Welsh daily life at different points in history. Seeing a reconstructed house from the 1960s in a museum was a sobering
thought... I was growing up then. It makes me realise, a) how
much things have changed in a relatively short time, and b)
how I need to keep moving in case I also get put into a
museum. The place was quite busy, as you'd expect in the
middle of a beautiful summer's day, but it was never too
busy. It was always easy to go inside the buildings and look
around at our own pace, which in our case wasn't rapid.
Museum staff, appropriately dressed for the relevant period,
waited patiently at many of the buildings to answer visitor's
questions. I loved it, especially the row of ironworkers'
cottages (and their gardens) originally built in Merthyr Tydfil
(Merthyr Tudful) in the 19th century. I can't think of anywhere
else in Britain to match St Fagans Museum on such a scale.
We had our late breakfast and then set off in search of our first
castle of the day.

We headed up the A470 towards Taff's Well (Ffynnon Taf)

and shortly after negotiating a roundabout that contained an area of land about the size of a small county, there it was on our right – Castle Coch (Red Castle). You can't miss it as you head up the Taff Vale; its imposing presence looks out from the hillside just north of the M4, that sinuous blue line on the map that snakes through South Wales and prevents Cardiff's urban sprawl from swallowing up places like Tongwynlais and Taff's Well.

Castell Coch was built by John Crichton-Stuart (1847–1900), the third Marquess of Bute. He was a Scottish nobleman who inherited extensive estates in South Wales and became a major figure in the history of Cardiff. His legacy includes many of the city's most iconic buildings and landmarks. One of his most notable contributions was his investment in the docks. Shipping coal from the Welsh valleys helped to make Cardiff one of the busiest ports in the world by the end of the 19th century and it also helped the Marquess of Bute to become one of the richest men in the world. He was a patron of the arts and had a penchant for Gothic Revival architecture. Between 1875 and 1891, he employed the renowned architect, William Burgess, to build Castle Coch in the style of a medieval fortress in stunning local red sandstone. I always think it looks like a Bavarian Castle, high on the steep valley side of the Danube. William Burgess also got the contract to renovate Cardiff Castle, turning it into one of the most impressive and ornate castles in Britain.

As we continued further north along Taff Vale, on the road towards Pontypridd, Nick and I were heading for one of the most iconic and well-known regions of Wales: 'The Valleys.' We were going to drive right up to the Heads of the Valleys road and into the Bannau Brycheiniog National Park. After that, we were going to make a quick dash up to Llanwrtyd Wells, before coming south again. The Valleys were going to occupy quite a large part of the rest of my *Journey through Wales*, so with that in mind, I should set the scene.

The Valleys of South Wales were heavily industrialised in

the 19th and early 20th centuries when they became the focus for mining coal and iron ore. They include the Rhondda Valley, the Cynon Valley, the Taff Valley, and others. They are characterised by tightly-knit communities in towns and villages that are often strung out along the valley floors. The South Wales coalfield played a crucial role in the growth and development of those communities, and cities like Cardiff, Barry, Newport, and Swansea. Its peak economic power was in 1913 when it produced a staggering 57 million tons of coal and employed over 234,000 miners working in hundreds of pits. The South Wales coalfield was the largest coalfield in Britain, and Cardiff and Barry became the two largest coal-exporting ports globally. Coal remained a crucial industry in South Wales throughout the 20th century, but its nationalisation in 1947 marked a turning point. The National Coal Board (NCB) became the region's largest employer. But by then, the industry was in decline. From the early 1970s, the industry faced further economic pressures, as oil became available as an alternative energy source and cheap coal was imported from abroad. The decline of the coal industry was further accelerated by the year-long miners' strike of 1984 to 1985. A sweeping closure programme ultimately ended coal's status as a significant employer in South Wales, leading to an economic and culture shock in the Valley's communities.

Nick soon got us to the village of Taff's Well, which is where you will find the only thermal spring in Wales. That unique status, along with my well documented left knee issues, seemed good enough reason to stop off and check the place out. The natural spring has a constant temperature of 21.1°C and has been famous for its healing properties for centuries. When the British Geological Survey researched the origin of the spring water, they found it had fallen as rain in the hills 15 miles to the north of Taff's Well approximately 5,000 years ago. Nick turned onto the old A4054 road that goes through the village, sandwiched between the river and the railway, and parked next to a small public park. A footpath leads towards the river, past a bowling green, to a modest stone building that houses the spring. There's an information board that explains the history of the well and the properties of the spring, but when we arrived, there was no one around, and no way of getting into the building. We could see inside, and there was a sign that read 'One of Wales' most unusual natural wonders.' Well, it probably is, but we couldn't see much of it. It felt like a visitor attraction opportunity going begging, but it was good to find out later that Ffynnon Taf Primary School now uses the warm spring water to keep its heating bills down.

Visits to Rockfield Studios, Bron Yr Aur, and the National Eisteddfod had provided an eclectic soundtrack to my journey so far, but I wasn't expecting the musical theme to continue into our next visit – a cheese company. Always expect the unexpected. Before we left the village of Taff's Well, Nick and I had an appointment to meet Tom Pinder, founder of The Welsh Cheese Company. We found the building near the middle of the village and Tom showed us around.

A Welsh cheese online retailer and wholesaler for the previous 5 years, Tom opened up a shiny new shop in Taff's Well in 2022, to become the first 100% Welsh cheesemonger in the UK. While he showed us around his premises, Tom told Nick and me about his background and how he ended up selling Welsh cheese. He went to Cardiff University at eighteen to study music. He left in 2002 and spent several years touring the world as a musician, playing trombone with his funk-punk crossover band from his university days, and later accompanying the Scottish singer, songwriter, and musician, Paolo Nutini. Tom neatly pulled together a couple of strands from my *Journey through Wales* when he told me he'd been recording with Paolo earlier in the year at the Rockfield Studios. Welsh readers might know Tom as a founding member of the national football team's official supporters' band, The Barry Horns. It's named after the Welsh footballing legend Barry Horne, who played fifty-nine times for the national team, won the FA Cup in 1995 with Everton, and later became chairman of the Professional Footballers Association. I might be biased, but from my point of view, the fifty-two appearances that the hard tackling box-to-box midfielder made for Southampton between 1988 and 1992 were the real pinnacle of his career.

Several factors combined for The Welsh Cheese Company to come into being in 2017. Tom popping round to sample the cheese at the dairy farm just down the road from where he grew up in Somerset might have had something to do with it. A self-confessed cheese fan, he enjoyed the wide range of amazing Welsh cheeses he found in Cardiff's delis and farmers' markets when he went to university in the city but became frustrated that he couldn't get them from a single source. He's a vegetarian and, like many of us these days, he began to pay more attention to the source and quality of the food he was eating. His solution to these combined issues was to plug the gap in the market himself by bringing together a dozen or so top-quality Welsh cheeses and promoting them from his own one-stop-shop. Sensibly, he started small and gradually scaled up as demand grew. He started in a small room, keeping the cheese in a small domestic fridge. At this point in the conversation, Tom showed Nick and me inside his latest refrigerated storage unit, which was considerably larger than the room he first started working in 5 years ago. It was spotlessly clean, and its neat racks contained over sixty varieties of cheese from fifteen different producers. His team now regularly sends out over a thousand orders a day to all parts of the UK. They could be individual cheeses, combinations, hampers, gift boxes, or cheese wedding cakes. At Christmas time, they even sell huge cheese advent calendars. Tom said the staff numbers vary according to demand, but he can usually bring people in at short notice when they're needed. Most of them are fellow musicians.

Tom puts the quality of Welsh cheeses down to the country's landscape and the long tradition of localised cheese production. All that Welsh rain produces superb rich pasture, whether it's on the high mountains or fertile lowlands. He was very modest in handing the credit to the producers, but he has been brilliant in putting together the one-stop-shop he first envisaged all those years ago. Speaking to Tom, and people like Rob Jardine of Halen Môn Sea Salt, Anne Parry of Felin Ganol watermill, and Nigel Smith of Gwaun Valley Brewery, it's the passion for their work that comes across so strongly. Perfecting the products, the traditional artisan food, and the drinks they're producing are like personal missions for each of them, and you can just see their enthusiasm gushing out as they talk.

Nick and I had spent most of our visit in the warehouse part of the business, but it will come as no surprise that we had one last place to visit before we left – the shop. It's no surprise either that we ended up with so much cheese that Tom had to post it back home for us. We drove away, playing our usual schoolboy game of making up our own song lyrics. Nick soon beat my version of the Eurythmics' classic, 'Sweet cheese is made of this' with some lyrics from a famous Carpenters' hit, 'So listen very Caerphilly.' It kept us amused, which doesn't take much, for the short drive via Pentyrch to the foot of Garth Hill (Mynydd y Garth)… or is it Garth Mountain?

Garth Hill lies on a small ridge of hills running from west to east at the lower end of the Taff Vale, bounding the edge of the floodplain for Cardiff's three rivers – the Ely, Taff, and Rhymney (Elai, Taf, and Rhymni). Garth Hill has two high points, the loftiest of which is 307 metres above sea level and lies on the Taff Ely Ridgeway Walk. The alignment of the ridge is unusual in a post-glacial landscape that has mainly left the rivers and valleys running north-south. There were at least two good reasons to climb the hill… so we did.

The first reason was the view; it is incredible for the relatively modest height of the hill and must be one of the best views in South Wales. Fortunately, we had a clear day, and we could easily pick out the Severn Bridges, the Bristol Channel, and the coastline of Somerset. Looking to the south, we traced the line of the Taff Vale into the city of Cardiff with its skyline dominated by Cardiff Castle, the Millennium Stadium, and the Pierhead Building (somewhere else we'd missed). In the west, the view extended over the Vale of Glamorgan, and to the north we could identify Caerphilly (Caerffili) and the Rhymney Valley. The second reason we climbed the hill was because of our background as OS cartographers. In 1995 there was a film, directed by Christopher Monger, called *The Man Who Went Up a Hill and Came Down a Mountain*. It was set in a small Welsh village during World War I and tells the story of a cartographer (played by Hugh Grant) who arrives in the village to survey a nearby summit. When his measurements show that the hill is just shy of the 1,000-foot mark needed to be classified as a mountain, the villagers decide to pile more earth on top to make it taller. The film was partly filmed on location in the village of Taff's Well and features scenes of Garth Hill.

After our usual burst of lairy photos, posing on and off the triangulation point, (which is decorated by a red Welsh dragon), we came down the mountain, which strangely enough, just felt like a hill on the way up. We continued towards Pontypridd.

The towns of Caerphilly and Llantrisant both lie a short distance either side of the Taff Vale. The former is about 2 miles to the east and the latter is a little further to the west. Sadly, Nick and I didn't go to either of them on this trip, but it would be rude of us to continue northwards without me mentioning a couple of things about each one.

Traditional, handmade Caerphilly cheese has a fresh, lactic, mildly lemony flavour, and a slightly crumbly texture. I agree with HV Morton (1932), who preferred to eat a simple meal of Caerphilly cheese with bread and butter in a field rather than the meals offered by most hotels (Morton, 1932).

'Caerphilly' was originally produced in the area from about 1830, to extend the shelf life of milk. It gained popularity by becoming the underground snack of choice for Welsh coal miners. Its thick rind made it easy to carry and its high salt content was handy for replenishing minerals (sweat) lost during arduous manual labour at the coal face. The importance and historical significance of Wales' most famous cheese was recognised in 2018, when it gained Protected Geographical Indication (PGI) status.

As well as being famous for its crumbly white cheese, Caerphilly is home to one of the finest castles in Wales. It is Britain's second largest after Windsor and the third largest in Europe. But although size matters, it's not everything. The castle's architecture is a stylish blend of medieval military magnificence and Gothic confidence. Its massive round towers, octagonal turrets, and intricate stonework are surrounded by a series of artificial lakes or moats, which are fed by the nearby River Rhymney. The strategic location of the castle, close to the border between Wales and England, made it a key stronghold for both sides during the relentless wars between the countries in the 13th and 14th centuries. Although the castle was partially ruined in the 18th and 19th centuries, it's perhaps no surprise to discover it was restored to its former glory in the early 20th century by the third Marquess of Bute. The magician and comedic genius, Tommy Cooper, was one of the town's most famous sons and his statue stands opposite the castle, '…just like that.'

Llantrisant is a small town in the county borough of Rhondda Cynon Taf, overlooking the Vale of Glamorgan and the River Ely. The 13th-century Llantrisant Castle and the 15th-century St Illtud's Church are evidence of its rich historical heritage. In fact, it's more than rich – the town is minted. The Royal Mint moved there in 1968 from London. It made a nice change. Llantrisant was chosen from a shortlist of contenders from elsewhere in Britain. Close enough to London to tempt existing staff to relocate, it had access to major transport routes, a stable workforce, and suitable land for the construction of a shiny new facility. At the time, James Callaghan was the MP for nearby Cardiff. His job as Chancellor of the Exchequer, and therefore Master of the Mint, probably didn't harm Llantrisant's chances of selection.

The next time you're thinking about hygienic and cost-effective alternatives to traditional burial, and we all do it, remember the name Dr William Price. He was an eccentric and flamboyant figure who lived in Llantrisant in the 19th century. There is a statue dedicated to his memory in front of the town hall and a plaque on the wall of his former home. He was a man of huge intellect and unorthodox dress sense, who became a member of the Royal College of Surgeons before the age of twenty-two. He was known for his unusual beliefs, including his rejection of Christianity in favour of Welsh Druidism, and his interest in cremation to dispose of the dead. His disapproval of eating meat led him to prescribe a vegetarian diet to his patients instead of medicines. As a no-nonsense, zero-tolerance kind of guy, he refused to treat any of his patients who wouldn't give up smoking. Price believed that marriage should be abolished and was a great advocate of free love, which resulted in him fathering several illegitimate children. It made him a figure of great controversy in those socially conservative times. When his five-month-old son sadly died, Dr William Price cremated the boy's remains, which landed the doctor in big trouble. He was arrested and charged with the illegal disposal of a corpse. His clever defence, which resulted in his acquittal, was that although cremation was not legal… it wasn't illegal. Although Price hadn't used a public crematorium, his son's cremation is considered to be the first recorded in Wales and the start of the modern cremation movement in Britain. Dr William Price died in 1893, but his legacy lives on. In 1862, the marriage rate in England and Wales (marriages per 1,000 people, per year) was 22.5. By 2019, the most recent year for which data are available, the marriage rate had almost exactly halved. We are regularly reminded of the need to eat our five fruit and vegetables per day, and to consume less meat. By law, cigarette packaging must warn about the dangers of smoking, and cremations now outnumber burials by nearly four to one… so maybe Dr Price was more ahead of his time than just plain crazy.

Because HV Morton passed through The Valleys way back in the 1930s, we can't blame him too much for not writing about Pontypridd's most famous son – the legendary Sir Tom Jones. 'The Voice' was born in Treforest, Pontypridd, in 1940, and he's sold over 100 million records. Aside from his successful music career, Sir Tom has also been a coach on the UK and US versions of the TV show, 'The Voice' since 2012. He presumably also has an unrivalled collection of female underwear, if the stories about women throwing their knickers at him at concerts are true.

HV Morton went to great lengths to describe the Pontypridd chain factory of Messrs Brown, Lenox, and Co. He described the factory, which was established in 1817, as looking like something from the beginning of the Industrial Revolution (Morton, 1932). It operated until 1939 and was a major producer of chains for coal mines, industrial machinery, and ships, including the RMS Mauritania, the RMS Queen Elizabeth, and the RMS Queen Mary. The iconic photo of Isambard Kingdom Brunel posing in front of vertical lines of enormous chains, wearing his 'stovepipe' hat was taken in 1857. The chains behind him were for the SS Great Eastern and were made at the Brown Lenox works at Pontypridd. Nick and I made our way to the site of the old factory, which is shown as, 'Newbridge Chain & Anchor Works' on the 19th century OS map of the town. We drove down Brown Lenox Road and parked in a retail centre car park next to Curry's, exactly where the old factory would have been. There's nothing to see now. The Taff Trail, just to the north of the car park, is the nearest you'll get to a link to the past as it runs along the alignment of the old Glamorganshire Canal. The waterway was used to transport finished chains from the Newbridge factory to the port of Cardiff. Maybe the town planners had a sense of humour when they looked at the old site, allowing a change of use from chain factory to chain store.

Nick and I shared a brief exchange of not very funny chain-related songs, but by the time we finished with 'Chain Reaction,' 'Unchained Melody,' and 'The Chain' by Fleetwood Mac, we had exhausted our very limited knowledge of the subject. After I'd consulted my spreadsheet to remind us of the agenda, Nick drove us less than 6 miles along the Cynon Vale (Cwm Cynon) to our next stop, at Mountain Ash (Aberpennar). Like many towns in The Valleys, it grew in step with the mining industry during the 19th century and had over eighty collieries at its peak. The town's population reached its height of around 30,000 in the early 20th century, but it also declined in step with the coal industry, and is now just over 7,000. We stopped in the town to visit the statue of Elaine Morgan OBE. She was a pioneering writer, evolutionary theorist, and the second woman to be honoured as part of a campaign called, 'Hidden Heroines,' created by the not-for-profit organisation Monumental Welsh Women. The campaign aims to highlight the contributions of women to the history and life of Wales by erecting five statues honouring five Welsh women. The other women on the list are Betty Campbell, who was the first black female headteacher in Wales, the suffragettes, Lady Rhondda (Margaret Haig Thomas) and Elizabeth Andrews, and Sarah Jane Rees, a Welsh language poet, novelist, and children's author.

Mountain Ash was a short diversion from our main route northwards up the Taff Vale and we dived back south again to get back on piste and continue towards Merthyr Tydfil. The name of our next stop is likely to send a shiver down the spine of anyone from my generation – Aberfan. The Aberfan disaster occurred on October 21st, 1966, when the waste tip from a colliery slid down the side of a mountain after heavy rain. A mud and waste landslide engulfed the village and resulted in the deaths of 144 people, including 116 children. It was one of the worst disasters in Welsh history. The tragedy led to a public inquiry and changes in mining regulations, as well as a wider discussion about the responsibilities of government and industry in protecting communities from harm. I can still remember, as a twelve-year-old, watching the black and white images on television at home, and the shock that everyone felt at the time.

Nick parked close to the Aberfan Disaster Memorial Garden, on the site of the former Pantglas Junior School, which was at the centre of the disaster. The Memorial Garden is beautiful. It is immaculately maintained and very peaceful. Low walls divide it into sections, showing where the original walls from the junior school would have been. While we were there, several other people dropped by. Like us, they read the tributes, absorbed the atmosphere, and quietly paid their respects. It is by no means a tourist attraction, but maintaining the memory of what happened in Aberfan is important, as is remembering those who died, and why it happened. The most poignant moment for both Nick and me was when we heard the squeals and laughter of young children coming from the neighbouring infant school playground.

We carried on, thoughtfully, along the A4054 to visit our second castle of the day, in Merthyr Tydfil. I remember being driven through the town as a child by my parents on a grey, wet, and windy day in the 1960s. I can't recall where we were going, but I remember thinking that it was surely the most depressing town I'd ever seen. Not that I could have seen that many in my short life up till then. Maybe it has changed, maybe it was the sunny weather of 2022, but I saw the town with different eyes this time.

But first the background bit. Back in the mid-1700s, Merthyr Tydfil was a small farming village at the head of the Taff Valley. It might have stayed that way if it wasn't for a history-changing combination of geology, human enterprise, and good timing. By the mid-19th century, those factors had turned this extraordinary place into the largest iron-producing town on the planet. The first railway locomotive to operate in the world did so in Merthyr Tydfil (the Penydarren Tramroad Locomotive, built by Richard Trevithick in 1804), and the area's long tradition of Puritanism, Chartism, and working-class community led the town to elect James Keir Hardie as the first Labour MP in Wales. This all came to light, for me, at the town's hugely impressive Cyfarthfa Castle, which I cannot praise highly enough. The castle, and the whole history of Merthyr Tydfil, was a revelation to me, and what I discovered there turned out to be one of the most memorable take-aways from my whole journey.

The Industrial Revolution began in Britain in the mid- to late-18th century. It had its roots in the textile industry, with the invention of the spinning Jenny by James Hargreaves and the water frame by Richard Arkwright. Those innovations were quickly followed by advances in power sources, particularly the steam engine, and the development of the transport infrastructure through railways and canals. There was a clamour for iron and steel, and for coal and coke to make and power the new machinery. To make iron, you need iron ore, coke (made from timber and coal), and limestone (to line the kilns). With all the raw materials on its doorstep, Merthyr Tydfil was the right place at the right time. It just needed the right people to make it all happen.

Enter, Anthony Bacon and William Brownrigg, who came down from Cumberland in 1765 to lease the land that eventually became the famous Cyfarthfa Iron Works. Brownrigg had experience in the iron trade. Bacon had built his fortune from the slave trade and was looking for new things to do with his money. They set up three furnaces, which thrived. After the death of Bacon, the Cyfarthfa enterprise was eventually taken over by Richard Crawshay. After some teething troubles, his considerable investment was richly rewarded. By 1797, Cyfarthfa's four blast furnaces were producing 7,000 tons of iron each year. Admiral Nelson even visited in 1802 to check out where and how his Navy's cannons were being produced. The writer Benjamin Malkin described the Cyfarthfa Works as 'The most extensive and important iron work in Europe, and in that case, as far as we know, the largest in the world.' (Malkin, B.H. 1804. The Scenery, Antiquities, and Biography, of South Wales: From Materials Collected During Two Excursions in the Year 1803. TN Longman and O. Rees UK. p154). Cyfarthfa wasn't the only ironworks in the area. Some sources (see England, 2019) describe how the nearby Dowlais Ironworks was, for a while, the largest and richest company in the world. It must have been the Apple of its day.

Nick and I spent a very enjoyable couple of hours visiting Cyfarthfa Castle. No expense was spared by the Crawshay family when they built the Gothic-style mansion in the early 19th century. Originally intended as a private residence, it was later used as a hospital during World War I, and as a school in the mid-20th century. Today, it is open to the public as a museum and art gallery, showcasing the history and culture of Merthyr Tydfil and the surrounding area. From its large bay windows, you can enjoy panoramic views of the town and valley. You can just imagine the Crawshay family standing in the same spot, looking across the valley at the vast expanse of their ironworks on the opposite side of the river, its huge mills and foundries belching out a constant cloud of thick smoke, and the sky glowing orange at nighttime.

Looking at the old town maps, Nick and I could pick out a few remnants of the original works in today's landscape. After a quick cuppa and a slice of Bara Brith (Welsh fruit loaf) each, we drove to the other side of the valley to see what we could find. We parked just off the A4102 and walked across some rough ground, back on the Taff Trail again (which we had seen in Pontypridd), next to the river. We came across a steep cliff face, into which was built several enormous brick arches. They were the features we had spotted from the castle. The flat valley floor on which we were standing was once covered by a huge railway yard. The rails would have gone through tunnels under the brick arches we were looking at, and into the hearths at the bases of the blast furnaces. As is tradition, Nick had a poke around in the dirt (geologists probably have a more technical name for it) and came up with a few handfuls of iron ore. It was another face-to-face encounter with a famous past.

The small village of Trefil is 7 miles north of Merthyr Tydfil and was a short diversion from our main route. Our overnight stopover there turned out to be the high point of our trip. Nick and I were drawn to the village for different reasons. When researching the route for my *Journey through Wales*, I discovered that OS had declared Trefil the highest village in Wales (409 metres). I'm always keen to bag another highest, lowest, biggest etc., so despite claims from other localities, I'm happy to accept Trefil as the loftiest amongst its peers. Nick was more excited about the quarries there. Since Roman times, the area has been an important source of limestone for the iron and steel industries.

A single small road leads in and out of the village. Before we found the quarryman's cottage, where we'd be staying overnight, we went looking for those quarries. I knew I might lose Nick there for days, but it was a risk I had to take. We drove through the village, past two chapels, a pub, a rugby club, and the last of the houses. The road went past an active quarry on our right, and as we continued to climb higher, we entered a more rugged and dramatic landscape. By then, we had entered the Bannau Brycheiniog National Park. We carried on until the road became a track amongst abandoned quarries, in a dramatic looking rocky area that resembled a lunar landing site. Those unreal looking surroundings attract a steady stream of location managers from the film industry. Box office hits such as *Wrath of the Titans* and *The Hitchhikers Guide to the Galaxy* have featured scenes from the lonely hills and quarries above Trefil, as have several popular TV productions, such as *Doctor Who*, *Merlin*, *Sherlock Holmes*, and *His Dark Materials*.

Nick drove us back towards the village a short distance, before parking by the side of the road. We set off on foot along the Cambrian Way, over the open moorlands. Our brief 1-mile-long walk was hardly of Proclaimers proportions, but it wasn't about the distance, it was all about our end goal. We were in search of another piece of Welsh history.

As we climbed higher onto the moors, we were met by a warm and gentle breeze from the south. There was near silence, except for the occasional screech from birds of prey. A steady flow of puffy white little 'Simpsons' clouds (I think the meteorologists would probably call them fair weather clouds) drifted towards the smooth outline of the Bannau Brycheiniog to the north. A big skies open landscape of heather moorland, gorse, and rocky outcrops, stretched for miles in every direction. It was a walk amidst raw natural beauty. Near a Bronze Age cairn named Garn Fawr, we came across a feature shown on the OS map as 'Ogof Fawr (Chartist Cave)'. Despite its remoteness (or maybe because of it) it had a starring role in the social history of Wales.

During the mid-19th century, Trefil played a key part in the Chartist movement, which advocated for political reform and social improvement for the working classes. The Chartists created a six-point People's Charter. The simple principles in the charter were not extraordinary by today's standards; you would expect to see them in any modern democracy, but some of those crazy ideas, like universal suffrage and secret ballots, clearly spooked those in power at the time. In November 1839, the Chartists organised a march to Newport to present a petition to Parliament, but it resulted in violent clashes. The Trefil miners used the Ogof Fawr cave to store and prepare weapons, including pikes, for the rally in Newport. When they were prevented from joining the march by the authorities, the miners responded by organising a protest that led to their arrest and charge for unlawful assembly. The trial of the Trefil Chartists became a famous case, attracting widespread attention and support for the Chartist movement. Although it wasn't an immediate success, the Chartist movement had shifted public opinion and played a crucial role in the development of democracy in Britain. Trefil's contribution is commemorated with a plaque in the village. The cave is regularly visited by walkers, historians, and the purely curious – like Nick and me.

Back on his highland estate on the Scottish northeast coast, Nick lives within sight of a distillery. It's so close, he's probably on a semi-high from the fumes most of the time. It would certainly account for a lot. Anyway, our next stop was my attempt to stave off any complications to our busy itinerary that might be caused if Nick started suffering from withdrawal symptoms. We were heading through the Bannau Brycheiniog, making our way to Mid Wales, and timing our run to be in Llanwrtyd Wells for the 2022 World Bog Snorkelling Championships. The village of Penderyn was on our route and it is home to the Penderyn Distillery. When it was established in 1998, it was the first Welsh distillery to produce single malt whisky for over 100 years. As luck would have it, we were able to tag along on one of their tours. Before it got underway, our guide left us for a while to look around the exhibition area, where we browsed our way through the history of whisky making in Wales. She then took us around the distillery, explaining the whisky production process, stage by stage, as we went along. We were shown the distillery's two copper-pot Faraday stills, designed by Dr David Faraday, a descendant of famous physicist Sir Michael Faraday. The copper and stainless-steel stills use a single distillation method that yields a high-quality spirit with a high alcohol content. We moved to a very photogenic area stacked high with white-painted barrels. They were mainly ex-bourbon and ex-Madeira wine casks, used to impart their own unique flavours to the end product. Our guide told us all about the unique flavours of the end products, which led inevitably to the tasting bar and the shop. You'll never guess what happened there.

Our roller-coaster ride through Wales continued to change topic every time we stopped. Poor Nick! At least I had my planning spreadsheet to give me some idea of what was coming up next. I kept telling him that change is good for you, especially as you get older; it keeps the mind flexible… it's all about neuroplasticity. Anyway, because I was driving to the next venue, I didn't have my two free samples at the distillery: Nick generously stepped up to the mark to drink mine as well as his, so I knew he'd be happy for a while… in fact, by the time he'd had four generous measures of whisky in the middle of the day, he was almost as neuroplastic as a newt.

The black dust hasn't quite settled on the story of coal in South Wales. Our next stop, as we continued to head west, was at the Aberpergwm mine, which has been worked since 1811 as a series of drift mines (horizontal mines accessed through a hillside opening). Its survival to this day is partly due to it being the only producer of high-grade anthracite in Western Europe. Anthracite is a high-carbon coal, which creates a clean burn with low emissions, low sulphur, and high efficiency. Although some of its output goes to the steel-works in Port Talbot, most of it gets finely crushed to produce a product used for carbon filtering in applications such as drinking water treatment and air purification. The colliery was the focus of controversy early in 2022 when the Coal Authority licensed it to produce another 40 million tons. Caught between the conflicting political aims of a Net Zero Strategy, energy independence, and regional support, there was a lot of blame shifting between the various parties involved. Whatever happened to the mine, someone was going to be disappointed. We drove in, trying not to look like climate activists, but expecting a cautious reception. The guy on the gate couldn't have been more friendly and welcoming. He gave us a name to contact for more information about the mine and was happy to pass on as much information as he was able to. There was no underground tour though; that would have to wait until our visit to the Big Pit National Coal Museum at Blaenavon, in a few days' time.

As well as cornering the market in famous pirates, Wales seems to have been a breeding ground for saints. Along with the famous ones I'd already come across so far on the trip, it also turns out that Ireland's own St Patrick could have been Welsh. Patrick was born around AD 387… somewhere. In one of his books, he wrote that he was from a town called Banna Venta Berniae, which is fine, but no one knows for sure where that was, except that it was somewhere in Britain. Possibly. Historical records regarding St Patrick's life are patchy. Some theories suggest St Patrick may have been born in Scotland or even France, but for this trip, he was definitely Welsh.

It seems to be agreed that he was captured by pirates when he was a teenager and sold into slavery. He worked as a shepherd in Ireland until he managed to escape, 6 years later, and found his way to Wales, or perhaps back to Wales. Some sources say he received his religious education at the monastic school of St Illtud, in Llantwit Major. Ordained as a priest, he returned to Ireland to convert the country to Christianity. So, what has all this got to do with my *Journey through Wales?* Well, some historians have identified St Patrick's place of birth as Banwen, about 12 miles northeast of Neath, and the next stop on our route north and westwards. Banwen was a geo-strategic location during the Roman occupation of Britain, and its Roman fort stood alongside the Roman Sarn Helen road. Many historians claim that Banwen was the Roman settlement, Bannavem Taburniae, (which may or may not be the same as Banna Venta Berniae) and the original home of St Patrick. The locals are convinced of this, and they hold an annual parade to celebrate their famous son. We drove past the village sign: 'BANWEN, birthplace of St Patrick' and inspected the St Patrick's Memorial Stone, which is next to the old Roman road. It all seemed plausible, but it's difficult to be sure.

Nick and I continued northwards, bumping along the edge of the Bannau Brycheiniog National Park. On another scorcher of a day, our next stop was going to be a cool place – Henrhyd Falls. It's one of a group of spectacular waterfalls in the area, all linked by the Henrhyd Falls and Nant Llech Trail. The Henrhyd Falls is the highest of the group and the most dramatic. And it's another site where you might well bump into another location manager from the film industry (I've been told films are now referred to as 'movies' by youngsters and cool older people).

Henrhyd Falls has been used as the 'Bat Cave' in *The Dark Knight Rises*, and features in the *Doctor Who* series. I was beginning to think the Doctor might be Welsh with all the time he must have spent in the area. As well as being a favourite spot for walkers and film location managers, the waters of the Nant Llech below the falls are popular with wild swimmers. With an ear-splitting cry of, 'To the bat cave,' the less than dynamic pensioner duo left the Nick-mobile in the small car park near the falls and wandered across to a café van. We cooled off in the shade with a spot of wild ice-cream eating.

It was a short walk to the falls, 15 minutes at most. We set off down the steep valley side, shaded by a dense woodland canopy. The path zig-zagged down into a world of damp emerald greenery and jutting rock formations. Halfway down the side of the valley, we met a local guy who told us he walks to the falls every day. Holy clockwork. He was a real character and was determined to give us his life history in about 3 minutes, without stopping for breath. He tipped us off about a route back that enabled us to turn our walk into a circuit rather than just going there and back. The path continued down the valley side and crossed the Nant Llech via a wooden bridge. Dense woodland, mosses, and ferns appeared to be thriving in a green and humid microclimate, even in the summer of 2022. The first thing you notice, as you're getting close to the falls, is the intense roar of rushing water, which gradually grows louder, adding to your sense of anticipation. You feel the power of the waterfall before you see it, but then it's there in front of you. The falls plunge uninterrupted some 30 metres, past horizontal bands of weathered sandstone. Lush, dense foliage either side of the falls provides a vivid contrast to the white cascading water. The mist rising from the foam created at the base adds to a slightly ethereal atmosphere.

A young couple stood embraced behind the falls, partially veiled by the wall of falling water. I'm sure the moment was a fleeting one for them, as they stood entwined, just them in their own world. Lucky them. It made a romantic scene but spoiled a perfectly good photo. At the risk of sounding unsentimental, I just wanted a photo of pure nature, without humans, and my wait seemed like hours. The couple's hands dropped simultaneously to their sides – great, perhaps they were leaving at last. Without averting my gaze from the falls, my left hand reached down to my utility belt to grab my camera. It was positioned in the usual place, sandwiched tightly between the Batmobile position tracker and the canister of shark repellent spray. But the couple re-engaged in another close embrace. Holy entanglement. Nick made his way closer to the falls and I decided to join him. I'd get the perfect photo of the falls as we left, as long as there was no one else in view by then. While Nick was examining rock formations, the loved-up couple finally left the space behind the waterfall, probably off to check some other film location. The place was temporarily deserted.

Standing behind the falls, almost enveloped by a translucent screen of falling water, is quite an experience. The sound is amplified in the enclosed space of the dark and shadowy

Batcave behind you, creating a deafening roar that seems to resonate as it fills the space. You feel the cool mist from the waterfall on your face, and it feels like the force of the water is vibrating the rocks on which you're standing. With your view of the outside world distorted by a curtain of water, you suddenly feel quite small compared to the overwhelming power of nature that's a couple of metres in front of you.

Feeling re-energised by the falls, we set off for the National Showcaves Centre for Wales, just over 7 miles further up the Swansea Valley (Cwm Tawe) from the Batcave. Like the Henrhyd Falls, the caves at Dan-yr-Ogof are another product of the remarkable geology of the area through which we were travelling. In a nutshell, the Bannau Brycheiniog National Park comprises successions of sedimentary rocks laid down between the late Ordovician period (for example, mudstones and siltstones) through to the late carboniferous time (for example, millstone, limestone, and coal). Add to that mix a slice of faulting and folding, and then a lot later, a scrape of glaciation. The result is a rounded mountain range of mainly Old Red Sandstone rock. Folds and faulting have created numerous waterfalls and the glaciation provides the classic U-shaped valleys, cwms, mountain ridges, and moraines. Carboniferous limestone has helped to produce numerous underground caverns and networks of tunnels, like those at Dan-yr-Ogof.

On our way to the caves, we stopped off at the small village of Abercrave (Abercraf). The village sits on the north side of the River Tawe opposite an incredible hole in the land-scape. I'm not sure how else to describe it. The sharp angular lines of the 700-hectare Nant Helen opencast site look strangely unnatural, and that hole in the hillside is just huge! We had a pit stop in the village café, which also turned out to be the village post office and a B&B. After making a first-class delivery of two coffees, the friendly owner told us about the history of the old mining village. It was a familiar tale of growth and decline in parallel with coal mining and iron-works, but with its location on the edge of the Bannau Brycheiniog National Park, the village has found a new lease of life through tourism. In between serving her other customers with teas, envelopes, coffees, and stamps, we heard about a new future for the old Nant Helen site, which had been one of the last opencast coal mines in Wales. Planning permission has been given to convert part of the old site into a £200m Global Centre of Rail Excellence. It will be trans-formed into a 'one-stop-shop' for railway innovation. The new site will include research and development facilities, all the usual admin stuff, and two large test tracks (loops of 4 and 2 miles long). With the potential for thousands of new jobs, it was good to hear about a positive development in the area as it continues to move away from its old dependence on extractive industries.

Nick and I had been to the caves at Dan-yr-Ogof many years earlier, in the days when he still had hair and my left knee was still fully operational. I think that shows how long ago we're talking. In those days, the caves weren't quite the commercial enterprise you see today. The National Show-caves Centre for Wales has been voted one of Britain's top beauty spots, ahead of attractions such as the Giant's Cause-way, the White Cliffs of Dover, and the Cheddar Gorge. In the old days, (as us old people like to keep reminding everyone younger), you could just walk around the caves. Nowadays, you have to negotiate your way past a toy train and life-sized dinosaurs. We weren't sure what to expect, but we went with open minds.

On balance, I think they've just about got things right at Dan-yr-Ogof. There are enough facts, figures, and information boards to explain the geology and physical geography of the area to serious-minded scholars like Nick and me. At the same time, the marketing guys have clearly focused on keeping the kids entertained, with what could be quite a dry subject for youngsters. If Nick and I rode on the red toy train and had silly photos taken looking out through the jaws of a triceratops – well, that's probably not so bad for a couple of old kids. We only had ourselves to embarrass.

The Dan-yr-Ogof cave is the largest of the show caves. There are over 12 miles of underground passageways in the cave system and although visitors only get to see a small fraction of that, there's more than enough to keep everyone occupied. It's a self-guided tour, so you can go at your own pace as you check out all the stalactites, stalagmites, and strange shaped rock formations. As my old geography teacher used to tell all the lads in his class, with a knowing wink, 'Remember tites come down.' It feels like a Sid James type comment from a *Carry on Caving* film that was never released (available underground). I'm sure our well-meaning teacher was just trying to provide us with a memorable mnemonic to help us with our identification of physical geography features – and given that I still remember it over 50 years later, he succeeded.

The pathways around the site (which is enormous) are well laid out and well maintained. They take you from one cave system to the next, each with its own unique underground surprise. One has a fast-flowing underground river. In the cathedral cave, you gasp in wonder at enormous caverns over 12 metres high, and you even get the chance to walk behind another waterfall. And you'll never guess what's in the Bone Cave. As well as the caves, the site has a shire horse centre and a recreated Iron Age farm. Nick and I wandered around a large outdoor area that resembled Jurassic Park, where over 200 life-sized and very realistic dinosaurs hang out in the grasslands, jungle, and swamps. I must reluctantly admit, it was great for kids of all ages, including pensioners.

Never, since my visit to the Houses of Parliament as a teenager, have I seen so many dinosaurs in one place.

We drove further west and north, still heading towards our date with destiny at Llanwrtyd Wells. While we were in Cardiff, Nick and I went to visit a guy called Simon, one of Nick's old university chums. When we told him about our route for the rest of the trip, and our objectives, he recommended: 'You must go to Castell Carreg.' It felt non-negotiable, and we still had to get out of his house, so we agreed. I'm very glad we did because it's the sort of place that doesn't get the same headlines as more famous Welsh castles, but it's special, and we might have missed it.

Carreg Cennen Castle is situated around 5 miles from the town of Llandeilo, on the western edge of both the Black Mountains and the Bannau Brycheiniog National Park. The castle dates to at least the 13th century, and its history features a classic cast list from Welsh history. The usual suspects include Sir Rhys ap Thomas, who owned the castle for what was a typically brief tenure in those days. As the script usually demands, it was, unfortunately, taken over by King Edward I, who turned up in 1277. The castle was gifted to one of the king's supporters, a soldier named John Giffard. He'd supported the king in his fight against the Welsh, particularly Prince Llywelyn ap Gruffydd. Giffard rebuilt Carreg Cennen into a powerful structure that came to dominate the surrounding landscape… although it didn't prevent a cameo appearance by Owain Glyndŵr, who attacked the castle in 1403.

As always, it's all about the location. The castle sits at 250 metres high on a limestone outcrop that towers over the Afon Cennen, with views for miles in every direction. Despite some gaps in its high, once-formidable walls, there's still plenty of castle left to see. We were lucky to be tipped off to visit the castle – it must be one of the most spectacularly situated castles in Wales. The BBC *Countryfile* magazine described it as 'The most romantic ruin,' in the country. As if the location isn't enough, the castle has its own mysterious cave. In one corner of the castle grounds, you can walk down a long, dark, and precarious set of steps to find it. It's pitch black down there, so take a torch… and watch your head. Nick and I had to check it out, of course, and at the end of the long tunnel we came across a small space that was presumably a cell or prison for previous unfortunate visitors. The cool, dark, and damp surroundings were a strong contrast to the gorgeous summer's day above, so it was nice to get back up top to the sunshine and warmth.

We had around 37 miles to drive from Carreg Cennen Castle to our overnight stop at Llanwrtyd Wells. We headed northwards, winding along narrow country lanes that meandered through the gentle hills of Carmarthenshire. Lush, green pastures stretched out around us, and the distant hills were covered in a hazy blue blanket. Approaching Llandeilo, the landscape started to change, giving way to the gentle curves of the River Towy as it meanders along its wide valley floor. Continuing northwards, the countryside became increasingly rugged. We left the Bannau Brycheiniog National Park behind us, and the road snaked its way gradually higher into the Cambrian Mountains. Eventually, we arrived in the small town of Llanwrtyd Wells, nestled in the heart of the Welsh countryside. The town is known for its quirky events, including the annual Man vs Horse Marathon, which sees runners competing against riders on horseback, and the World Bog Snorkelling Championships, where competitors don snorkels and flippers to race through a peat bog – can you imagine anyone being stupid enough to do that!

14

LLANWRTYD WELLS TO TREFIL

Parts of my *Journey through Wales* involved events that had fixed dates, so I had to plan my trip around them. These included the National Eisteddfod, the World Bog Snorkelling Championships, and a visit to meet the Treorchy Male Choir. Each one was big. I had the National Eisteddfod in the bag, and the second big event would soon be in the bog.

I couldn't persuade my great friend Nick to enter the World Bog Snorkelling Championships with me, but he kindly offered to act as my right-hand man for the event. It also gave him the opportunity to witness sporting history and the chance to spend a couple of weeks touring the land of his childhood. So, there we were in Llanwrtyd Wells on the eve of the big day – ready for the event that Lonely Planet has described as one of the top fifty 'must do' things from around the world. It's hard to imagine there are forty-nine other things as good. Destiny beckoned. I could have been less than 24 hours from one of the most prestigious titles in international sport.

Arriving in Llanwrtyd Wells the night before the event was a rare display of forethought for two senior gentlemen. The plan to have a pasta rich macaroni cheese dinner that evening was equally impressive. It was all about marginal gains. Nick and I followed that eve-of-race carbohydrate fix with a tour of the town's hostelries. Arguably, that last bit didn't add to the marginal gains. Some would consider it sub-optimal race preparation the night before a major international sporting event. We ended up at the famous Neuadd Arms Hotel, birthplace of the bog snorkelling competition, and a place revered by followers of the sport. Hung around the walls of the bar are wooden honour boards listing the previous winners of the event, and the famous 'man versus horse' competitions. By chance, we sat at a table with a local couple, Kathy, and Paul. He is a builder, and she is a former nurse and now an author, but the following day they were going to be two of the timekeepers for the bog snorkelling championship. What serendipitous toss of the dice by the gods of fortune brought us all together that night? In hindsight, I should have upped my offer of £15 and two pints of Guinness for an agreed understanding on my finish time, but I could tell Paul and Kathy were incorruptible – well, at least at the level I could afford.

And so to the big day! Gareth had already named his squad for Qatar. Ollie Pope seemed to have made the England number three batting position his own and my golf handicap of thirty-six had left me, once again, just outside the quali-fying criteria for the Open. At sixty-eight, I didn't think I could still be a sporting world champion at anything. And I was right. On 28th August 2022, however, I was a tantalising 1 minute 19 seconds away from that coveted title, and global fame. So close, it hurts. This is how things panned out…

We were up bright and early. I didn't want to be the one thinking myself accursed or holding my manhood cheap because I was still abed when battle commenced on the muddy fields of Powys. A medium dish of plain soy yogurt with a diced apple and half a cup of low-fat granola, topped with a tablespoon of honey, followed by three scrambled egg whites cooked with olive oil spray and seasoned with pinches of both black pepper and Halon Môn sea salt. That's a breakfast high in carbohydrate, moderate in protein, and low in fat; one that enables easy digestion and long-term energy release. It would have been the perfect way to start my race day. Instead, I opted for the full Belle Vue Hotel fry-up, including black pudding. Time would tell if my choice would be inspired left-field thinking, or just bloody stupid. I was leaning towards it being the latter by the time I'd followed up with a couple of rounds of toast and marmalade, and a second cup of strong coffee. In that wide awake but well stuffed state, however, I sensed a win-win situation. I could be rocket-fuelled to victory, or on the off-chance I didn't get crowned world champion, at least I had one of my excuses already lined up. As soon as breakfast was over, along with other pre-race routines that we won't dwell on, there was no time to lose. With the scent of victory already in my nostrils, I was keen to get to the site of my imminent triumph.

Nick and I must have been two of the first people to arrive at the Waen Rydd bog, about a mile south of the town. The bog lies within a site of special scientific interest, containing within its soggy ecosystem many examples of rare flora and fauna. It's something about which the organisers of the bog snorkelling event are very conscious. They have to seek permission for events, and someone regularly assesses the site. The experts agree that some limited footfall and stirring of the bog water is not harmful and can be beneficial to the area.

Immediately behind us, as we drove into the car park, were timekeepers, Paul and Kathy. I apologised profusely for any misunderstanding from the previous night, and I upped my offer to £25 and two pints of Guinness. I grabbed my kit – swimsuit, flippers, and snorkel – and walked with Nick across a large grassy field towards the competition area. Stalls were being set up to cater for the steady stream of spectators that were arriving. There were food and drink stalls, a bouncy castle, and people selling a comprehensive range of bog related merchandise.

A short distance past the volunteers setting up their equipment in the registration tent, we found the two official ditches that had been cut into the Waen Rydd wetlands for the 2022 Bog Snorkelling World Championship. We gazed in incredulity at those twin aqua-theatres of glory, mindful of the battle that lay ahead, and the global acclaim reserved for those who emerged victorious from the murky waters.

The bog was a glorious sight early on a Sunday morning (an observation Nick makes most weekends). As bogs go, the Waen Rydd is relatively modest, stretching only a few hundred yards from the Cledan, a stream that flows into the River Irfon, which winds through Llanwrtyd Wells on its way to joining the River Wye at Builth Wells. To the south of us, fields randomly dotted with sheep stretched upwards towards the northern end of the Crychan Forest. A green patchwork of fields and woodlands on the hills surrounding Garn Wen provided a picturesque backdrop on the northern side of the valley. Blue skies and sunshine set the scene for a glorious day… and a day of glory.

We were there so early that there were hardly any other competitors to be seen. A small army of local volunteers dressed in high-vis jackets were attending to last-minute preparations. It was the perfect moment to 'walk the course' and assess the conditions. The two ditches were about 5 metres apart. Each ditch is 60 yards long, about 4 feet wide, and about the same depth (I think they are measured in imperial units rather than metric). They were exactly the same – you could probably call them bog standard.

The way they had been labelled Bog 1 and Bog 2 appealed to my sense of order; it was a pleasing display of methodical sequencing at an emotionally fragile time for a competitor. A waist-deep soup of brown water containing a variety of plant and animal life filled each ditch. Wooden posts marked the ends of the two muddy troughs of water, and ropes and bunting lined the sides, ready to hold back enthusiastic spectators.

Competitors have to start by holding a wooden post that marks the start end of the ditch. They then snorkel (no recognised swimming strokes are permitted) up to the post at the other end. After touching it, they turn around and snorkel their way back to the start. The timekeeper's stopwatches are stopped when the competitor touches the wooden post back at the start. The fastest there and back is the winner.

More competitors and spectators arrived and found their way to the two ditches. Nick and I discussed the marginal gains possible through the latest thinking on tumble turn techniques. It's always comforting to know you've got a good bog roll available when you need one. As we chatted, we looked back to see a line of people stretching back from the registration tent. We dashed back to join the queue and got talking to some of the other competitors. Jim had entered before and wasn't sure why he'd come back. Perhaps he just liked that heady mixture of Hawaiian skirt and pearl beads he was wearing, along with a few minutes of floundering in cold ditch water. Suzi, like me, was a first-timer. She was an experienced snorkeller, but her training had mainly taken place in the clear, warm waters of the Caribbean. Well, that's much the same as the Waen Rydd bog. No problem there. A couple of guys walked past in outrageously skin-tight one-piece swimwear that left nothing to the imagination. I think it was the lads' flamboyant choice of funky rainbow costume design that Suzi was referring to when she commented, 'They've got some balls.' She was brilliant company and before we knew it, we were at the registration tent and signed up – there was no going back now! I asked Nick if he'd had any second thoughts; the organisers were taking entries on the day, and spare snorkelling gear was available. He said something about rather poking his eye out with a fork, so I sensed he was still not quite mentally ready. By the time we returned to the two ditches, it was time for the first competitor to start the 2022 event.

A lovely, larger-than-life lady called Berni (aka Lady Lily

Pink) wandered around with a microphone all day, calling competitors to the line, commentating on the event, interviewing people, and entertaining the crowd. She was dressed to be noticed, mostly in shades of pink, from her Dr Martens boots to the shiny pill-box hat on her curly pink hair. Berni's style and energy, which she somehow kept going all day, were amazing. As well as doing the important stuff, organising the competitors, etc., her commentary was hilariously entertaining. She made sure she mentioned all the various charities being supported and was empathetic and encouraging for those competitors who needed it… if you know what I'm saying.

Berni called the first competitor to Bog 1, and to great cheers from the crowd, Superman, who leads a secret life as Dave, began his swim. He looked about the same age as me and I went into a downward spiral of despair when I heard his finish time of only 2 minutes 30 seconds. OMG, that's amazing, I thought. I'll get nowhere near that. Oh, but hold on a second, he's got superhuman powers.

The next few dozen snorkellers all achieved similar times, with one or two torpedos and the occasional person who didn't finish. As they got out of the bog, each competitor emerged with a thin layer of reddish-brown residue on any exposed skin, which for most people was most of their bodies. Some came out wearing a few bits of grass and some long straggly weedy hair attachments.

I was so absorbed watching the other competitors that I got a bit of a shock when I realised it was almost my turn. I dashed back to the changing tent and emerged a couple of minutes later, ready for action. By now, the crowds of spectators had grown to maybe a couple of hundred, and I had to shuffle my way through them towards the starting line. As the competitor countdown moved inexorably towards my number, I began final preparations. I sat on the wooden bridge over the end of the strip of muddy water in Bog 1 that was surely about to witness sporting history.

When Paul, the timekeeper, shouted my name, I stepped into that murky ditch of destiny and entered that special state of mind that elite athletes call the flow (in this case more like the flow country) – total concentration on the task at hand, the rest of the world blocked out, a synthesis of mindful movement and focused awareness while maintaining complete control. I was up to my waist in cold water, but the temperature didn't register at the time; I was in the zone.

I experienced a split second of self-doubt as the burden of a lifetime's sporting mediocrity draped itself around my shoulders like a heavy cloak of chain mail. That wasn't going to help. But this was my moment. I cast that mental burden aside with barely disguised disdain, placed the snorkel in my mouth, checked the breathing tube was upright and held the wooden starting post ready for the off. Destiny beckoned. I was (potentially) 1 minute and 17 seconds away from sporting immortality – a new world record and a place in the Guinness World Records.

Paul asked if I was ready. Of course I was bloody ready – my whole life had been building towards that moment. I nodded, and he gave me the countdown. 'Three, two, one, GO!' I felt the adrenalin coursing through my veins as I surged forward into the murky depths of the bog. My first reaction was 'Oh shit! I can't see a thing.' I knew it would be like that, but somehow it still came as a shock.

I left the outside world behind. Gone were all the people, the colour, and excitement. Gone was the loud cheering, Berni's banter, and the babble of the crowd. I could see nothing apart from watery dark brownness on the other side of my face mask. All I could hear was the steady whoosh, whoosh of my breathing and the babbling rush of water passing my ears. Re-capturing my composure, I entered the zone occupied by those who achieve sporting greatness. Bannister, Pele, Bradman, Spitz; they'd all been this way before. I felt their presence. I was in complete and effortless control. My legs were kicking strongly in a good, steady rhythm. I stretched my arms out forwards and slightly outwards, waiting for the first sign of weeds on the sides of the channel so I could correct my course and maintain a straight line for the marker post at the end of the bog. I reminded myself not to go too fast at the beginning. It felt like a co-ordinated surge, and it was brilliant. All those weeks of mind training, my practice swim in the warm clear seas off Burton Bradstock, and watching that Neil Rutter (serial world bog snorkelling champion) YouTube video were all proving their worth. I made a couple of mid-course corrections and continued, like a laser, for my appointment with destiny, and the white post at the end of the first length. Maybe it was the first signs of oxygen starvation, but I began to fantasise about the film and TV series about my rise to sporting fame. *One Man and his Bog* sprung to mind as a working title.

I hadn't felt the side of the ditch for a while, so I looked up to check my progress; surely I was getting close to the end post and I didn't want to go piling into it – not at that speed! To my dismay, I was less than halfway down the course. Suddenly, the end of the ditch seemed a mile away. My legwork felt heavy, and my breathing was no longer under control. I hit the side a few times, thrashed wildly, and somehow struggled to the turning post… which I head butted. I couldn't get enough air and was feeling awful, but somehow I stopped myself from standing up and taking a long breather.

I turned and started out for the finish line, but it was *so* far away. About then, I heard Nick shouting out, 'Come on Mark! you're doing great.' It was about the only thing I remember hearing and it might have saved me. I hit the sides again and again, and looked up several more times, desperately willing the end post towards me. Each time I looked up, it hardly looked any closer than the previous time. By now, my breathing was frantic and the sound of it, in my private underwater world, was deafening. I somehow floundered my way back to the start, my uncoordinated limbs randomly flailing in all directions. I threw in a few inelegant doggy paddle strokes over the last couple of metres, desperately clawing at the water to pull myself home. My lungs were bursting. I had a flashback to the graffiti in the St Briavels Castle prison – 'My days are weary, my time has come…'

By then, my ambitions had shifted from achieving international glory to not troubling the emergency services. I was so grateful to reach out and grab that finish post, and for the ordeal to be over. Getting to my feet with a bit of a wobble, I was telling myself to look cool and untroubled. I somehow summoned sufficient breath to say, 'Well, that was bloody tough.' Timekeeper Paul was very generous with his comment of 'You did 2 minutes 39 seconds Mark. Well done! Anything under 3 minutes is excellent.' He added 'You'd have been in the overall lead by now, if you hadn't kept touching the sides.'

Holding the finishing post for support… the world record safe for another year

As my breathing stabilised, the desperation of trying to complete the course without having a heart attack soon turned to elation at just being part of the event. I wore my competitors' medal with pride for the rest of the day – I'd done it!

The competitors kept coming. Amidst the few sensible ones were Father Christmas, Shrek, Fred Flintstone, a Brazilian lifeguard, a Viking, a shark, a man dressed as a bride, several fairies, and someone who identified as a bar of soap. Competitors had come from across the globe, with Australia, Belgium, Canada, China, Ireland, Italy, Poland, Sweden, South Africa, The Netherlands, and the US all represented. There were two 'celebrity' snorkellers: the reigning world champion and sporting legend, Neil Rutter, and BBC Wales weatherman, Derek Brockway, who was putting himself through the ordeal as part of his long-running BBC Wales series, *Weatherman Walking*.

The arrival at the start line of Neil Rutter marked the beginning of one of the highlights of the day. The crowd had swollen at the end of Bog 1 and in stark contrast to my effort, there was an excited buzz of anticipation. Neil looked as though he meant business as he entered the ditch, with his skin-tight wet suit, nose clip, goggles, and a professional-looking snorkel. His own world record was under threat. A roar went up from the spectators as he burst from the starting post and sped towards the far end of the ditch. With a dolphin-like whole body wave movement, he was at the turn and heading for home in way under a minute. I couldn't believe how fast he was moving through the water. He touched the finishing post to an enormous roar from the crowd, for a time of 1 minute 20 seconds – easily the winning time for 2022, and just one second outside his previous world record. Incredible.

Neil was a man in demand after his swim, followed around by a small pack of well-wishers, friends, photographers, and a film crew. I caught up with him eventually and he was kind enough to spend a few minutes chatting about how he got involved with the competition and his approach to the event. I told him he was lucky – I'd had an off day.

Maybe it was the black pudding. Asking for a friend, I enquired whether he had any tips for a near middle-aged elite athlete looking to improve his time. 'It's all about the legs,' he said. 'Try to keep going straight and have something left in the tank for the final few metres.' Wise words, and tactics that my coach and I will work on in my high-intensity training camps over the next 12 months.

As Nick and I were leaving the car park, we almost drove past two other niche sporting events. We stopped to watch the closing stages of the wife-carrying and husband-dragging competitions. It was a day that kept giving, and a tremendously enjoyable experience – apart from about 2 minutes 39 seconds in the middle.

The heady excitement of the day continued in the evening as many of the competitors and spectators crowded into the lively Neuadd Arms. To background music provided by a live band, the friendly banter and tales of what might have been continued well into the night. We bumped into Berni (Lady Lily Pink) again and she told us a string of hilarious stories about the bog and the event. A steady stream of celebrities have been filmed there, including Chris Tarrant, Paddy McGuinness and Rory McGrath (*Rory and Paddy's Great British Adventure*), Griff Rhys Jones (*A Great Welsh Adventure*), Steph and Dom Parker (ex Gogglebox, now radio), and Warwick Davis and family (*Weekend Escapes*). It came as no surprise to hear that the bog had seen a stag weekend and a marriage proposal. I think my favourite story was the one about the guys dressed as a pantomime horse one year – apparently, they hadn't considered that the rear end of the horse would also need to breathe.

With its calendar of crazy sporting events, the town of Llanwrtyd Wells is one of the wackiest places you will ever visit, but its lovely people are also among the friendliest and most welcoming. They had put on a spectacular, eccentric, and hugely enjoyable event and until August 2023 at least, I could place myself in that elite band of athletes that comprise the world's top twenty over-50 bog snorkellers. I like to think I have a good claim to the title of number one in the much-coveted over-68, left hander from Dorset class… but I can't be certain.

I'm sure I will be telling my bog snorkelling story to anyone unfortunate enough to be within earshot for years to come. It will evolve with each telling, getting more extreme, death-defying, and record-breaking with every new telling. That's what happens to stories if there aren't too many indisputable facts (I might dispute my finish time). Going back in time, before written records, it's easy to see how word-of-mouth stories changed as they were repeated over time. Back in prehistoric times, the spiritual leaders of the Preseli bluestone removals team would have spun a good story about the stars at night, the changing seasons, and the need to get those bloomin' stones shifted. Stories inspire beliefs, influence opinions, and keep cultures alive.

Much of what we understand about Wales from centuries ago is in the form of stories. During the research for my trip, I came across stories about people such as King Arthur, Branwen, Blodeuwedd, Rhiannon, Merlin, Barti Ddu, Llywelyn, and Owain Glyndŵr. Some are magical, others are inspiring. The content of the stories ranges from factual to mystical and everything between. Eventually, I came across the Welsh equivalent of England's Robin Hood and Scotland's Rob Roy. His name was Thomas Jones, otherwise known as Twm Siôn Cati. As a cultural re-set, the day after the craziness of bog snorkelling, Nick and I went off to discover more about this colourful character. The cave where this outlaw hid from the law and stashed his booty back in the 16th century was about 25 miles from our stopover in Llanwrtyd Wells.

We were back on the road again, and I was back on my *Journey through Wales*. Leaving Llanwrtyd Wells, we headed southwest along the A483, and climbed slowly up the picturesque Cledan Valley. At a height of 250 metres above sea level, just before the road wound itself around the Sugar Loaf mountain, we passed the 150-year-old single-track railway halt called Sugar Loaf station, one of the most geographically remote and quietest stations in Wales. We turned right off the main road and headed west, along pretty country lanes to reach the River Towy. We had wandered into Carmarthenshire again, and into the southern part of the Cambrian Mountains. To the east of us, on the other side of the Towy Valley, was the Mynydd Epynt, and to the south, beyond the town of Llandovery, lay the Black Mountains.

We headed north along the upper stretches of the beautiful River Towy, on a perfect summer morning (yes, another one). Although the weather undoubtedly helped, I recall commenting on what an amazing part of Wales we were driving through. And why hadn't either of us been there before? The valley landscape was picture postcard perfect and, on either side, hills covered in rough grass and forest rose dramatically to touch clear blue skies. The accolade 'hidden gem' is overused, but it certainly applies to the Towy Valley. As the country lane wound its way towards the Llŷn Brianne Reservoir, we passed through the village of Rhandirmwyn. It's hard to imagine it now, but that quiet little rural village was once the centre of the largest and most productive metal mine in South Wales. The Nantymwyn lead mine closed in 1932, but at its peak, it employed over 400 people.

The cave of Twm Siôn Cati on Dinas Hill is about 2 miles further up the valley from Rhandirmwyn. I was expecting a bit of a struggle to find it, but in the event, it was super easy. An information board in the car park at the RSPB Gwenffrwd-Dinas Nature Reserve told us the Twm Siôn Cati story, and a signpost pointed us towards the beginning of a well-marked path that encircles Dinas Hill and leads to the cave. To walk right round and back to the start takes about 2 hours.

The car park was empty when we arrived, but we were soon joined by Paul, who had just ridden up from Llandovery on his Suzuki V-Strom 600cc motorcycle. On Paul's back was a rucksack, inside which was a border collie called Molly. She looked quite chilled, despite her lack of safety apparel, but the speed with which she crouched down for a wee as soon as Paul set her free suggested she was quite pleased to be back on *terra firma*. Immediate needs attended to, Molly had a good run around to stretch her four legs. She travels like that all over Wales with Paul apparently, and loves her biker days out.

Nick and I set off along the well-maintained boardwalk. When that ran out, the path was easy to follow, but quite rough going in places. We followed it anticlockwise around the hill and before long, we were walking through woodlands of ancient oak and alder, along the banks of the fast-flowing River Towy. We'd arrived in the greenwood. A carpet of mosses, lichens, and liverworts covered the trees and boulders, giving everything a verdant, and slightly damp feel, even in midsummer… like Henrhyd Falls. It looked like fairly dense Celtic rainforest, and it was a beautiful place to be on a stunning day. The serenity of the woodlands was the perfect antidote to the adrenalin infused mayhem of the previous day in the bog.

Our route to the cave was mainly through dappled shade, but sunlight occasionally burst through the green canopy where it thinned out by the riverbank. A tubby looking dipper bird whirred from boulder to boulder in the middle of the river doing what dippers do. The river rushed on past us, impatient to get to its appointment with the Celtic Sea at Carmarthen Bay. As it did so, it chuckled to itself at the sight of two more cave seekers. The surface of the water twinkled brightly, like a watery glitter ball, scattering the rays of the midday sun. Almost halfway round the trail, one mad dog and one Englishman scrambled up a short steep section of the hill that takes you up to the cave of

Twm Siôn Cati. It didn't hold us up for long. So, before we enter, who was he?

Twm Siôn Cati has a bit more historical legitimacy than Robin Hood, who emerges in English medieval folklore as a green-clad, bow-wielding leader of merry men. The stories, poems, and songs about the outlaw of Sherwood Forest may or may not be based upon a real person, but Twm Siôn Cati *was* real, and his name was Thomas Jones. He was born in Tregaron around 1530, an illegitimate boy with noble blood. He died in 1609. Those few points seem to be generally accepted, but there are many versions of the rest of his life. Tales of Twm's colourful exploits were passed down over the years by word-of-mouth and began to appear in books in the early 19th century. The stories probably became more exaggerated and romanticised as they were re-told, like those of his English and Scottish partners in crime... and my bog snorkelling achievements.

Seemingly intelligent, Twm is described as a tall and handsome gentleman farmer. He is also described as a womaniser, a bit of a cad, and a semi-successful outlaw who lived during times of political uncertainty and violence. Henry VIII's Act of Union in 1536 created legal confusion in parts of Wales, which people like Twm used to their advantage. His criminal career appears to have progressed from dishonest chancer to common thief, through to dandy highwayman, and then crafty conman. One famous story tells how he stole a prize bull (or bullock, or chestnut horse, depending on which story you read) from a farmer and then disguised the beast with dye and a false tail, before selling it back to the same farmer. As the original owner took his 'new' bull home from the market, it rained, and the dye washed away. The farmer realised he'd been conned. Back at his farm, he grabbed his gun and galloped off to Twm's house for retribution. Sat outside Twm's house was a poor beggar dressed in rags. The farmer instructed the beggar to hold his riding crop and the horse's reins for him. The farmer then entered Twm's house with his gun primed, ready to put matters right. As soon as the farmer was inside, the beggar jumped up and threw aside the old clothes he'd been using as a disguise. He mounted the farmer's horse and galloped away – it was Twm. He rode at speed to the farmer's house where he told the farmer's wife that her husband was in trouble and had instructed him to ride back to the farm for help. She must find 50 guineas for Twm to take back to her husband… and make it quick. The obedient wife soon found the money and Twm rode off into the sunset – or more accurately to London, where he lived it up for as long as the money lasted. When things got hot and the law threatened to catch up with him, he moved to Geneva, where he stayed on the run for a few more years. Other versions say Twm was a fervent Protestant, and he fled to Switzerland to escape persecution by the Catholic Queen Mary. In that version, he returns to Wales eventually with a royal pardon from Queen Elizabeth I. There are also different accounts of why Twm used his cave. It might have been his highwayman hideaway and loot store, which seems likely. Other stories suggest that it was where he hid to avoid religious persecution, or that it was where he kept low for a while when he returned to Wales from Geneva, using it as a base while wooing a rich heiress who lived nearby. I suppose it could have been any of those, a combination, or all three. Some stories credit Twm Siôn Cati with helping the poor, like his English counterpart. Some stories tell how he used his trickery to fight against the injustices faced by ordinary people. He also gained a reputation for not hurting or killing his victims – he would fire an arrow to pin his victims to their saddle, for example, which was a neat trick and very considerate.

Back at Dinas Hill, Nick and I clambered up to reach the entrance to Twm's cave. Nick stood tall and puffed his chest out, looking meaningfully into the sky above the woods. It brought a smile to my face when he waved a pretend pistol in the air and burst into a very loud 'Staaand and deliver!' I asked him if he really needed to be going round with a white stripe painted across his face, but he remained defiant, and in character… he was adamant. It seemed only right to join in with a chorus of: Da diddly, qua qua, da diddly, qua qua.

It was a short scramble to get inside the cave. You have to slither over some large slabs of rock to reach the main chamber – if you can call it a cave without its roof, which must have collapsed many years ago. As it stands, it's a decent size but a bit draughty. If you're a highwayman looking for somewhere to hide away in relative comfort, the cave delivers. It's easy to see how it would remain unseen from the surrounding area. Carved into the rock walls of the cave, there are the initials of scores of previous visitors. Once you get your eye in, you see them everywhere (the carved initials). We found some going back to the beginning of the 18th century. A few members of the Pembrokeshire Yeomanry travelled to the cave on horseback just before the outbreak of World War I and carved their names with bayonets.

There was something special about that walk to and from the cave. It had some Shinrin-Yoku but something extra. I think the combination of the forest calmness, the babbling river, and the historical mystery has left a bit of magic in the air. I've seen the walk described as one of the most beautiful in Wales, and I wouldn't argue with that. With a Sir Walter Scott style makeover, I'm sure Twm Siôn Cati could become a Welsh icon and national hero. I look forward to the books, the movies, the walking trail, the visitor centre, tea-towels, fridge magnets, and the Twm Siôn Cati Welsh whisky. Nick and I couldn't help thinking of the Towy Valley as a bit of a secret treasure. At the end of my *Journey through Wales*, I looked back at this valley as one of the most beautiful places I'd visited in Wales.

We set off southwards, along the valley of the Afon Cothi, towards Dolaucothi. It was about 10 miles away and we were in no hurry. In fact, we were so relaxed that the jukebox in my head thought it appropriate to cue up Sunny Afternoon by the Kinks. My brain isn't content with just playing songs in my head based on some random outside influence. Sometimes, thankfully not too often, I get a touch of pareidolia. It's that thing where you see a familiar pattern or shape in something. Surely, I'm not the only person who can spot the outline of India in their poppadom? OK, maybe I am. With a background in geography and map-making, my version of the affliction usually manifests itself in country outlines, although I remember the Isle of Wight, Florida, the Kintyre Peninsula, and a frying pan all making guest appearances. And so it was that Nick was driving us through the beautiful Carmarthen countryside while Ray Davies sipped his ice-cold beer and a cloud the shape of Australia was performing tectonic manoeuvres at a height of 3,000 metres in the skies above us. I didn't want to distract Nick; his driving is bad enough when he's looking where he's going, so by the time he could stop to admire and verify my observation, Australia had morphed into Ireland. Back down to Earth, we were heading for the village of Pumsaint, home to the National Trust-owned Dolaucothi Estate, which includes extensive woodlands, a network of walking trails, and… a gold mine.

The Dolaucothi Mines are a scheduled ancient monument (an archaeological site of national importance, legally protected), and the only known Roman gold mines in Britain. Is there anything the rocks of Wales haven't provided? Coal, copper, iron, slate, and now gold. I can't think of another country that packs so many remarkable natural resources into such a relatively small area. Anyway, back to the gold. Just like the Spanish in South America, the Ottomans in Europe, and the British just about everywhere, the Romans were keen on flexing their military muscle, expanding their empire, and stripping out whatever assets they could lay their hands on.

The British Isles had a lot to offer the Romans, although they clearly weren't coming for the weather. As well as slaves, taxes, and good agricultural land, Britain offered valuable natural resources, including tin, lead, iron, and even coal. The Romans were particularly interested in the Cornish tin mines, which were a valuable resource for the production of bronze. But in the Welsh hills they also found gold.

Although the Romans arrived in Britain in the 1st century AD, it took them a few more years to pluck up the courage to venture into central Wales. When they found out about the gold at Dolaucothi, they called in the mining experts. The gold wasn't exactly easy pickings. It came in the form of tiny dust-sized particles in the quartz veins that they found running through the shale rock at Dolaucothi. To begin with, the gold was dug out from a large opencast pit, using Welsh slave labour. They followed the quartz veins underground, through tunnels that reached a depth of at least 50 metres. The Romans then brought in the high-tech guys with their state-of-the art hydraulic mining techniques. Aqueducts were used to transport water several miles to the site, where it was collected in tanks. Periodically, the water was suddenly released and directed to a specific location on the site. The watery blast swept away the topsoil and exposed the gold-bearing veins in the underlying rock. When the Romans threw the towel in and went home in the 5th century, the mine was abandoned and left to gather gold-dust and cobwebs. It wasn't until the 19th century that the mine was revived using new mining techniques. Extracting the gold was once again economically viable and by the 1930s, there were over 200 men employed in the mines. The mine continued to operate until the outbreak of World War II, when it was closed due to labour shortages and wartime restrictions. The National Trust took over the mines in the 1980s, restoring the site, and making it one of the most popular tourist attractions in Wales.

Visitors are shown around the neat and tidy site by knowl-edgeable guides. After being told some of the historical stuff and looking around some of the buildings on the surface, you get to do what everyone wants to do – go underground. After walking down a long tunnel, you enter a large cavern. Roman pick-marks from 2,000 years ago can still be spotted on the cave walls in some parts of the mine. After a good look around, you climb back out again, blinking into the bright light of day. Nick and I had a go at gold panning. We were very productive, both ending up with a very nice slurry of mud and grit. The children next to us had much better results… but they had better equipment and they were quite lucky.

Less than 12 miles from Dolaucothi is the mighty Defynnog Yew, an ancient tree that could be over 5,000 years old, and the oldest in Britain, or even Europe. I know what you're thinking – we've already met one oldest tree in Britain back in Llangernyw in Chapter Five. The Fortingall Yew in Perthshire, Scotland, also has a claim to the title 'oldest,' which I may have endorsed if I'd been on a journey through Scotland. But I wasn't. There was only one thing to do – pop into the churchyard of St Cynog's Church in the village of Defynnog, Powys, and see what was going on.

The drive from Dolaucothi to Defynnog is a journey through a landscape that has been shaped by centuries of human activity. As we worked our way through rural Carmarthenshire and Powys, back to the Bannau Brycheiniog National Park, the hills rose around us, their slopes thick with heather and gorse. The road winds its way through the rolling hills and verdant valleys, past fields and hedgerows that speak of a rural way of life that has changed little in places for generations. The afternoon sun beat down on the landscape, casting deep shadows across the fields. Like so many parts of Wales, it was a land that had been fought over, conquered, and colonised time and time again. The ghosts of the past were everywhere, from the Roman forts and camps, the crumbling ruins of castles, and the ancient standing stones that dotted the countryside. As we approached Defynnog, just south of Sennybridge (Pont-Senni), we could see the pretty little village perched on the valley side next to the Afon Senni. And there, in the churchyard of St Cynog's Church, about the size of a large dark green double-decker bus, was the ancient Defynnog Yew. Nick was ahead of me as we entered the churchyard. I took a leisurely stroll around the majestic and gnarly old timer, and then continued on to the tree.

It's a long walk around the Defynnog Yew because the trunk, which looks like two trees split down the middle, is approximately 11 metres in circumference. As keen amateur dendrochronologists, Nick and I employed a variety of non-invasive dating techniques and extensive evidence-based research to conclude that the ancient yew is 5,611 years old. We based this mainly on an estimate made in 2011 that said the tree was 5,600 years old.

The Defynnog Yew is so much more than just a tree. It was possibly planted originally to honour a tribal leader. It could have represented a connection from our world to the spiritual one, and from heaven to Earth – the 'axis mundi' for the local tribe. Yew trees were held sacred by the druids and were central to their ceremonies. It's also a breathing art installation, with its sinuous gnarled brown trunk, leathery bark, twisted branches, and dark green leaves forming a living sculpture over which visitors have marvelled for thousands of years. Think of the dramas the tree has witnessed, the scandals it was party to, the secrets it has kept, the gossip it could tell us! Nick and I took a while to admire the tree from a distance. It looked rather stately, with an air of mystery. It was surrounded by an exhausted support cast of tumbling gravestones in a sleepy, very sleepy, old graveyard. Maybe the oldest tree title is in the eye of the beholder, but the challenge is out there: is *this* the one?

But hang on, this is missing the point. It's not the extreme label that makes the tree special or magical. We would not get a better view from Garth Hill, if we said we were standing on a mountain. The essence of a place or something is not its name, its age, or its physical dimensions. The yew tree at Defynnog existed for thousands of years before there was anywhere called Defynnog. It was revered by a community of people for thousands of years before people built a church there. The Defynnog Yew was a symbol of the timelessness of nature compared to the fleeting existence of man long before we came along with our new-fangled Christian beliefs a mere 2000 years ago. It wouldn't matter even if there was an older rival; it's what the tree represents to each of us, and to the local and wider community that is important. This type of philosophical musing can turn a pensioner's thoughts to cheese on toast.

We were dashing from dandy highwayman to gold mine to yew tree, whatever next? Most of the places I'd visited on my *Journey through Wales* were nicely spaced out, at least several miles apart. With such rapidly changing themes, my fellow travellers and I just about had time to get our heads round one stop before arriving at the next one. Defynnog allowed us no such luxury to re-set our brains – we had two places to visit in one village. After a short walk of 270 metres from the gate of the churchyard, you come across a Victorian former school building (there are some nerdy ex-land surveyor types who still feel the compulsion to measure distances like this). The former school building is The International Welsh Rarebit Centre. Nick and I had arranged to meet Rose Geraedts, the owner of this unlikely rural gastro hotspot.

The centre with the important sounding name draws visitors from all around the country and abroad, earning itself a string of five-star reviews. Lonely Planet has given it a starred 'must see' recommendation. They're not wrong. It's a lovely old building full of character and the charm and warmth of the place strike you immediately you walk in. Rose has hit just the right spot with cool furnishings and decor that are in equal measures old world, comfortable, and chic. There were cakes, coffees, and all manner of teas on the menu, chalked up on a school blackboard, but it is the rarebit dish that has earned the centre its reputation since it opened 7 years ago, and that's what Nick, and I had come to sample.

We ordered two traditional Welsh versions. Exotic looking Patagonian, Spanish, Bengal, and Irish variations were on the menu but given the setting, it only seemed right to go old-school. Dutch born Rose, who started work as an occupa-tional therapist, settled in Wales after meeting her Welsh part-ner, and found herself working in cafés and delis in Brecon. Welsh rarebit wasn't on the menu, but so many people asked about it that she sensed a gap in the market. From there to opening a specialist restaurant in Defynnog 7 years ago was quite a leap of faith, but the venture has been a great success. People in the village may not have initially understood Rose's crazy rarebit-centric vision, ('What, you won't you be doing Sunday roasts?') but they soon learned that the dish is much more than cheese on toast. Now locals, which means people from as far afield as places like Cardiff, Merthyr, Neath, and Swansea, form a loyal, and regular customer base. Tourists, cyclists, and walkers also manage to seek the place out and keep it busy. The warm welcome provided by Rose and her staff is a massive part of the place's attraction. You can see the enthusiasm in her smile and hear it in her voice, which has picked up a gentle Welsh lilt. What may have seemed like a bit of a gamble has paid off because the centre is something different, with something unique and memorable to offer.

So, before I rabbit on any further, what is this classic Welsh dish? Rose went through the basic ingredients: Welsh cheddar cheese, mustard, Worcestershire sauce, other seasoning, all mixed together, and grilled on thick toasted bread. The mixture needs to be in a thick liquid form, maybe with a bit of milk or cream to help it along. It sounds straightforward enough, but I suspect the version she dishes up now results from years of fine tuning.

Rose told us some of the background to the 'rarebit' name, stories that were also on posters decorating the walls of the upper classroom. HV Morton spent a couple of pages on the subject, quoting a poem from 1613 that referenced the dish (Morton, 1932). It might have originated as an inexpensive meal for people who couldn't afford meat. Some texts speculate that the Welsh dish was the source of mild mockery by the English back in the 16th century. Let's not go down that rabbit hole. Speaking of which, had Rose experienced any confusion with that name over the years?

She may have added to the potential for confusion by mischievously writing, 'The International Welsh Rabbit Centre' on one side of the sign outside the Centre. 'Oh yes, we sometimes get people stopping off expecting to look at rabbits,' she said. 'We even had someone phone up once asking if we could re-home some rabbits they couldn't keep any longer.' Nick and I wanted to hear more and Rose was happy to chat, but the place was getting busy. I sensed I was running out of tenuous links to rabbit puns, so we decided to hop it and let Rose look after her customers.

As well as a restaurant, the centre is also an art gallery and cultural hub, so before we left, Nick and I popped upstairs to check out the gallery. Much of the work on display was by Janis Fry, a local artist and yew expert. She has done more than anyone to bring the Defynnog Yew to people's attention and has campaigned energetically for its protection. Defynnog had provided us with food for thought and food for lunch. It was an unusual combination for sure, but totally in keeping with the crazy variety of things we were witnessing on our travels. What a great place, delicious food, and lovely people.

Nick and I were meandering our way back gradually to Trefil for another overnight stop before continuing down The Valleys for the final part of the journey. We had two more visits to complete before Trefil. The first was another reminder of Roman Britain, at Y Gaer, near Brecon, and then our final stop for the day, further along the northern edge of the

Bannau Brycheiniog National Park, would be Llangorse Lake (Llŷn Syfadden).

The Roman fort of Y Gaer was built around AD 75, as part of a chain of similar forts strategically placed along the River Usk to conquer and rule over the lands occupied by the Silures. Up to 500 horses and their riders would have been housed in the fort. Being recently new to the world of allotments back home, my thoughts immediately turned to the soil enrichment opportunities that would be brought about by 500 horses.

The stables and the basic accommodation for the Roman soldiers would have been made of wood, and the rectangular encampment would have been protected by clay banks topped with a wooden palisade. All that wood in the original build means there's not a huge amount left to see today. Nick parked the car at the side of a narrow country lane, and we walked down a public footpath, across a couple of cow-filled fields, to Y Garn Farm that overlooks the River Usk. We saw some remains of the fort, but there's not much left to admire, to be honest. It's possible to pick out the remains of the North Wall and the foundations of the gates that stood at the south, east, and west edges of the fort. I think archaeologists like Nick always manage to see more of the original scene than me. In my mind, I'm seeing the spatial stuff – polygons of tribal areas, natural resources, and farmland, linear networks of Roman roads, and dots representing standing stones.

We skirted around the market town of Brecon and were soon parked in a large free car park next to the reed fringed Llangorse Lake. It's about 6 miles east of Brecon, between the Central Bannau Brycheiniog and the Black Mountains. Situated at 154 metres above sea level, Llangorse Lake is the largest natural lake in South Wales. It has a surface area of approximately 132 hectares with a perimeter of just under 4 miles and an outline like a slightly floppy Africa. It lies in a hollow formed by glaciation and has an average depth of just over 3 metres. Those are the stats, but we had come to see one of the most remarkable archaeological sites in Wales – the country's only confirmed crannog site.

Crannogs are ancient man-made island settlements, typically constructed in shallow water, near the shore of a lake or river. They were built by piling up a mound of stones, earth, and timber. The structure was then topped with a wooden or stone building that could have been a dwelling, or used for storage, or a defensive position. Access to the crannog was usually via a wooden bridge or causeway. They typically date from late prehistoric times to the medieval period, and the Llangorse crannog, discovered in the 1860s, is estimated to be from the early medieval period (AD 800 to AD 900). It lies approximately 40 metres from the northern shore of the lake. When you can see the remains peeping above the water, they form a rectangular shape roughly 30 by 40 metres in size, but in the winter the crannog often disappears altogether. Artefacts and historical records discovered on and around the crannog show that this was no ordinary room with a water view – it was a royal residence for the Kings of Brycheiniog. Much as I'd like that to be a Welsh punk band, The Kings of Brycheiniog were a dynasty of rulers who governed the Kingdom of Brycheiniog, which was until recently called the Brecon Beacons area, during the early Middle Ages. They descended from Irish and Welsh noble families, which provides a neat link to Ireland, where crannogs were a common feature of the landscape.

Anything that old is guaranteed to come with a good set of myths and legends, and Llangorse does not disappoint. There are several tales featuring King Arthur, his knights, and assorted beautiful princesses. Could it be that King Arthur's sword, Excalibur, was thrown into Llangorse Lake after Arthur's death? And is it still there, guarded by the Lady of the Lake? Nick and I saw several Excalibur posters and even the end of a sword sticking suspiciously out of a boulder.

Nick and I liked the look of Llangorse; there was a lot going on. At the Welsh Crannog Centre, you can walk out over a causeway to look at a reconstructed thatched round-house. There is a viewing platform around the outside, from which there are great views of the lake and the surrounding mountains. As well as the historical interest, the lake was a beautiful spot to enjoy nature and there were plenty of water sport activities going on.

It was time to head back to Trefil. It was the end of another hectic day on the roads of Wales. There weren't many of those days left on this journey, however. I had mixed feelings as I sensed the adventure coming to its conclusion. In some ways, I just wanted the adrenaline rush of so many amazing places and people to continue – but it felt like I'd been travelling for a long time and my poor brain was running out of little corners into which I could stash memories and bits of information.

The corpulent diva had already commenced her warbling as far as my *Journey through Wales* was concerned. With Nick by my side, I just had a final run through The Valleys left before I ended up in Chepstow, back where it all began. But we had unfinished business in the Gower, and it had been niggling me. It would require a small detour, but I reckoned we could still squeeze in a return trip to Paviland.

It wasn't a small detour at all; it was a huge one. The effort would be worth it, though. I checked to get the timing right, making sure the low tide was a proper low spring tide. Under a cloudless sky, Nick drove us back down to the Gower faster than a speeding bullet that was keeping within the speed limit. More by luck than judgement, we arrived at our usual car park spot at Pilton Green at the perfect time. We were down the footpath and sat on the rocks looking at the waves with 15 minutes to spare before low tide. Perfect.

As soon as we arrived, we knew it was different to our previous visit; we could almost cross the short stretch of sandy beach already. Spring-tide-tastic. Our friendly seal was there to welcome us back, and high on the cliffs behind us, an imperious-looking peregrine falcon preened his feathers and looked very pleased with himself. Nick and I tippy toed across the wet rippled sand, in a very manly and rugged explorer way, and scrambled carefully over the razor-sharp rocks up to Paviland Cave. It was the size of a very large and especially tall living room. On a bright sunny day outside, the shaded cave walls were very rough, cold, and damp. Someone had respectfully left a few candles and some wild-flowers in a neat arrangement on the cave floor. Hats off to whoever chose the oldest known ceremonial burial site in Europe: it is quite a location. The view from the cave 30,000 years ago would have been over vast plains. The melting of the glaciers at the end of an Ice Age flooded the area that is now the Bristol Channel. It's hard to imagine a more perfect day than the one we had chosen. Looking out from the dark-ness of the cave, the sun was blindingly bright, reflecting off the gently rising and falling rollers as they came in from the Atlantic. I took a photo of Nick silhouetted against the sun in his best Indiana Jones pose. Inside, the cave felt understand-ably solemn, but as I've observed before at places like this, there was something in the air. Maybe a bit of multi-dimen-sional quantum time entanglement, who knows?

We took our time to absorb the Paviland atmosphere before slowly walking back to the car. On our way back along the footpath, we feasted on wild blackberries again before getting covered from head to toe in clouds of powdered Pembrokeshire soil by the local farmer as he ploughed his bone-dry fields. It was time to dust ourselves down and move on to the final leg of the journey.

15

TREFIL TO CHEPSTOW

My *Journey through Wales* had been a crazy rollercoaster of travel experiences. I knew it would be. Keeping all the historical events and sites in perspective was hard enough, but into that mix I'd thrown some beautiful landscapes, a dollop of cultural heritage, musical icons, a pinch of sporting diversity, and some mustardy cheese on toast. The last leg of the journey would continue the trend of unpredictable variety, starting with the final UNESCO World Heritage Site of my trip before taking in some workers' rights history, some red paint, a Roman garrison, and a male choir.

There are four UNESCO World Heritage sites in Wales, and I'd already visited three on my *Journey through Wales* (The Slate Landscape of Northwest Wales, Castles and Town Walls of King Edward I, and the Pontcysyllte Aqueduct and Canal). Nick and I were on our way to the fourth.

The Blaenavon Industrial Landscape UNESCO World Heritage Site is a powerful reminder of the contributions made by the people of South Wales to the world-changing events of the Industrial Revolution. This area, and the valleys that Nick and I had seen further west such as Merthyr and Taff, were once the hub of iron and coal production in the late 18th and early 19th centuries. Visiting Blaenavon is like stepping back in time. Well-preserved old ironworks, such as the original blast furnaces and foundry, show off the technological innovations and advances made during the Industrial Revolution, and a collection of preserved terraced houses provides a glimpse into the daily lives of the people who lived and worked in the area. The jewel in the crown is the Big Pit Coal Museum – and that's where Nick and I were heading first.

The Big Pit was a working coal mine during the hundred years from 1880 to 1980, and during the early decades, coal was hacked out of the ground manually. At its peak, the Big Pit employed 1,300 people and produced over 250,000 tons of coal per year. Those are the cold facts, and although impressive, they are just numbers. The industry dictated the day-to-day lives of thousands of people and the communities in which they lived. The Big Pit has a new role today – to tell the story of those people, and the area in which they lived and worked, within the bigger picture of the massive economic and social changes that affected the whole of Britain over those hundred years.

The ex-mine opened to the public as a museum in 1983, run as a charitable trust, and in 2001 it was incorporated into the National Museum and Galleries of Wales as the National Mining Museum of Wales. Later in the morning, Nick and I had a meeting arranged with Ceri Thompson, the curator of the museum, but we timed our arrival at the pit so we could take a trip underground first.

After collecting our tickets, we were shown to a holding area. We sat patiently with about thirty other visitors awaiting our turn to go down the mine. They take groups of twelve to fifteen visitors at a time, to see the old mine workings, and we were soon being kitted out with miners' lamps, helmets, and emergency breathing apparatus. The first two were essential, and although the breathing apparatus wasn't, we had to take it because the mine is still classed as a working pit and the safety gear is required by HM Inspectorate of

Mines. And anyway, it meant we could pretend to be real miners.

Our group was prepared for action by a team of orange clad stand-up comedians who the museum employs as underground guides. They are mostly former underground workers, so they know what they're talking about, but their line in banter soon had everyone chuckling and in good spirits. As our group was being prepared for our trip to the coal face, we all enjoyed a few minutes of rapid-fire jesting from the miner celebrities:

'Where you from?'

'Dorset.'

'Oh, Sandbanks is it? …Yeh, you look like millionaires.'

'Where you from?'

'London.'

'Oh, I've been there… nice little place… give my regards to the queen.'

And so it went on. They asked us to hand over our cameras, phones, and anything else capable of making a spark; items called 'contraband' in mining terminology. Kitted out and sparkless, our group, helped by our guide, Andrew, was led to a metal cage that slowly rattled its way down a vertical shaft. We left the bright light and warmth of summer behind us. Our new world felt very enclosed, cold, slightly damp, and very dark.

We must have been underground for about an hour, gradually working our way along tunnels known as 'roadways' in miner-speak, at one point finding ourselves 90 metres below the surface. Most of the roadways were a couple of metres wide and about the same height, although in many places the roof was much lower. Grownups must adopt a strange crouch-walk in places, which is probably good for core muscle toning, but difficult to keep up after just a few metres. We slowly ducked and dived our way through low passageways lined with thick wooden pit props. Most of us had a couple of occasions to be thankful we were wearing protective helmets. As the lamps on our heads illuminated the way along tight passageways and chambers, our guide stopped regularly to tell us about the history of the mine and the life of the miners. He modestly claimed that he wasn't really cut out for the job of guide; he'd be more comfortable with a pickaxe in his hands. In reality, he was a natural communicator, as so many Welsh people are, and his stories kept flowing with great humility and good humour.

We eventually squeezed into a narrow passageway that took us to where miners would have been working not so many years ago – literally at the coal face. We were looking at what looked like a black, slightly shiny, rough wall of rock, about 2 metres high. Andrew pointed out the subtle geological banding and flaws in the seam that miners would have exploited to help them extract the precious black stuff. A weary-looking conveyor system ran along the floor away from the coal face, and a couple of discarded pneumatic hammers lay on the floor of the shaft, as if waiting to be picked up to continue their job. We heard how these were used to chip away at the coal face section by section. I think most of us were imagining ourselves in that job – sweating, caked in thick coal dust, a deafening noise rattling around the confined space as you desperately try to carve out enough coal to meet your daily quota. I think I'd have been fine with that… for about 5 minutes.

A miner's life was harsh, to put it mildly, and not for the fainthearted. Although there was a strong camaraderie, there was also a brutally hard side to it – it was a place where young men grew up fast and had to become strong minded as well as strong bodied. There was no nostalgic romance as far as Andrew was concerned. 'We only did it for one thing,' he said, rubbing his forefinger and thumb together. 'Money, that's all it was… it was a job.'

Softies like Nick and me could never know what it was really like, but seeing the coal face, feeling the claustrophobic atmosphere in that dark and confined space, and hearing

Andrew's description of life underground gave us a glimpse into the world in which the miners had to live and work for large parts of their lives. It was a thoughtful group that waited patiently for 'the cage,' which then clanked its way up to the surface, taking us back to the dazzling light of day.

Someone pointed Nick and me towards the administration block, where we were told we would find Ceri Thompson, the curator of the museum. Our pre-arranged 10-minute scheduled chat lasted for nearly 2 hours, but I blame most of that on Ceri and Nick's regular and lengthy digressions into Welsh rugby. Ceri was another natural communicator and once into his stride, the stories flowed. I'm tempted to call him a mine of information but, in his case, it's more of a bottomless pit.

I think Ceri's initial sentence was the most succinct and perfect summary of South Wales history that I've come across: 'Well in 1800, there was nothing much here, then in 1900 there was a hell of a lot here, and by 2000 it was heading back the other way.'

He then unpacked that brilliant précis, explaining how places like Blaenavon and the Rhondda valley were once part of the largest continuous coalfield in Britain, and how the high quality of its coal had made the area a key part of the Industrial Revolution. He described how the population of the Rhondda valleys, previously inhabited by small farming settlements, jumped from 900 in 1830 to over 185,000 by the end of that century. The picture painted by Ceri was of a Welsh version of the gold rush… only blacker and much dustier. It was mostly men who were drawn to the area looking for work, initially from other parts of Wales, but also from Somerset and Gloucestershire. The mine owners became very rich while those working in the mines endured horrific working conditions and pitiful pay. Drinking and fighting were rife, but in contrast, there was also a temperance movement. There was a lot more to tell, but first, I was interested to find out about Ceri himself. What was his background?

Born in the Rhondda Valley into a family with six

previous generations of miners, he'd started work underground at the Cwm Colliery at sixteen, straight from school… like most of his pals. He was clearly a bright lad, but for him, like so many others, there was no alternative. Ceri told us a story about his parents being asked to see the junior school headmaster, who had become concerned with the young boy's progress. The headmaster asked Ceri's mum and dad if their child ever read at home. 'Yes, his head is never out of a book,' came the reply. 'Well, what sort of things is he reading – comics?' asked the headmaster. 'Well no,' said Ceri's father. 'Right now, he's reading *Bismarck and the Reunification of Germany*.'

The Cwm pit employed a thousand men, had the widest shaft of all the surrounding mines, and the best coking coal in Europe. It became the flagship of the NCB, the statutory corporation created to run the nationalised coal industry in 1947. Ceri worked at the coal face for 16 years until just after the miners' strike of 1984 to 1985. He used the spare time provided by the strike to educate himself further and get some qualifications. He learned Welsh and went to Workers Education Association classes in Pontypridd, where they encouraged him to go to the Coleg Harlech. The education certificate he got there enabled him to study history at Cardiff University. A series of jobs and volunteering opportunities eventually led to him being appointed as curator of the National Coal Museum in 1999. It's a heart-warming story of a boy who was clearly brilliant but whose only option as a lad was to become a miner. Through his own drive and hard work, he has become the curator of a museum that won World Heritage status in 2000, and then in 2005, the coveted Gulbenkian Prize (and £100,000) for the museum of the year.

I asked Ceri about the Big Pit National Coal Museum, and how it came about. The story went back to the 1980s. Even before the mine was closed, they identified it as a potential heritage attraction. Seeing the success of the Llechwedd slate mine in North Wales, a working group of experts (NCB, local government, the National Museum, the Welsh Development Agency, and the Welsh Office) was established to find somewhere similar for South Wales. A coal mine was the obvious choice and the Big Pit almost selected itself. The priority was safety – ideally a shallow mine with no chance of methane gas. 'Shallow? Well, you could practically jump down the Big Pit,' said Ceri, 'and it was both self-draining and self-ventilating.' Ceri told us how the former Welsh rugby international fly-half, Billy Cleaver ('Billy the Kick'), became involved with the Big Pit project. In those days, Rugby Union was a sport for amateurs and even international players had full-time jobs. The NCB employed Billy Cleaver as Chief Mechanisation Officer and he played rugby in his spare time. Billy could have described the requirements for ventilation at the Big Pit as being minimal, but being Welsh, he had a more poetic version: '…Big Pit could be ventilated by a moth flexing its wings.'

As its first curator under the National Museum of Wales, Ceri went about his task thoughtfully, visiting as many museums as possible to pick up best practice ideas. His aim was to produce a world class mining museum for Wales. From the outset, his goal was to focus on the human aspects of mining history. Although the Big Pit has plenty of buildings to look round, and mining equipment to examine, Ceri says 90% of the exhibits are about human beings: 'The people who worked the machinery are more important than the machinery itself.' Funding from the Welsh Government allows the museum not to charge for entry and the visitor numbers prove its success. It was an absolute treat to have so much time with Ceri. He is so dedicated and passionate about this work and mixes hard work with a terrific sense of humour. I think it's fair to say he's completely nailed his aim of producing a world class mining museum for Wales.

When HV Morton visited the area in the 1930s, he also went down a working pit. He dedicated over ten pages to his trip underground and his colourful description really brings home both the horror of the miners' lifestyle and the cama- raderie they enjoyed. HV Morton likened that bond to that experienced by a regiment in the firing line. Nick and I ended our visit to the Big Pit with a quick look around the old pithead baths. You might think I'm pushing the boundaries of extreme tourism here, but the building is significant for two reasons. The architect, Percy Thomas, designed the Grade II listed building in 1939, in the International Style, which was associated with the Bauhaus School of Architecture. Charac- terised by functional design and the absence of ornamenta- tion, the focus was on the use of new materials and technologies. It's not something you would normally associate with a coal mine… a bit like Christian Dior producing safety boots. Design enthusiasts from all around the world presumably converge on the Big Pit baths to admire the subtle architectural integration of clean lines and clean bodies. The other important point is that the baths represent a marker point in social history. Before the pithead baths were built, miners had to travel home covered in coal dust, and wash in a metal bathtub, either in front of the fire or outside in the yard. Their wives had to boil tubs of water for the bath, and to wash the dirty clothes… a long time before automatic washing machines came along. The magnitude of the trans- formation that the pithead baths provided is difficult for most of us to grasp, given our current pampered lifestyles.

Heading south towards Newport, Nick, and I were again driving through the distinctive and unique landscape of The Valleys. Rows of standard grey terraced houses appear abruptly and line the valley sides. They snuggle down in the valley floors for collective security, as if trying to evade the harsh winds of economic misfortune that have blown their way. Terraces of identical small houses line the road, inter- rupted every now and again by a chapel, a miners' institute, a scrap of waste ground, a general store, or a random field of sheep. If you're travelling through the area, stop a while and listen… it's OK, the natives are friendly. Faint echoes of colliery whistles, the rattle of a lift cage, and the clopping of pit ponies still linger in the air, a reminder of a time when the area hummed with mining activity, the pride of Britain's industrial strength.

Without exception, every valley has been touched by despair and misfortune from that famous past; each one has its tales of tragedy, and the suffering is measured by hundreds of lives lost – not just jobs. It can feel as if the very fabric of The Valleys' landscape is suffering a collective loss, about which you are regularly reminded when you come across the many memorials. Nick and I stopped off at the village of Six Bells to visit a miners' memorial called 'The Guardian', which was unveiled on 28 October 2010.

The 20-metre-high statue of a miner is constructed from 20,000 strips of corten steel, which has oxidised to give him a natural rusty brown colour like that of the Angel of the North. Sculptor Sebastian Boyesen was commissioned to design the monument to honour the forty-five miners who lost their lives in the Six Bells Colliery Disaster in 1960. An explosion trapped many of the men underground and despite the efforts of rescuers, only one miner survived. The disaster had a profound impact on the local community, which is still felt to this day. Sadly, every one of the valleys can tell similar stories, but it is memorials like The Guardian that ensure that the miners who lost their lives will never be forgotten. The steel memorial towers over the site of the former Six Bells colliery, looking down on the village and the valley below. It's hard to stand underneath it and not be moved by the thought of the forty-five victims whose names are cut into the steel band that surrounds the plinth of the statue.

Nick and I were shown The Guardian by Hywel Clatworthy, who volunteers at the local Tŷ Ebbw Fach, a community building run by Six Bells Regeneration Limited to provide support and encouragement to locally run volunteer groups. Profits from their business facilities and restaurant are ploughed back into the local area. I had arranged to meet

Hywel to find out about the memorial and the work done at the centre. He and another volunteer, Lucy Wilkinson, showed us around the Tŷ Ebbw Fach building, a former pub, which includes a heritage centre (which was opened in 2011 by our current king), office accommodation, a conference room, and an impressive forty-seater café. Hywel and Lucy were two more of those super-enthusiastic people who seem to ooze passion for their work.

One thing I was particularly keen to find out about was the story of 'Six Bells Red.' When the local coal mines were closed back in the 1980s, the pumps that kept the underground workings clear of water eventually had to be switched off. The inevitable happened and the iron-rich water from the flooded mines found its way to the local river, starving it of oxygen and turning it red. The discharge from the mine was bad news for anything living in or around the water, so a bore hole was drilled into the ground to intercept the polluted material and divert it into settling ponds in a mine water treatment site. It's the next bit which is different, clever, and makes the story unusual.

While studying for a PhD at the University College London, in 2017, artist Onya McCausland came up with the idea of converting that coal mine sludge (there will be a more scientific name for it) into pigment for use as paint. After visiting forty-six similar ex-mine sites around Britain, she chose Six Bells to try out her bright (red) idea. The mine water treatment site, a short walk from the Tŷ Ebbw Fach centre, is central to the process. It even has a plaque to acknowledge it as the source of the 'Six Bells Ochre.' The waste residue from the mine is collected there and gets processed into a tan coloured pigment powder. Burning the powder at a specific temperature creates the distinctive Six Bells Red colour, which makes a fitting link to the fire and heat of the old mines. Onya set up the Turning Landscape Community Interest Company (CIC) in 2020 with Hywel and Lucy Harding to produce the paint at Six Bells. Based in the Tŷ Ebbw Fach building, the

CIC secured lottery funding to facilitate a series of events, workshops, talks, and demonstrations on the art of making paint in this way. The company is slowly developing a range of five colours using materials from other mines around Britain. Each one is derived from its own distinct landscape and topography, providing characteristics that are unique to each source. Working with architects, Turning Landscape CIC uses the paint for innovative architectural projects, and Onya uses the paint to make large-scale wall painting installations.

The paint and the hands-on production process symbolise both the industrial heritage and the uncertain environmental future of the planet. On a positive note, this environmental legacy has been turned into something creative which serves as a reminder of the industrial past. As the four of us sat discussing Six Bells Red in the Tŷ Ebbw Fach restaurant, Hywel told us about his background in digital mapping – we could easily have been there chatting for the rest of the day, but Nick and I had to be on our way, continuing on our journey down The Valleys and on to Newport. Not for the first time, we felt humbled by the welcome and friendly reception we had been given. We continued winding our way south, through a ribbon of old mining communities in the Ebbw Vale.

Now, you know what they say about pithead baths? You wait all your life to see one, then two come along the same day. We stopped at a bend in the B447 in the village of Llan-hilleth to look at some more pithead baths in the flesh. These were the raw, unadulterated, real thing, another building that has somehow survived from the industrial past – and another one designed by Percy Thomas. The massive red-brick block, once a key part of the defunct Llanhilleth Colliery, has not been polished for the benefit of tourists. Rather it remains at the roadside, an unadulterated testament to the past, a nearly empty husk of a building, its windows shattered, gradually being overtaken by the forces of nature. Nick and I clambered up a brick wall to peer inside, where a solitary row of less than pristine porcelain toilets remained (I know, it's quite an image) surrounded by walls of broken tiles, embellished in places by the artwork of modern vandals. In its raw state, it felt even more poignant than the cleaned-up version at the Big Pit. It was easy to conjure visions of the days when it offered the miners of Llanhilleth a warm and safe place to clean up and unwind. I hope that some enterprising soul will undertake the challenge of converting the old shell into a grand architectural abode, instead of consigning it to the dustbin of history through demolition.

Our journey through the valleys of South Wales was brief, resulting in impressions that, while impactful, could only scratch the surface of the region's rich complexity. There was undoubtedly a gritty exterior, and to be frank, some places still look bleak. But there was a steely character and an honesty about the area, if that doesn't sound too pretentious. The valleys have a subtle charm that's hard to put your finger on. As old mining areas are reclaimed, fields and woodland are gradually returning to the valley sides and tops, adding colour to an otherwise grey canvas. Everyone Nick and I met there was warm and welcoming, and despite all the changes the valleys have seen, and the economic blows they have suffered, there is a sense of community that is probably unmatched anywhere else in Britain.

The city of Newport is one of the largest in Wales. It lies along the River Usk near its confluence with the Severn Estuary and is home to around 140,000 people. After our brush with the Chartists at Cyfarthfa and Trefil, Nick and I were keen to visit the historic Westgate Hotel, which was at the heart of the Newport Rising on 4th November 1839. The uprising was the last large-scale armed rebellion against authority in Great Britain. We found the hotel, which now looks like a music venue, near the city centre, and it still looks much the same as it did on that historic day in 1839. Those events were little over a century before I was born, so in some ways they don't seem so far back in history, even though the world in which they took place seems so different to the one in which we live today. Led by John Frost, a group of about 3,000 Chartists and working-class people marched to Newport to fight for improved voting rights and parliamentary reform – as laid out in their simple six-point charter. They gathered in front of the Westgate Hotel to protest peacefully, but things took a turn for the worse when the authorities attempted to arrest the leaders. This sparked a violent clash between the protesters and the authorities, and the Newport Rising turned into a bloody uprising. Tragically, at least twenty-two protesters were shot dead outside the hotel. The Newport Rising is considered a turning point in the social history of the nation and is remembered and celebrated as a proud part of Welsh heritage and history.

The next time you get a quiz question asking what York, Chester, and Caerleon have in common, you will now be ready (if you didn't know already): they were the three permanent Roman Legionary Fortresses in Britain. Chester was known as Deva Victrix, York was more familiar to legionnaires as Eboracum, while Caerleon, established in AD 75, was known as Isca Augusta.

The fortress at Caerleon dominated the South Wales area for the following 200 years. Imagine that – for us today it would be like having had a foreign army dictating daily life in Britain since the 1820s. Since at least medieval times, Caerleon has been linked to the myth of King Arthur. The idea was given a boost by the writings of our old friend Geoffrey of Monmouth (if you can remember back to Chapter 2) in his Kings of Britain book (*Historia Regum Britanniae*). According to Geoffrey's account, the Round Table where Arthur and his knights convened, was in Caerleon, although it should be noted that Cadbury Castle, Somerset, and Winchester also have claims to the site of Camelot and the Round Table.

Invited to look for evidence of Arthurian legend, the renowned archaeologist, Sir Mortimer Wheeler, went digging up bits of Caerleon in the 1920s. Although Wheeler's team didn't find evidence of a court or a table, they made some remarkable other discoveries. Most notable was a 2nd century, 6000-seater Roman amphitheatre, considered by some to be the best-preserved example in Britain. Also brought to light were a large Roman barracks and an associated civilian settlement, where families and tradespeople supporting the military community would have lived.

A familiar sight in Wales - two teams enjoying a game of rugby

Nick and I spent an enjoyable couple of hours or so looking around The National Roman Legion Museum, the Baths Museum, and the open-air ruins of the amphitheatre and barracks. While I watched someone flying a drone around the turf-covered terraces of the amphitheatre, Nick had the unexpected bonus of watching half a game of rugby between Caerleon and Bedwas seconds. Caerleon is right up there with Chester, Bath, York, and Hadrian's Wall for giving visitors a great insight of what Roman Britain would have been like. It has a good balance of formal 'museum' places where everything is explained, and open-air spaces left for visitors to just look around on their own.

My summer-long *Journey through Wales* was nearly over. It had been a long, hot summer. A record breaker. In Caerleon, the dryness had even caused some leaves to turn to their Autumnal yellows and browns by early September. As Nick and I left the town, I looked up and saw a skein of geese heading south to their wintering grounds. Maybe that was a sign – but in any case, I was about to do the same. If I'd just headed east and over the Severn Bridge at that point, it would have brought a satisfyingly simple conclusion to the journey, but things were slightly more complicated. Nick was going to take me back to pick up my motorcycle, and then he'd head back up to Scotland while I rode home via Chepstow, where my journey had begun. Before that, we had one last stop on the journey to make.

It meant making a dash back to the Rhondda Valley. It was breaking the overall pattern of an anticlockwise tour around Wales, but one extra night, out of sequence, was going to be worth it. Listening to the Treorchy Male Choir at one of their weekly rehearsal sessions would be a very special climax to my adventure through the Land of Song. There couldn't be a more fitting way to end it.

Choirs are one of the defining cultural features of Wales. Every valley and most villages have their own choir and they've been around in the Rhondda Valley for over 150 years. Treorchy had one of the first, although the present Treorchy Male Choir didn't come into being until 1946, when it was reformed after World War II. Nowadays, it is recognised as one of the greatest choral ensembles of all time and has been described by Sir Tom Jones as simply 'the finest.' It has a record eight National Eisteddfod wins and enjoys international fame and acclaim. In more recent times it was the first male choir to venture into the field of popular music, collaborating with a 'Who's Who' of international celebrities, including Sir Tom Jones, Dame Shirley Bassey, Ozzy Osbourne, Sir Cliff Richard, and McFly, to produce over fifty recordings. The choir has a very full touring schedule, but where better to see and hear these amazing choral superstars than in their own backyard, on rehearsal night?

In the weeks before my Welsh adventure, I'd corresponded with David Bebb, the choir's secretary, to explain my trip, and my *Journey through Wales* book. He invited me to make myself known to the boys when I went along to the rehearsals, and maybe join them for a pint afterwards. The prospect of the choir, in full voice, sent a shiver of anticipation through me every time I thought about it. I was pretty smug about the brilliant trip scheduling that was going to deliver the perfect finale for my Welsh adventure. It also felt great knowing my pal Nick, a diehard Welshman, would be there with me as well… it was going to be absolutely perfect (the usual precursor to something that doesn't end up absolutely perfect).

Treorchy looks like many other towns and communities in the South Wales valleys. Lines of grey terraced houses run parallel to each other along the contours of the hills, neatly stepping up the valley sides in rows, like the terraces of the Principality Stadium. Beyond the back fences of the highest rows of houses lie the moorlands and trees of the mountainside. And sheep. The valley towns fell upon hard times when the coal mines closed through the 1980s. Some Treorchy residents began commuting to places like Cardiff and Bridgend for work, but unemployment rates in the town became eyewateringly high, despite vast amounts of investment capital from Britain and overseas. At either end of the valleys, new factories and enterprises have sprung up, but in between, unemployment remains high. Unlike some other valley towns, however, Treorchy has picked itself up like a phoenix from the coal ashes.

Nick and I arrived at our Treorchy hotel for the last night of our adventure in the early evening. We checked in and went for a walk down the High Street (more precisely, Bute Street, but the two roads run into each other). It looked good, and it was bustling. There was an impressive mix of old and new businesses. There were a few of the usual national chains, but plenty of independent shops and unique businesses. We shouldn't have been surprised because Treorchy has become recognised as a retail success story, with its main drag being voted UK High Street of the year in 2020. The turnaround is testament to the community spirit and entrepreneurial imagination of the people of Treorchy and if I was a Chamber of Trade leader from one of the many boarded up towns across Britain, I'd want to know how they did it.

With my Welsh adventure nearly over, I would soon be heading back to Dorset for the green, green, grass of home, and right on cue, Nick and I came across a barber shop with the sign: 'Tom Jones Gents' Hairdresser.' It was maybe our last opportunity for a childish burst of corny puns. Nick kicked off with a far from tuneful, 'Down the road I look at heads so hairy.' I couldn't respond with anything tuneful (no change there) or even untuneful, but I remember saying how sad it was to see an international singing legend having to resort to a second job to supplement his pension. Nick pointed out that 'it's not unusual' but I had to rule his effort out immediately and tell him I'd already done that joke in Chapter Four. I felt the pain of his pun and we laughed no more.

After sampling the delights of the chippy, we walked the short distance to the primary school, where, for many years, the Treorchy Male Choir has rehearsed twice a week. We got there early, having built in even more contingency time than usual to our planning... we didn't want to miss this one! The blue plaque on the wall of the school confirmed we were in the right place. You can probably see where this is going.

The rehearsals were due to start at 7:00 pm but by 7:15 pm

no one had turned up. We quizzed an elderly gentleman walking past. 'Oh, yes; every week they're here, regular as clockwork.' Well, not that week. The clock must have stopped. We waited another half an hour before finally admitting defeat. By then, I'd treble-checked the date and time. I checked them one more time. I even checked the tide times. What could have happened? I phoned the secretary of the choir but got no response. We sloped off to The Lion pub on the corner of the award-winning High Street, despondent and confused. That was that then.

Unlike us, The Lion pub was buzzing. It was quiz night, and as soon as we sat down, someone presented us with an answer sheet and a blank map of Treorchy High Street. We knew it wasn't our night when, for the first round, we had to label twenty shops or businesses on the map. By the time we'd marked up the chippy, the pub, and the Tom Jones hairdresser, we'd exhausted our local knowledge and were at least seventeen points behind everyone else. It made me think about how much sensory data our brains process all the time, without us being conscious of it. Nick and I must have seen every one of those shops and businesses on the High Street. The central processing units in our brains had received the data but chosen not to store it for later retrieval – prioritising other inputs and processes, such as thinking about where to eat, finding the primary school, and recalling the lyrics to the power ballad Delilah, which Sir Tom Jones took to number two in the UK singles charts, and number one in eight overseas charts, in March 1968.

After a few more rounds of the quiz, there was a break for everyone to get more drinks, and it was about then, just after 9:00 pm, we noticed quite a few men coming into the pub wearing Treorchy Male Choir polo shirts and blazers. Nick and I looked at each other with a mixture of confusion and horror. Uh oh… had we missed something? Had they skipped rehearsals and just come out for a pint? I asked one guy if he was from the choir and he told me, 'Yes; we've just had a brilliant night of rehearsals… the first after our summer break. It was good to be back… the boys were in fine voice, and we had a few visitors watching us.' I was so pleased for them. I explained how the choir might have had two more fans in the audience, but we'd waited in vain outside the primary school for almost an hour. 'Oh no, we don't rehearse there anymore. We've been rehearsing at the chapel ever since COVID.'

That explained everything. I found David Bebb, the choir secretary, at the bar, and introduced myself. The mix up was all my fault because David had explained the switch to the chapel in one of his emails a couple of months earlier. I'd completely forgotten about it, and with my laptop out of action for the previous week, I wasn't able to look back and check my old emails. He said that in normal circumstances, he'd get the boys to strike up a song for us in the pub, but they couldn't really do that with the quiz going on. I suggested they should do it anyway; we weren't doing very well in the quiz. Looking back, I can tell how disconsolate I must have been because I went on a real bender that night by having a second pint.

My phone rang when we got back to the hotel. It was Selwyn, the former choir secretary, responding to the missed call he'd received earlier in the evening. When I explained the debacle of the evening to him, he sympathised, told me a bit more about the choir, and asked if we could come along to the next rehearsals. I explained how we'd already extended our trip once to be in Treorchy that night. We had to go home the next day. He asked me where I lived and suggested a cunning plan.

The curtain had come down on my *Journey through Wales*, if not exactly in the way I had expected. The following day, Nick and I went our separate ways; he returned to Scotland, and I returned to Dorset. My journey was over. Time for some reflection on an incredible adventure, to remember so many unbelievable places visited, and all those wonderful people I'd met. I needed to get my laptop repaired and start writing.

But there was one more twist to this plot, and for the final encore we have to move forward two weeks to the seaside town of Lyme Regis on the Dorset coast, just a short drive from my home.

Jan and I arrived at St Michael's Parish Church that evening in good time for the evening concert. Standing around chatting outside in twos and threes when we arrived were members of the Treorchy Male Choir – I recognised the blazers. Great! I was in the right place this time. We got talking to a couple of the choir members and they told us how pleased they were to be there, and how much they enjoyed touring. They told us how they'd been singing with other choral groups recently, back in Treorchy, and on the road. In a lovely Welsh melodic lilt, one of them said, 'Last week, we were singing with a choir from Iceland,' and then with perfect comedy timing, he added, 'next week, we're singing with a choir from Tesco.'

The lads introduced me to their former choir secretary, Selwyn, and I was able to thank him personally for his return phone call on that fateful night in Treorchy. It was his kind thought to ring me back that had enabled Jan and me to see the boys in concert in Lyme Regis that evening. Selwyn and I had a good chat and by then I could even laugh about the rehearsal incident.

The choir, led by award-winning musical director, Stewart Roberts, provided a performance every bit as fantastic and moving as I knew it would be. Along with guest soloist, Angharad Morgan, they put on a magnificent show, and I will always remember the occasion as being the first time I sang God save the King, instead of God save the Queen. What a special group of people to be singing it with. On a technicality, I can now say that I've sung with the Treorchy Male Choir. Towards the end of the performance, Selwyn moved to the front of the choir to make a few announcements. He's another Welshman, who could easily have made a career as a stand-up comedian. He told the audience about an incident that happened a couple of weeks ago, back home in the valleys. 'A chap called Mark came to Treorchy with his friend Nick, and they waited patiently at the primary school to hear us rehearsing... while we sang just down the road at the chapel.' The audience found this highly amusing for some reason. Scanning the audience as the laughter subsided, he then called out, 'Mark, are you out there?' I stood up, feeling suitably embarrassed, while the audience clapped enthusiastically... presumably in sympathy. I think at this stage Jan was sinking as low as she could in the pew, trying to hide between the prayer mats. Selwyn continued, 'That was really unfortunate, but we thought, well, if you can't find us in Treorchy... then we'll come down here and find you in Dorset!'

The last row on my spreadsheet could be ticked off. My journey was over.

REFLECTIONS

I knew my *Journey through Wales* would be an amazing and incident packed experience, and I knew many of the best incidents along the way would be the unexpected ones. The trip was always intended to be a light-hearted travel experience; I wasn't trying to come up with a ground-breaking anthropological thesis – I just wanted to explore the country with the eyes of a stranger, enjoy the ride, and see what happened along the way. I still went with a few considerations in mind, however. How did Welsh people feel about being Welsh? How was their country looking in 2022 compared to the one HV Morton drove through all those years ago? After I'd unpacked my panniers, washed my smalls, and caught up with a few jobs, I had to unpack my experiences – what had moved me, what had surprised me, and had the trip changed me at all?

Thinking of the things that moved me… Côr Dyffryn Dyfi reducing me to tears at the National Eisteddfod was the most emotional moment of my journey, quite a moving experience. The day with Scott and Ruth at Bron yr Aur left Sarah, Dan, and me all feeling stunned and grateful for such incredible hospitality… and that happened a lot. On a slightly selfish note, my day in the mountains with my daughter was very special, as were those quiet few days of calm I spent on the Llangollen Canal with Jan… they were timely reminders of the important things in life. The chance to have a couple of unsupervised weeks of irresponsibility with my old pal Nick is always to be treasured.

You probably yawned at the number of times I wrote something like, 'the builders of these prehistoric sites knew how to pick a good spot.' Just about every one of those sites was stunning and provided food for thought about the builders, the occupants, their lives, beliefs, and motivations. Pontnewydd Cave and Paviland Cave are both mind-boggling in terms of their age. It's hard to get your head around the timescales, but both are incredible when you think about what they represent on the timeline of human life in Europe. From a historical perspective, the Tudor period is incredibly significant and influential – so seeing the quiet rural backwater where Owen Tudor came from, unleashing that dynasty on England and the world, made me think. I already knew about the role Wales had played in the Industrial Revolution, but the scale of that role was eye opening and more than once I found myself shaking my head in disbelief at the amount of natural resources that Wales has provided to Britain and the rest of the world. I found myself moved and slightly angry at the plight of the many ordinary people who were exploited in that process. Sitting in the room where the notes of Bohemian Rhapsody were first heard is quite a thought, and my spine tingled similarly in Bron Yr Aur, thinking about Robert Plant tinkering with the opening lines of Stairway to Heaven. Those experiences, and trips to Tregaron and Treorchy, ensured that music was a constant companion on my travels through the Land of Song.

The BBC film crew Sarah and I met in the mountains of Snowdonia, a long hot summer, and a watermill without water, made me think seriously about the effects of climate change.

Without exception, I met lovely, friendly people. Many

gave up a lot of their time and were incredibly hospitable. By definition, my trip brought me into contact with nice customer-facing people in the tourism and hospitality industries, but I also met so many other people from many other walks of life. The warmth of their welcomes was very heartening. One of the most memorable days of the trip was when I walked around the National Eisteddfod and bumped into so many friendly and happy people – considering I was an outsider at their party. Maybe I was just lucky, but if so, I'll take it – thank you.

The natural beauty of Wales did not surprise me, although seeing virtually all of it without getting wet was something I hadn't expected. I'd visited most regions of the country many times previously, and knowing those amazing mountains, hills, and coastline was a big reason for choosing Wales for my big adventure. The Welsh landscape is stunning. The one area that caught me out was Mid Wales. I really enjoyed exploring the area around Rhayader and the central Cambrian Mountains for the first time.

Everyone knows that Wales has lots of castles and abbeys, but seriously… how many!?

Before I started researching this trip, there were many aspects of Welsh history that I hadn't come across. I'm ashamed to say that I hadn't realised that the Welsh people are some of the most British people of our islands, and their language is the most British. By the way, we should scrap the English legal system right now and start again, based on the Laws of Hywel Dda – they were a revelation to me. I couldn't help but wonder how different things would have been if Wales had found its way through life without the burden of being England's handy next-door treasure chest. The information I learned in Cyfarthfa about the sheer size and importance of the iron, steel, and coal industries left quite an impression on me, especially coming so soon after learning about Copperopolis in Swansea. It's sobering to think of all those natural resources being found at such a pivotal moment in history.

I learned about a few characters I'd not come across before. Sir Pryce Pryce-Jones and Robert Owen from Newtown, Bill Frost from Saundersfoot, Twm Siôn Cati from Tregaron, The Reverend William Morgan of St Asaph, The Reverend Griffith Jones of Carmarthenshire, Dr William Price from Llantrisant and Hywel Dda should all be more well known than they are, alongside the towering names of Owain Glyndŵr, Llywelyn ap Iorwerth, and Llywelyn ap Gruffydd. To my shame, the Nant Gwrtheyrn Welsh Language and Heritage Centre on the Llŷn Peninsula, and the National Library of Wales, Aberystwyth, both surprised me. They are both hugely impressive, but my surprise came mostly from not being aware of them before my visit. The Willow Theatre at Rhayader and the Carreg Cennen Castle were also both completely new to me and delightful discoveries. Laverbread, less so. Sorry, but I tried.

Welsh people came across as being very patriotic and rightly proud of their country, their fellow countrymen, and their history. Everyone wanted me to write about their love of their country and about how their part of Wales was best. The newcomers to the country were often its most enthusiastic advocates and the ones most keen to learn the language. The problem of affordable homes for local people still needs a solution (as in other parts of Britain) as does the degradation of rural communities through the purchase of land by outsiders. While my journey gave me a feeling of great joy, I came home with a deep sense of unease at how England has treated its near neighbour over the centuries, and how that unjust relationship continues. My trip has turned me into an ambassador for Wales and I feel protective towards it. I find myself telling people about the Welsh history that non-Welsh people don't normally hear about, how the country fuelled the Industrial Revolution… and so on.

People outside Wales already know about its magnificent

mountain scenery and castles. They don't generally know so much about its superb coastline, beaches, traditional regional food, and dark skies. I don't say too much about the Glyders, the Preseli Mountains, Anglesey, The Llangollen Canal, or the Pembrokeshire Coast because I don't want too many people to know about them. Luckily, no one will be reading this.

I had another look at those Seven Wonders of Wales, previously rather northeast-centric. I've come up with my own slightly clumsy updated version, but I'm sure everyone will have their own favourites.

> *From Snowdon's peaks to Pembrokeshire's shore,*
> *So much beauty to explore.*
> *Harlech Castle, and six hundred more,*
> *Can hear the mighty Pistyll Rhaeadr roar.*
> *While Menai's bridge spans waters wide,*
> *St Davids Cathedral gives national pride.*
> *The Laws of Hywel Dda, so good and fair,*
> *These seven wonders are so rare.*

Being able to go on such a trip is a privilege and I count myself extremely fortunate. After taking *Another Journey through Britain* on my own in 2018, and then a *Journey through India* with my best friend in 2020, I decided to share this latest adventure with some more people, and that provided another type of experience, a more shared one, and I will treasure those memories for as long as the old grey matter holds out.

Searching for Wales almost a century after HV Morton highlights the remarkable changes that have taken place within the country, particularly with its big industries. The once dominant coal and steel sectors, which in places, literally shaped the landscape, are gradually giving way to new and thriving economic sectors such as digital technology, natural sciences, and tourism. Amidst these significant transformations, the enduring elements of Welsh culture that HV Morton so colourfully portrayed continue to thrive. Music, poetry, and a strong sense of community (not to mention the love of a good natter) remain integral to the Welsh identity, exemplified by cherished traditions such as the renowned Eisteddfod festivals. According to the 1931 census, just before HV Morton's visit, the percentage of Welsh speakers in Wales stood at 36.8%. While the figure in the 2021 census shows a decline to 17.8%, it represents a rise from a low point in 1981. In my informal conversations, most people I asked expressed a desire to identify as Welsh first and British second. Although a small sample in statistical terms, this sentiment resonated strongly. It appears that the inclusion and subsequent withdrawal from the European Union have not necessarily clarified issues of national identity in a country that has long aspired for self-reliance.

Although some aspects of Wales have changed dramatically, some things never change. The natural landscape, mountains, and coastline remain beautiful and despite the freak weather of the summer of 2022, it still rains a lot (although even that might be changing), and there are still lots of sheep. The people of Wales still make us outsiders welcome, love a good chat or a song, and love a game of rugby. Even without this book to remind me, I will always remember my Summer of 2022 in Wales as a joy and a huge privilege. Thank you – Diolch yn fawr iawn.

WELSH HISTORY

Journey through Wales includes a lot of places of historical interest. But it's a light-hearted travel memoir, not a history book. The order in which the places appear in the book has been decided by a geographical reference frame rather than a chronological one – historical sites just turn up along the route. To make sense of this random stream of historic places, it might help to have a simplified overview of Welsh history to refer to. The following paragraphs provide that overview. It is intentionally brief and takes huge liberties with both the choice of key events and with its sweeping generalisations. Fortunately, there is an inexhaustible supply of books and Internet sites available to provide clarification and fill in the inevitable gaps.

Known in Welsh as Cymru, meaning 'fellow countrymen' or 'land of the Welsh' depending on the source, Wales is a nation with a rich history. The name 'Wales' itself has Germanic origins, derived from the words 'Walh' or 'Walhas,' used by the Anglo-Saxons to refer to outsiders such as the Celts or Romans. Wales did not exist as a unified nation in the distant past. The land was divided between kingdoms with ever-changing borders as tribes fought to gain more territory and defend their holdings. The rugged, mountainous terrain of Wales deterred invaders like the Romans, Vikings and Anglo-Saxons, limiting their influence. This allowed the Welsh people to maintain their distinct genetic identity as the most ancient Britons, quite distinct from much of mainland Britain.

Celts - The early settlement of Wales is still debated, particularly regarding the origins of the Celtic people. It was long thought that Wales was first settled by people from the Iberian peninsula, with Celtic tribes from mainland Europe gradually taking over. However, more recent DNA evidence proposes the opposite - that a common Celtic culture emerged along the Atlantic coasts of Europe, including Iberia, Ireland, and western Britain. From around 5000 BC, Celtic ideas and culture spread eastward, blending with those moving west. This suggests the ancient Celts on Europe's western edge developed the Celtic language. Wherever the early Celts origi-nated, it seems agreed their language diverged into two branches over time. Goidelic or Gaelic developed into Irish, Manx and Scottish Gaelic, while Brythonic evolved into modern Welsh, Cornish and Breton.

Romans – The Roman invasion started in modern-day Kent in AD 43, but it took them another 5 years to reach Wales. The Silures and Ordovices tribes of what is now Wales put up strong resistance, but by AD 80 almost all of England and Wales was under Roman control. There is evidence to suggest that the far northwest lands of the Ordovices (mod-ern-day Gwynedd, Conwy, and Isle of Anglesey) were never completely subdued. The Romans built their roads and forts but apart from its mineral wealth, Wales was never really attractive to them because the terrain made it difficult to move around, its climate wasn't quite southern Italy, and there was a distinct lack of places flat enough to cultivate. The Romans began to abandon Wales towards the end of the fourth century AD, in a bit of a huff, claiming they'd kept the lid on foreign invaders, invested more heavily in the national road system than any previous occupier, and got all the big calls right. Over the course of 300 years, their effect on Wales varied in different localities. Their influence was minimal in the remote northern hill settlements, but the people of South Wales absorbed some elements of the Roman way of life. Although Latin did not replace the native Brythonic language, many Latin words were absorbed and can still be heard in the Welsh language today, for example church (Welsh eglwys, from Latin *ecclesia*) and bridge (Welsh pont, from Latin *pons*).

Middle Ages – The departure of the Romans brought about a power struggle between the individual Welsh kingdoms. The largest and most powerful ones were Gwynedd in the north and Powys in the east. The leaders of these kingdoms fought each other for the upper hand, with the hope of eventually uniting and leading all of Wales. A map of Britain in AD 500 shows a considerable area occupied by Brythonic speaking Britons. Their lands extended well beyond the current borders of Wales, up the west side of England into southern Scotland (Strathclyde), and down to Cornwall.

Roman rule had brought Christianity, but the power vacuum of the Romans' departure saw pagan Anglo-Saxon tribes gaining control of increasing amounts of England. In Wales, the period AD 500 to AD 700 is known as the 'age of the saints,' a time of religious activity, when several monastic settlements were established across Wales. Several influential Christian figures emerged, such as St David (Dewi Sant), St Dyfrig, St Illtud, and St Teilo.

Amid a long period of perpetual warfare and aggression, the boundaries of Britain were constantly shifting, with some realms unifying, and others breaking apart. King Offa of Mercia, the kingdom bordering Wales, decided he had to draw the line somewhere. Between AD 757 and AD 796, he oversaw the construction of a remarkable earth wall and ditch, running from 'sea to sea' to keep out the unruly Welsh tribes. Perhaps Offa's Dyke also helped to unify the Welsh, because by the middle of the 9th century, Rhodri ap Merfyn, known as Rhodri Mawr (Rhodri the Great) emerged as the first leader to rule all of Wales. His grandson, Hywel Dda (Hywel the Good), best remembered for his laws of medieval Wales, is also said to have ruled most of Wales in 942 CE. Towards the end of this period, Gruffydd ap Llywelyn also achieved the remarkable feat of becoming King of Wales, but his death in 1063 was soon followed by the history changing arrival of the Normans.

Vikings – Those rough-and-tumble Scandinavian seafaring folks just couldn't resist the allure of Wales. From AD 856 to AD 1066, they just kept coming back for more. The long western coast of Wales was like a buffet of easy pickings, especially for those vulnerable but rich monasteries. Vikings probably did some trading too, but let's be honest, most of their visits were probably raids. Though they never set up any permanent homes, they did leave their mark on Wales in the form of place names like Fishguard (which was originally 'fiskigarth,' or 'enclosure for catching or keeping fish'). By the time the Normans rolled in, the Vikings had long since sailed back home, but their impact on the Welsh language lives on in words like 'bardd' (bard), 'caer' (fort), and 'dyffryn' (valley).

Normans – Although the Normans came from the northern part of France, they were originally Vikings, or Norsemen. Getting fed up with regular Viking raids in the 10th century, King Charles III of France, who had the unfortunate epithet 'Charles the Simple,' came up with a characteristically uncomplicated solution. He thought he could keep the invaders under control if he just gave them some land and asked them to behave. The Vikings went along with the crazy idea for a while and kept themselves busy by speaking French, inter-marrying with the locals, farming, and converting to Christianity. Their new homeland name of Northmannia, became shortened to Normandy. Old habits and behavioural genetics die hard though, and eventually the Normans felt the urge to invade somewhere. They overran parts of southern Italy in 1030, and in 1066, as we know, they turned their attentions to Britain. William the Conqueror was also known as William the Bastard, although I dare say all his soldiers were similarly referenced by those whom they conquered. The illegitimi arrived in Hastings in 1066, but it took them another 4 years to get to Wales and take on the tribes of the Welsh kingdoms. Rugged terrain and the guerrilla tactics of the Welsh proved to be problematic, leading to the construction of many castles and fortified settlements, and the creation of the semi-autonomous states of the Welsh Marches. The Normans claimed the fertile land for themselves, pushing the native Welsh population into the uplands. Welsh resistance to the Normans lasted for nearly 200 years, a testament to the fierce spirit of people determined to hold on to their land and culture.

Late Middle Ages – The post Norman period is best remembered for the heroics of three men who become national heroes: Llywelyn ap Iorwerth, also known as Llywelyn Fawr (Llywelyn the Great), his grandson Llywelyn II ap Gruffydd (also known as Llywelyn the Last), and Owain Glyndŵr (Owen of the Glen of Dee Water).

Llywelyn ap Iorwerth became the 'Prince of North Wales' by 1200 and by 1216 he was ruler of most of the nation of 'Pura Wallia,' the self-ruling kingdoms of Wales not under the control of the Marcher lords (March Wallia). He achieved a degree of national unity and political power that was never to be equalled again. His son Dafydd took over the role of Prince of Wales from 1240 to 1246, and then Llywelyn II ap Gruffydd held the title from 1246 to 1282. When Edward I became king of England in 1272, it was very bad news for Wales. The serial castle builder embarked upon three major military campaigns to subdue the Welsh. His overwhelming military resources were decisive. It provided the Welsh people with no doubt who was in control, yet the unexpected upside all these centuries later is some of the most spectacular castles in Europe.

Owain Glyndŵr, was a Welsh nobleman, and descendant of Llywelyn ap Iorwerth. He was born into a wealthy family around 1354. He received the best of educations and married the daughter of an Anglo-Welsh judge. His transformation from being part of the Anglo-Welsh establishment to rebel leader seems to have stemmed from an unresolved land dispute at a time when his country was looking for someone to take up their grievances with the English. His supporters declared him Prince of Wales in 1400 and they set out to topple the English king. Owain Glyndŵr was the leader the Welsh people had been looking for since Llywelyn ap Iorwerth. In time, all northern and central Wales came under his control. The English fought back however, and the battle of Pwll Melyn in 1406 was the beginning of the end for Owain Glyndŵr. By 1410, he had become a hunted outlaw in his own land. He was never captured or betrayed, and his place of hiding remains a mystery to this day. His name now symbolises Welsh pride and independence, and legend has it that he will one day rise again to defeat the English.

Tudors – The Tudor family, the most remarkable royal dynasty in British history, ruled England between 1485 and 1603 – and its origins were Welsh! The green and white in the background of the modern Welsh flag are the heraldic colours of the Tudor family standard. The exiled Henry Tudor (Harri Tudur), who was born in Pembroke Castle, returned to Wales in 1485 and marched north to defeat Richard III at the Battle of Bosworth Field. He became King Henry VII and ruled England until his death in 1509. The honeymoon period of Welsh influence on the English Crown didn't last long. Henry VII's successor, Henry VIII, brought about monumental changes to Wales. His 1536 and 1542 Acts of Union meant Wales was joined with England, not just annexed to it. It brought about a system of counties, removed the independence of the Welsh Marches, and brought Wales under the common law of England. Despite coming under increasing English influence, a strong Welsh cultural identity remained over the following two centuries, with most Welsh people continuing to speak Welsh and worshipping in nonconformist chapels.

Industrial Revolution – In the mid-18th century, Wales became the world's second industrialised country. If coal was the energy source that fuelled the Industrial Revolution, iron was its key new material. Wales had plenty of both. The demand for coal skyrocketed with the invention of coal-powered steam engines. Iron was needed for engines, ships, factory machines, trains, and railway lines.

Metalworks, potteries, cotton mills, coal, and lead mines sprang up in the north of Wales, alongside copper and slate mining. But it was the south of Wales that had vast reserves of iron and the black gold which powered the British Empire. The region saw the rapid development of its iron industry, especially in the Merthyr Tydfil area, which for a while was called 'the iron capital of the world.' The Cyfarthfa Ironworks became critical to the success of the Royal Navy at a time when the British Empire was expanding rapidly, and the Dowlais Ironworks became the largest steel producer in the UK. When it opened in 1789, the Blaenavon Ironworks was the most advanced in the world. Cities such as Cardiff, Swansea, and Newport expanded rapidly as trade boomed and goods were transported from their docks. The demand for copper made Swansea the most important port in the world. In central Wales, new technology brought factory methods to the existing wool industry. By the end of the 19th century, the Elan Valley Reservoirs had been constructed, and Pryce-Jones had begun the world's first mail order business in Newtown. Exploitation of the natural resources of Wales also involved exploitation of its workers, however, and this period is also notable for the rise in worker unrest, the formation of unions, and the Chartist movement.

Post Wars / 20th Century Onwards – Industrial unrest in the 19th century continued into the 20th century and is partly responsible for the Labour party reaching a dominant position in Welsh politics between and after the two world wars. Early in the 1900s, the radical social reforms of Welshman Lloyd George (Chancellor of the Exchequer and then Prime Minister) made him one of the most influential British politicians of the 20th century. Two more Welshmen, James Griffiths and Aneurin Bevan, worked hard to create the Welfare State and the National Health Service, and attended the birth in 1948.

The Welsh coal industry peaked in 1920 with 271,000 people employed. Demand fell away because of foreign competition and some industries turning to oil as their energy source. Many of the mines became financially unviable. Fifty were closed between 1957 and 1964. The decline had set in and a couple of decades later, with another round of closures threatened, the miners went on strike. It was the beginning of the end for the coal industry in South Wales and the rest of Britain. Subsequent UK and foreign investment in Wales has had mixed results, and employment rates are still high in many areas. Although the Welsh economy now generally reflects that of the UK, there are some subtle differences. Wales has a higher proportion of people employed in agriculture and forestry, manufacturing, and government. Foreign and UK investment supports a variety of high-technology industries such as life sciences and renewable energy. Prior to Brexit, the European Union provided significant resources to Wales, and it now appears to be one of the regions hit hardest by the loss of those structural funds. In terms of politics, Wales has two governments: one in the UK and one in Cardiff. The devolved Senedd Cymru (the Welsh Parliament) can now decide on many areas of domestic policy, set some taxes, and make and pass laws to be implemented by the executive, the Welsh Government.

ACKNOWLEDGMENTS

I'm going to begin with someone who I normally leave until last, for dramatic effect. For even more weeks than on previous occasions, Janice Probert let her husband go off and do lots of silly things. At least she was there to witness some of those silly things this time. I should follow quickly with my other travelling companions, Sarah, Danny, and the indefatigable Dr Nick Lindsay. It was such a pleasure to be with you all, and having you around enhanced my experience considerably. I should also add HV Morton to my list of fellow travellers. He came with me all the way, in the form of his book *In Search of Wales* and provided much inspiration for places to visit.

Once again, I must give huge thanks to Kirstie Edwards, my editor, for turning my manuscript into something you were able to read, and to Tom Probert for creating the stunning book cover, which, let's face it, is the real reason you picked up this book. I must also thank Jonathan Williams of the Welsh History Podcast for casting a knowledgable eye over the summary of Welsh history that I've included at the back of this book.

Occasionally, I thought ahead to set up meetings with people before I left home (let's not dwell on the Treorchy incident). Everyone involved was incredibly supportive and helpful, and I have a long list of people to thank. Other meetings cropped up along the way and the people involved are also on the list below. Some of the people listed here were contacted after the trip to provide information or clarification about something I'd seen.

I've listed people in alphabetical order (roughly). Everyone was amazing in their own ways. I apologise to anyone whose name is missing and can assure you its nothing to do with your impact on my journey. I can't blame it on the sunshine. The moonlight, good times and even the boogie are all similarly blameless - any omissions are totally down to the condition of my brain.

Thank you all, so much:

- Bebb, David, Treorchy Male Choir
- Benton, Berni, Llanwrtyd Wells
- Biggs, Kathy and Paul, Llanwrtyd Wells
- Buttler, Simon, Cardiff
- Clatworthy, Hywel, Turning Landscape CIC
- Davies, Bessie, Dyffryn Arms, Pontfaen
- Gee, Sarah, Windy Wick Bakery, Llantwit Major
- Geraedts, Rose, International Welsh Rarebit Centre
- Hall, Jenny, Trysor Heritage Consultancy
- Hood, Cheryl and Andy, Llanwrtyd Wells
- Jardine, Rob, Halen Môn, Anglesey
- James, Professor Christine, Gorsedd Cymru
- Jones, Selwyn, and all of Treorchy Male Choir
- Jowett, Nick, Great Orme Mines
- Lewis, Captain Beryn Charles Martin, Felinfoel Brewery
- Linda, warden at St Briavels Youth Hostel
- Louise, Jacquie, and Sue, Willow Globe Theatre
- McCausland, Onya, Turning Landscape CIC
- Nigel and Gay, Cardiff, guests at St Briavels Youth Hostel
- Owen, Llio, Welsh Language Statistics
- Parry, Anne and Andrew, Felin Ganol Watermill
- Pinder, Tom, The Welsh Cheese Company
- Reading Room Team, Gladstone's Library
- Reed, Mary, Blackwood
- Rees, Siwan Lona, Blackwood

- Roe, Scott and Ruth, Bron Yr Aur, Machynlleth
- Smith, Nigel, Gwaun Valley Brewery
- Sambrook, Paul, Trysor Heritage Consultancy
- Thompson, Ceri, Big Pit National Coal Museum
- Ward, Lisa, Rockfield Studios
- Wendy, Felinfoel Brewery
- Wilkinson, Lucy, Turning Landscape CIC
- Williams, Jonathan, Welsh History Podcast
- Wilson, Suzi, Bog-Snorkeller
- Woolard, Arthur and Lesley, often found in Amroth

Lastly, there are so many people I came across along the way for whom I have no names. Hotel and B&B owners, garage attendants, people serving in pubs, and cafés, YHA volunteers, shopkeepers, fellow travellers, librarians, other bog snorkellers, and random people with whom I spoke for maybe just a few minutes along the way – you all added to the rich experience of my *Journey through Wales* and whether you remember me or not, I thank you all!

ABOUT MARK PROBERT

Mark Probert has spent most of his life as a mapmaker. His early career with OS, the national mapping agency, allowed him to travel widely in Britain. He set up his own company in 2003 and over the following 16 years, he travelled extensively overseas, working on five continents. Now retired, and living in rural Dorset, he spends his time writing, walking, cycling and motorcycling. Mark and Jan have a daughter, two sons and a granddaughter.

Mark published his first book in 2020. In *Another Journey through Britain,* he uses gentle humour to describe a two-week motorcycle ride through the back lanes of Britain. Along the way, Mark compares what he comes across with the Britain of 50 years ago, as described in the book *Journey through Britain*, written by John Hillaby.

To catch up with Mark's latest writing, view his gallery of images, and purchase his other books, please visit his website at mgprobert.com

ALSO ON THE JOURNEY

One of my goals in publishing the 'Journey through' series of books is to inspire people of a certain age to embark on their own adventures. I've had the pleasure of meeting many like-minded seniors during my travels but I know that some may feel intimidated by the idea. I hope that readers of my books will think to themselves, 'If that old duffer can do it, so can I!' If you're fortunate enough to have reasonable health and fitness, you certainly can.

My first book describes a solo journey from Land's End to John o'Groats—thats one way to do it. For *Journey through India*, I travelled with my best friend—a different experience. For this third book, I've brought together a mix of friends and family as my travelling companions. By describing these various ways of travelling, I hope readers can find an option that inspires them to try their own journey.

Some readers may feel excited about travelling to India (and you can!), while others may prefer the familiarity of exploring closer to home, like Wales… it's all possible.

In the following pages, I would like to introduce you to my travelling companions on my *Journey through Wales*.

Janice Probert

Jan was born in Rochdale in 1957 but moved to rural Shropshire for most of her childhood and teenage years. She married Mark in Oswestry, in 1981 when life was mainly still in black and white. She somehow maintained a career in Environmental Health while juggling with three children and a husband who has had a habit of going off to obscure places around the world and doing silly things. It was usually at those times that the domestic dramas took place, all to be sorted out by the time Mark returned home.

Jan and Mark have lived in many places since 1981, including Leicestershire, Ayrshire, Cornwall, Hamble, near Southampton, Fontainebleau, Hamble again, and Shropshire.

They now live in very rural Dorset where Jan enjoys gardening, walking, yoga, keeping up with the various village societies and activities, and spending time with Sarah (below) and grand-daughter Lyra.

Sarah Page

Sarah is Mark Probert's 'middle child', born in 1991 in Southampton. She says she has been brought up with an agreeable balance of parental influences; her Dad's spirit of exploration & adventure, and her Mum's sage guidance to 'not go off and do anything silly.'

She followed her childhood love of dancing and movement into her career where she trained to teach dance and Pilates, before embarking on a behind-the-scenes role in marketing for theatres and arts venues for several years. Having settled in rural Dorset with her 5 year old daughter Lyra, Sarah has recently opened a Pilates studio and is embracing the balance of running a business and teaching movement.

In her spare time she loves reading, the arts, cooking, wellbeing and has a life-long ambition to 'do more travelling.'

Danny Silvestri

Danny is Sarah's partner in life, silliness, and adventures, delighting in the shared joy of those activities with Sarah and her family.

He's a barber to the stars, serving many elite athletes, musicians, actors, and others in his barbering studio. His deep passion for wellbeing is now steering his life in a new direction. Danny plans to use complementary practices to holistically support others in their search for wellbeing.

As a guy of balance and stillness, but with a cheeky restlessness, he values mindful time usage while seeking exhilarating experiences.

Surfing, wild swimming, skate-boarding, and motorbiking are complemented by camping, nature, meditation, walks, and good food. The combination brings solace and stimulates deep and heartfelt conversations... often over a bottle of red.

Dr Nick Lindsay

Born in Cardiff in 1957, proud Welshman, Nick Lindsay, began his working life with OS, the national mapping agency of Great Britain. He left in 1980 to continue his education with a degree, followed by a PhD in geology at the University of Liverpool. Employment as a geologist gave him the chance to travel extensively. Now retired and living in the Highlands, he spends his time as chairman of Clyne Heritage Society, running, writing, and walking in his beloved Scottish mountains. Nick is married to Ellen, and they share their house with four cats.

Nick published his first book in 2010, *Cape Wrath to Brora: A walking adventure across Sutherland*. His second book, *Clyne, Loth & Golspie place names*, was published in 2016, and his third, a biography of a larger-than-life character from Doll: *We had nothing, but we had everything: George MacBeath's memories of growing up on a croft, at Doll, Brora*, was published in 2020.

ABOUT HV MORTON

HV Morton, born in Lancashire in 1892, was a British journalist and renowned travel writer of his time. His captivating travel books, known for their light-hearted and engaging style, achieved widespread acclaim. One of his early works, *In Search of England*, published in 1927, propelled him to literary fame. In this captivating book, Morton embarked on a journey across England, exploring various towns and villages while immersing himself in their rich history and vibrant culture. The book, celebrated for its historical accuracy and vivid portrayal of the past, quickly became a bestseller and played a pivotal role in popularising the genre of travel writing.

Building upon his success, Morton continued his explorations with similar searches in Wales and Scotland, further solidifying his reputation as a prolific writer. Throughout his lifetime, he published over 50 books, each contributing to his legacy as an influential figure in the realm of travel literature.

Despite his literary achievements, Morton's personal life and political beliefs were complex, often evoking controversy. He was known for his right-wing views and controversial support for fascism.

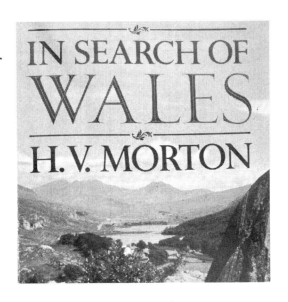

Morton's contribution to travel writing remains very significant and his books continue to resonate with new readers. In order to delve deeper into the life and works of this remarkable writer, those interested can explore the HV Morton Society's website at www.hvmorton.com. The society serves as a platform to foster interest, exchange information, and promote the legacy of HV Morton, facilitating a comprehensive understanding of his enduring impact as a writer and journalist.

BIBLIOGRAPHY

England, J., (2019). *Merthyr: The Crucible of Modern Wales*. Parthian Books.

Malkin, B.H., (1804). The *Scenery, Antiquities, and Biography, of South Wales: From Materials Collected During Two Excursions in the Year 1803*. TN Longman and O. Rees UK.

Morton, H.V., (1932). *In Search of Wales*. Methuen UK.

Parker, M. and Whitfield, P., (2003). *The Rough Guide To Wales*. Rough Guides. Penguin House UK.

Tacitus, C., (1996). *The Annals Of Imperial Rome* (Vol. 60). Penguin UK.

UNESCO (2021). *Man and the Biosphere (MAB) Programme*. UNESCO. Retrieved February 28, 2023, from https://en.unesco.org/biosphere/

Wright, S., (1948). *Up the Claerwen*. Cornish Brothers UK.

.

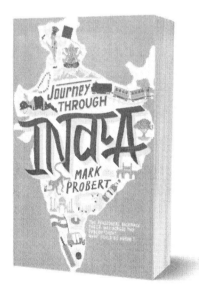

'Be happy with what you have and are, be generous with both, and you won't have to hunt for happiness'
— William E Gladstone

·

Printed in Great Britain
by Amazon